OPERATION LONG JUMP

Operation Long Jump

STALIN, ROOSEVELT, CHURCHILL, AND THE GREATEST
ASSASSINATION PLOT IN HISTORY

Bill Yenne

REGNERY
HISTORY

Regnery History™ is a trademark of Salem Communications Holding Corporation; Regnery® is a registered trademark of Salem Communications Holding Corporation

Library of Congress Cataloging-in-Publication Data

Yenne, Bill, 1949- author.
  Operation Long Jump : Stalin, Roosevelt, Churchill, and the greatest assassination plot in history / Bill Yenne.
    pages cm
  Includes bibliographical references and index.
  ISBN 978-1-62157-346-3 (alk. paper)
  1. Operation Long Jump. 2. World War, 1939-1945--Secret service--Germany. 3. Conspiracies--Iran--Tehran--History--20th century. 4. Conspiracies--Germany--History--20th century. 5. Teheran Conference (1943 : Tehran, Iran) 6. Roosevelt, Franklin D. (Franklin Delano), 1882-1945. 7. Stalin, Joseph, 1878-1953. 8. Churchill, Winston, 1874-1965. I. Title.
  D810.S7Y46 2015
  940.53'141--dc23
                              2015015710

Published in the United States by
Regnery History
An imprint of Regnery Publishing
A Division of Salem Media Group
300 New Jersey Ave NW
Washington, DC 20001
www.RegneryHistory.com

Manufactured in the United States of America

10 9 8 7 6 5 4 3 2 1

Books are available in quantity for promotional or premium use. For information on discounts and terms, please visit our website: www.Regnery.com.

Distributed to the trade by
Perseus Distribution
250 West 57th Street
New York, NY 10107

Contents

Cast of Characters

DMITRI VASILEVICH ARKADIEV: the NKVD man who coordinated Soviet logistics for the Tehran Conference

GENERAL HENRY "HAP" ARNOLD: the commanding general of the USAAF, and a participant in the Tehran Conference

ELYESA BAZNA: a German asset in Turkey, called Cicero because the intelligence he provided spoke so eloquently

LAVRENTY BERIA: head of the Soviet NKVD and a probable participant in the Tehran Conference, though he kept to the shadows

CHIP BOHLEN: the first secretary at the American embassy in Moscow and Roosevelt's translator in Tehran

GENERAL ALAN BROOKE: chief of the British General Staff, and a participant in the Tehran Conference

READER BULLARD: the veteran foreign service man who was the British ambassador to Iran

ADMIRAL WILHELM CANARIS: the head of the Abwehr, the German military intelligence organization

KHALIL CHAPAT: a French-Iranian high school teacher and a fixture of the expat community in Tehran

WINSTON CHURCHILL: the Prime Minister of Great Britain and one of the targets of Operation Long Jump

GENERAL DONALD CONNOLLY: the engineer who headed the U.S. Army's Persian Gulf Command

ADMIRAL ANDREW CUNNINGHAM: chief of the Royal Naval Staff, and a participant in the Tehran Conference

JAMES DOWNWARD: an agent of the U.S. Office of War Information in Tehran

PERCY DOWNWARD: a covert agent of the British SOE operating in Tehran

LOUIS GOETHE DREYFUS: the veteran foreign service man who was the American ambassador to Iran

MISBAH EBTEHAJ: a practitioner of Pahlevani, a form of Iranian martial arts and someone who seemed to know everyone in Tehran

ANTHONY EDEN: foreign minister of the United Kingdom, and a participant in the Tehran Conference

ERWIN ETTEL: the veteran foreign service man and loyal Nazi who was the prewar German ambassador to Iran

PETER FERGUSON: an American adventurer and OSS man who hatched a scheme to thwart Long Jump

ROMAN GAMOTHA: an agent on the ground in Iran of the German SD spy agency

GEORG ALEXANDER HANSEN: the chief of the Abwehr counterintelligence component

AVERELL HARRIMAN: the American ambassador to the Soviet Union, and a participant in the Tehran Conference

STURMBANNFÜHRER RUDOLF VON HOLTEN-PFLUG: an aggressive and ambitious SS officer and a Long Jump team leader

HARRY HOPKINS: special assistant to President Roosevelt, and a participant in the Tehran Conference

GENERAL PATRICK HURLEY: Roosevelt's personal troubleshooter in Russia and the Middle East, and a participant in the Tehran Conference

OBERGRUPPENFÜHRER ERNST KALTENBRUNNER: the head of the German Sicherheitsdienst (SD) domestic and foreign intelligence agency

ARCHIBALD CLARK KERR: the British ambassador to the Soviet Union, a participant in the Tehran Conference

NASR KHAN: the warlord leader of the powerful Qashqai, a nomadic people who saw the Germans as liberators

ADMIRAL ERNEST KING: United States Chief of Naval Operations, a participant in the Tehran Conference

DANIEL KOMISSAROV: a Farsi-speaking translator and key figure within the Soviet embassy in Tehran

IDA KOVALSKA: a well-educated Polish refugee, part of the expat community in Tehran, and a confidante of spies

NIKOLAI IVANOVICH KUZNETSOV: a legendary NKVD double agent specializing in covert operations

ADMIRAL WILLIAM LEAHY: Roosevelt's military chief of staff, also the Chairman of the Joint Chiefs of Staff, and a participant in the Tehran Conference

GEORGE LENCZOWSKI: the press attaché at the Polish embassy in Tehran

FITZROY MACLEAN: a legendary soldier of fortune and British covert operations master

GENERAL GEORGE MARSHALL: Chief of Staff of the U.S. Army, and a participant in the Tehran Conference

MIKHAIL MAXIMOV: the Soviet ambassador to Iran, he replaced Andrei Smirnov in 1943

FRANZ MAYR: the longest-serving agent of the German SD spy network on the ground in Iran

ADMIRAL ROSS MCINTIRE: Roosevelt's doctor

ERNST MERSER: a Swiss double agent operating for the SIS and the Abwehr in Tehran under cover as a businessman, he became the central figure in Operation Long Jump

ARTHUR MILLSPAUGH: the American fiscal genius who became Administrator General of Finances of Iran

VYACHESLAV MOLOTOV: the Soviet foreign commissar, and a participant in the Tehran Conference

SYDNEY MORRELL: a British Security Coordination agent under cover as a public affairs man

HABIBULLAH NOBAKHT: a pro-German Iranian politician, he gave aid and comfort to German spies

STURMBANNFÜHRER WINIFRED OBERG: the handler of German spies in the Middle East for the SD

STURMBANNFÜHRER HANS ULRICH VON ORTEL: an SS hit man, clever and aggressive, but he talked too much

MOHAMMAD REZA PAHLAVI: the timid son of Reza Shah who grew up to be a despot

HAROLD PETERS: an agent of the U.S. Office of War Information operating in Tehran

WANDA POLLACK: a young Polish refugee who was taken in by Ernst Merser, and who was to play an unwitting pivotal role in the Long Jump story

PAUL POURBAIX: a Belgian NKVD informant and a fixture of the Tehran expat community

MICHAEL FRANCIS REILLY: the head of the Secret Service White House Detail and Roosevelt's bodyguard

LIEUTENANT (JG) BILL RIGDON: the U.S. Navy officer who was Roosevelt's personal secretary at the Tehran conference

FRANKLIN ROOSEVELT: the President of the United States and one of the targets of Operation Long Jump

BRIGADEFÜHRER WALTHER FRIEDRICH SCHELLENBERG: the head of SD-Ausland, the foreign espionage wing of the SD

UNTERSTURMFÜHRER JOSEF SCHNABEL: a young and energetic SS man who was part of the Long Jump team

LOTHAR SCHOELLHORN: a ruthless criminal recruited by the Abwehr for his skills as a hired killer

MAJOR JULIUS SCHULZE-HOLTHUS: the agent on the ground in Iran of the Abwehr, German military intelligence

GENERAL HERBERT NORMAN SCHWARZKOPF: the crime buster from New Jersey who headed the Iranian gendarmerie

REZA SHAH: the iron-fisted ruler of Iran until deposed in 1941

STANDARTENFÜHRER OTTO SKORZENY: the legendary SS special forces commander, known for accomplishing the impossible

ANDREI SMIRNOV: the Soviet ambassador to Iran, replaced in 1943 by Mikhail Maximov

JOSEF STALIN: Marshal of the Soviet Union, and one of the targets of Operation Long Jump

GEVORK VARTANIAN: an NKVD man in Tehran who described Long Jump to the international media sixty years later

ANDREI MIKHALOVITS VERTINSKI: the NKVD resident agent in Tehran

MARSHAL KLIMENT VOROSHILOV: Stalin's senior military man at the Tehran Conference

MERVYN WOLLHEIM: an American amateur archeologist and a fixture of the expat community in Tehran

GENERAL FAZLOLLAH ZAHEDI: a pro-German Iranian general who gave aid and comfort to German spies

Acronyms

Abwehr: German "defensive" military intelligence
AFHQ: Allied Force Headquarters
BND: Bundesnachrichtendienst (German Federal intelligence service)
BSC: British Security Coordination
CCS: Combined Chiefs of Staff (Anglo-American Allies)
CIA: Central Intelligence Agency (United States)
CIC: Counter Intelligence Corps (U.S. Army)
ETOUSA: European Theater of Operations, U.S. Army
FDR: President Franklin Delano Roosevelt
FHO: Fremde Heere Ost (Foreign Armies East) (Germany)
FSB: Federal'naya Sluzhba Bezopasnosti (Federal Security Service) (Russia)
Gestapo: Geheime Staatspolizei (Secret State Police) (Germany)
GKO: Gosudarstvennyj Komitet Oborony (State Defense Committee) (Soviet Union)
JCS: Joint Chiefs of Staff (United States)

KGB: Komitet Gosudarstvennoy Bezopasnosti (Committee for State Security) (Soviet Union)

MI5: Military Intelligence, Section 5 (United Kingdom internal security)

MI6: Military Intelligence, Section 6 (United Kingdom foreign intelligence)

MID: Military Intelligence Division (U.S. Army)

MIS: Military Intelligence Service (U.S. Army)

MTOUSA: Mediterranean Theater of Operations, U.S. Army

ND: Schweizer Nachrichtendienst (Swiss Intelligence Service)

NKVD: Narodnyy Komissariat Vnutrennikh Del (People's Commissariat for Internal Affairs) (Soviet Union)

ODESSA: Organization der Ehemaligen SS-Angehörigen (Organization of SS Retirees)

OKW: Oberkommando der Wehrmacht (Supreme Command of the Armed Forces) (Germany)

ONI: Office of Naval Intelligence (U.S. Navy)

OSS: Office of Strategic Services (United States)

OWI: Office of War Information (United States)

PGC: Persian Gulf Command (United States)

PGSC: Persian Gulf Service Command (United States)

PID: Political Intelligence Department (United Kingdom)

PWE: Political Warfare Executive (United Kingdom)

RAF: Royal Air Force (United Kingdom)

RSHA: Reichssicherheitshauptamt (Reich Main Security Office) (Germany)

SA: Sturmabteilung (Storm Troops) (Germany)

SD: Sicherheitsdienst (Security Service of the SS) (Germany)

SHAEF: Supreme Headquarters Allied Expeditionary Forces

SIME: Security Intelligence Middle East (United Kingdom)

SIS: Secret Intelligence Service (United Kingdom)

SOE: Special Operations Executive (United Kingdom)

SS: Schutzstaffel (Protection Squadron) (Germany)

USAAF: U.S. Army Air Forces

VOKS: Vsesoiuznoe Obshchestvo Kul'turnoi Sviazi ([Soviet] All-Union Society for Cultural Relations)

Prologue

What Might Have Been

THE BRITISH EMBASSY, TEHRAN, NOVEMBER 30, 1943:

Michael Francis Reilly stifled a yawn and glanced at his watch. It was nearly midnight and the bigwigs were still toasting, still trying to outdo one another with fawning praise, cynical accolades, and clever witticisms that came across more and more lame with each round of high octane Russian vodka.

Reilly yawned.

These two dozen or more high-ranking generals, admirals, politicians, and diplomats could sleep off tonight's hangover, but Reilly knew that he and his team would be up at dawn—again.

Maybe it was the elevation. Tehran was nearly as high as mile-high Denver. Maybe it was the breakneck schedule. A Secret Service man's day—especially when the Boss is on the road *and* overseas—is long, tiring, and filled with worry. For Mike Reilly, in charge of Franklin Delano Roosevelt's protection detail, you could multiply all that by at least ten.

Three times in the past week, Reilly had flown into this dusty medieval metropolis at the edge of nowhere while Otis Bryan, the president's pilot, was trying to prove that he could make the entire six-hour flight from Cairo below 8,000 feet in the unpressurized C-54 so that it would not put undue strain on Roosevelt's weary ticker. This he did, but flying that low put the big airplane at the mercy of updrafts that Bryan called "thermals." These tossed the plane—and Reilly's gut—around like willow leaves ahead of a thunderstorm.

Everyone in the room had a sense that tonight, the third big sit-down dinner of the Big Three, was the climax of the whole show. It was Winston Churchill's sixty-ninth birthday; the President of the United States was on his right; Josef Stalin, the master of Russia and Marshal of the Soviet Union, on his left.

When the prime minister raised his glass to toast the short man with the big presence and the big moustache, he called him "Stalin the Great," suggesting that he was just like "Peter the Great" and all those other "great" czars and czarinas that they had in Russia back in the olden days. The "great" man didn't argue.

He had been born Ioseb Besarionis Dze Jughashvili, but he renamed himself "Stalin," because it is the Russian word for "steel." He wanted to be known—in Russian, tellingly, not in his native Georgian—as the "Man of Steel." In private, the Boss and Churchill called him "Uncle Joe."

It was an historic meeting. Churchill said it was "the greatest concentration of power that the world had ever seen"; he added that between them, the three "controlled practically all the naval and three-quarters of all the air forces in the world, and could direct armies of nearly 20 millions of men."

The Big Three were confident of victory. They were here to discuss exactly *how* they were going to finally defeat Hitler, and attending with them was an unprecedented array of officers and advisors. Both Churchill and Stalin had brought their foreign ministers, Anthony Eden and Vyacheslav Molotov, while Roosevelt had Harry Hopkins, his special assistant and closest confidant, as well as Admiral William Leahy, his military advisor and the Chairman of the Joint Chiefs of Staff. The Boss had also brought the rest of the Joint Chiefs, General George Marshall of the U.S. Army, Admiral Ernest King of the U.S. Navy, and General Hap Arnold of the U.S. Army Air Force.

Churchill, meanwhile, was accompanied by General Sir Alan Brooke, chief of the Imperial General Staff; Admiral Sir Andrew Cunningham, First Sea Lord and Chief of the Royal Naval Staff; and Air Chief Marshal Charles "Peter" Portal of the Royal Air Staff. At Stalin's side was Marshal Klim Voroshilov of the omnipotent State Defense Committee that helped the Man of Steel rule the Soviet Union.

They sure could drink, these two dozen or more brass hat generals, admirals, politicians, and diplomats who had come together here in god-forsaken Tehran to plot Adolf Hitler's demise. The Boss, who was not shy about his fondness for a dirty martini or three, could barely keep pace. Despite the bright, legendary Roosevelt grin, Reilly could see the weariness in his Boss's eyes. Stalin, on the other hand, seemed to possess an infinite capacity for Russia's native spirit, or any other alternative to vodka that might be offered. As for Churchill, Reilly had watched him on numerous occasions over the past couple of years, and had observed in his own diary that they had not yet made enough alcohol to dull his biting wit.

He looked around the room. Security was tight. Though tonight's dinner was in the British embassy, the Russians had packed the place with their NKVD goons. They outnumbered Reilly's own detail, and they outnumbered the Brits on their home turf.

Most of the security guys, even the Russians to whom Reilly had talked, were guardedly optimistic about the security arrangements—though there was a definite threat. Reilly was aware the Russians and the Brits had, for many months, been tracking Germans who had parachuted into Iran. The Germans wanted to sabotage the railroad the Americans were using to run Lend-Lease supplies from the Persian Gulf into Russia.

This place, Tehran, with its open sewers and dusty streets crowded with characters like nobody had ever seen outside the pages of *National Geographic*, seemed about as far from Germany as the South Pole, but the Krauts had been busy in Iran for decades. They had built the railroads and many other public works. They used to run the airlines.

When the Reds and Brits invaded the place two years ago, they rounded up the Germans—or at least most of them—but the Germans kept coming back. When he had flown into Tehran a week ago on his second visit, Reilly had been met at the airport by General Dmitri Arkadiev of the NKVD, the Soviet secret police, who told him that thirty-eight Nazis had flown into Iran to kill the Big Three and that a half dozen of these would-be assassins were still at large.

Reilly raised an eyebrow at Arkadiev's peculiarly precise number, but he took him seriously. The Russians had offered to let Roosevelt stay in a detached house within the heavily guarded Soviet embassy compound, rather than at the American legation on the edge of town, and after initially declining, Roosevelt finally accepted.

Reilly had breathed easier.

That would keep the Boss off the street, because the British embassy was practically next door to the Russians, and both were surrounded by Allied troops. Security bordered on overkill, and the Big Three meeting had been kept pretty hush-hush, so nobody considered it realistic to suspect that a few saboteurs would have the gall to try to break in *here*.

Now that the circus was almost over, most of the security guys were feeling more relaxed. At dinner on the first night, the NKVD thugs never took their fingers out of the trigger guards on their submachine guns. Tonight, Reilly could see them yawning just like everybody else.

At the head tables, everyone had to toast everyone else, so after a while, Reilly and the other bodyguards in the room stopped listening.

None of the layers of security men paid much attention when Roosevelt waxed nostalgically of a time, back in the previous century, when the father of General Sir Alan Brooke had called on the president's father, James Roosevelt, at the family home in Hyde Park, New York.

Just as he was finishing, and Brooke was thinking what an easy time he should have replying to such kind words, Stalin rose abruptly, interrupting Roosevelt, startling Brooke, and announcing that *he* would finish the toast.

The attention of the room abruptly refocused on the head table. The dignitaries and the bodyguards, who had been generally relaxed and somewhat distracted, all now turned their eyes toward Uncle Joe.

The Russians listened to Stalin, but other heads turned toward Arthur Birse, the British translator, as he relayed Stalin's assertion that Brooke had failed to show real feelings of friendship towards the Red Army, that he was "lacking in a true appreciation of its fine qualities, and that he hoped in future he should be able to show greater comradeship towards the soldiers of the Red Army."

Brooke, who had risen to his feet to thank Roosevelt for his remarks, remained standing, having seen enough of Stalin by then to know that if he sat down under these unexpected insults, he would lose any respect Stalin might ever have had for him.

"Now, Marshal, may I deal with your toast," Brooke said, turning to the Man of Steel. "I am surprised that you should have found it necessary to raise accusations against me that are entirely unfounded. You will remember that this morning, while we were discussing cover plans, Mr. Churchill said that 'in war truth must have an escort of lies.' You will also remember that you yourself told us that in all your great offensives your real intentions were always kept concealed from the outer world. You told us that all your dummy tanks and dummy aeroplanes were always massed on those fronts that were of an immediate interest, while your true intentions were covered by a cloak of complete secrecy."

Here, he paused as Vladimir Pavlov, Stalin's interpreter, related what had been said, and every Russian in the room hung on every word.

"Well, Marshal," Brooke continued, "you have been misled by dummy tanks and dummy aeroplanes, and you have failed to observe those feelings of true friendship which I have for the Red Army, nor have you seen the feelings of genuine comradeship which I bear towards all its members."

As Pavlov translated, all eyes were on Stalin's inscrutable expression.

When Brooke had finished, Stalin whispered something to Churchill, as Pavlov translated.

"I like that man," Stalin said. "He rings true."

Everyone was so focused on the standoff between Brooke and Stalin that they scarcely paid a second thought to a crash which came from the direction of the kitchen.

Someone, Reilly thought absently, was going to pay dearly for dropping a tray of embassy dinnerware.

Looking around, he noticed that there were at least a dozen more uniformed Russian troops in the room than there had been a few moments before. The ones who had been standing guard all night seemed confused as the others filtered into the room from several doorways.

No one else seemed to notice. Over the past three days, everybody had grown used to seeing large numbers of armed and uniformed Russians lurking about.

Over his shoulder, Reilly heard the unmistakable *pop* of a gunshot.

As he turned, there was suddenly the clatter of submachine gun fire from every direction.

Russians were killing Russians!

What the hell is going on?

As he drew his own Smith and Wesson, and began pushing through the crowd toward the Boss, Reilly noticed a group of about a half dozen men in business suits. They *weren't* U.S. Secret Service. Were they Brits? More Russians?

At the head table, the expressions ranged from Roosevelt's stark bewilderment to Stalin's appearance of complete terror. In a split second, Reilly remembered that when the Germans had invaded the Soviet Union back in '41, Stalin was so paralyzed with panic that Molotov had to take charge and address the nation on radio.

If Stalin *appeared* helpless, Reilly knew that Roosevelt *was* helpless. Confined to his wheelchair, he could not leap to his feet and run for cover, as others were starting to do.

Just as he reached the front of the room, Reilly saw, out of the corner of his eye, General Brooke's head spattering blood.

Reilly reached Roosevelt and the president clasped his hands behind his bodyguard's neck.

Reilly was about to lift him up when he felt himself stumble. Someone was crawling across the floor.

As he turned to keep himself and the president from falling, Reilly could see that the mystery men in business suits were all around the head table, barking orders in German.

"*They're damned Krauts,*" Reilly exclaimed.

One of the business-suited Germans pointed a Walther P38 directly at Winston Churchill, who glared at him defiantly before his head exploded in a shower of blood and bone.

Tears rolling down his cheeks, Stalin begged for mercy.

Reilly awkwardly raised his own sidearm, which was not easily done with Roosevelt's arms grasped around his neck.

The Secret Service man squeezed off a round at the German who had just shot Churchill.

It was hard to miss at this range, and Reilly didn't.

He took aim at a German threatening Stalin, winging the would-be assassin in the arm, forcing the German to drop his gun. But almost immediately, Stalin's upper torso was shredded in a burst of submachine gun fire. One round clipped Uncle Joe's chin, pulverizing his lower jaw.

Reilly staggered to his feet, threw the thirty-second president of the United States over his shoulder, and ran like hell for the nearest doorway.

It seemed to take an hour, although it was probably no more than a few seconds.

On the way, Reilly recognized the lifeless body of Admiral Leahy. Sir Reader Bullard, the British ambassador whose embassy was the scene of this bloodbath, was writhing on the floor with a horrific leg wound.

Reilly smelled the acrid stench of burnt powder and spilled alcohol; his ears were deafened by the roar of guns, screams, and breaking glass. But Reilly made it through the door, and kept running.

Now he was in some sort of vestibule. He heard his shoes clattering on a tile floor, which gave him a sense—though he knew better—that he was out of danger.

He felt the coolness of the night air on his face and saw a door ajar at the far end of the hallway.

Sprinting through this second doorway, he found himself outside.

Beyond a nearby hedge, he thought he heard troops racing to enter the main door of the embassy, but the little garden was eerily empty—except for Reilly and the Boss.

The Secret Service man dropped to his knees and looked into the face of the man he had just carried to safety.

As he watched, the life flickered quietly from the eyes of Franklin Delano Roosevelt.

That night [November 27, 1943], late, I got word from Marshal Stalin that they had got word of a German plot.

Well, no use going into details. Everybody was more or less upset, Secret Service, and so forth. And he pleaded with me to go down to the Russian Embassy [in central Tehran]—they have two or three different buildings in the compound—and he offered to turn over one of them to me, and that would avoid either his, or Mr. Churchill's, or my having to take trips through the streets, in order to see each other.

So the next morning I moved out [of the United States embassy compound], down to the Russian compound. I was extremely comfortable there, and it was just another wall from the British place, so that none of the three of us had to go out on the streets, for example.

But of course, in a place like Tehran there are hundreds of German spies, probably, around the place, and I suppose it would make a pretty good haul if they could get all three of us going through the streets. [Laughter] And of course, if your future plans are known, or if they can guess the time because of departure from one place, they can get German pursuit planes over the transport plane very easily.

—President Franklin D. Roosevelt at a news conference
(Washington, D.C., December 17, 1943)

Introduction

A Pretty Good Haul ... If

This is the story of what is probably the greatest assassination conspiracy in history. *If* it had succeeded, it would have been, in Roosevelt's folksy understatement, "a pretty good haul." Had Roosevelt, Churchill, and Stalin all died in Tehran on a cold winter day in 1943, it would have changed the course of world history.

The Prologue of this book is, of course, "alternative history," although the exchange between Brooke and Stalin actually *did* take place in Tehran at Winston Churchill's birthday dinner as described. The actions attributed to Michael Reilly, chief of the U.S. Secret Service White House Detail, represent what he almost certainly *would have* done. The rest represents the methods and the goals of *Unternehmen Weitsprung*, or Operation Long Jump, as it was planned behind closed doors in Berlin.

Conceived at the highest levels of German covert operations, Long Jump was a conspiracy whose stranger-than-fiction twists and turns are so unlikely that were it not for the fraying of wartime secrecy, it could still be written off as improbable.

This is the story of how the three most powerful men in the Allied world came together in a relatively obscure backwater that was a nest of spies, wannabe spies, and double agents, beneath which was a morass of ancient rivalries, incomprehensible fiefdoms, and competing ideological interests, from Iran's pro-Soviet Tudeh faction to the fervently pro-Nazi Melliyun-I-Iran.

Why did the Big Three gather here? Because Stalin willed it. Churchill did not want to go to Tehran and suggested a series of alternative sites. Roosevelt flatly refused to go to Tehran, and in a series of personal coded memos, he and Stalin argued about this for months. But Stalin was paranoid. He did not want to travel far from the Soviet Union and he was afraid of flying. Roosevelt eventually relented in order to ensure that the meeting of the Big Three *would* actually take place, and the three leaders traveled to Tehran.

The Big Three conference succeeded, and the assassination conspiracy did not. This would allow Operation Long Jump to quietly slip beneath the opaque shroud of wartime secrecy, where it would remain hidden from the daylight of historical memory for decades. Many of the secrets are gone forever, while others have reemerged from time to time in the form of rumors and whispered recollections. This is the story of a distant place and time, a story assembled from events chronicled and filed away, but later found; and from secrets long ago hidden beneath the sands of time, but later revealed.

Iran, the Remote Fastness

ran was one of those places about which one might have said, "It is not at the ends of the earth, but one must pass *through* the ends of the earth to get there."

For a snapshot of Iran in those days, we squeeze into the back seat of John Gunther's car as he drives into Iran in the late 1930s. Gunther's hugely popular and influential book *Inside Europe* was published in 1936; its sequel, *Inside Asia*, was published in 1939, and Iran was one of his stops.

"Entrance into Iran," he wrote, " ... is explosive. Here is the real Asia, here is Asia naked. This is the magnificent and impregnable inner fastness of the Moslem world. For two days, three days, your car bounces and slithers, writhes and groans, climbing the terrific passes between Baghdad and Tehran, wallowing in stones and mud, leaping crevasses and landslips, penetrating villages which can have changed very little since the days of Xerxes, and cutting across country the color of Gorgonzola cheese and the consistency of pumice stone."

Geographically, that cheese-colored land stretches from the arid steppes of Central Asia to the Persian Gulf, a place that had been on the way to almost nowhere else since the heyday of the Silk Road a thousand years before. Historically, Iran stretches back to the Elamite days in the fourth millennium B.C., giving it roots in one of the world's oldest civilizations. Religiously, Iran has been Islamic since the seventh century, though the influence of the mullahs has both risen and ebbed through time.

Politically, Iran reached the high water mark of its international greatness in the sixth century B.C. when Cyrus the Great hammered together the Achaemenid Empire, and Xerxes hammered Greece into submission a century later. The empire deteriorated after the Greeks retook Greece, but lasted until Alexander the Great defeated Darius III in 333 B.C. From that point forward, Iran—it was the Greeks who named it Persia, the name that stuck in the West—declined gradually into obscurity. By the nineteenth century, Iran had devolved into one of the pawns on the chessboard of the "Great Game," a buffer state—Afghanistan was another—in the great strategic rivalry between the Russian Empire to the north and the British Empire which ruled nearby India.

Iran's ruler, at the time Gunther's car bounced into the country, was Reza Khan, an illiterate shepherd boy who joined the army and went on to command a Persian Cossack Brigade. In 1921, a group led by a journalist named Sayyid Zia ud-Din Tabataba'i (a.k.a. Zia'eddin Tabatabaee) engineered a coup against the reigning sovereign, Ahmad Shah. Reza led troops on Zia's behalf.

Less ambitious than the average coup-master, the democracy-minded Zia wanted not to overthrow the Qajar Dynasty and become the shah, but merely to become the shah's prime minister, which he became, but only for a few months.

Ahmad Shah, on the job since 1909 when he was just eleven years old, was as lacking in ambition as Sayyid Zia, and was simply uninterested in his job and his country. He wasn't even around. As Gunther reports, Ahmad spent little time in Iran, but instead "lived in Deauville [France] and gave fortunes in rubies to chorus girls. He was called the Grocer-Boy Shah, when he wasn't called something even less complimentary, because he bought the entire grain crop of the country during a famine and then sold it to the starving people at fantastic prices."

In 1923, having spent two years putting down revolts and consolidating his political power base, Reza Khan became prime minister. Two years later, Iran's rubber-stamp parliament deposed the old shah and declared Reza Khan the new sovereign. Reza Khan was now Reza Shah Pahlavi, the Shah-in-Shah (King of Kings), and variously known as the Shadow of the Almighty, or the Vice Regent of God. As the Qajar Dynasty gave way to the Pahlavi Dynasty, playboy Ahmad simply remained in Europe, where he died in suburban Paris in 1930.

Reza would graciously describe himself to foreign diplomats as a "simple soldier," but he was a ruthless man, giving no quarter to political opponents—or to dogs, whom he had slaughtered in villages where he stayed, because he was a light sleeper.

Reza was fond of French wine and pipes of opium—and of rights for women, including the right to vote and doing away with the veil, which put him at odds with the Muslim clergy. Once, when a mullah scolded Reza's wife, the Shah descended upon the mullah's mosque accompanied by an entourage of armored cars, and personally beat the sanctimonious holy man half to death. Reza was a harsh reformer who curbed the power of the mullahs, wiped out banditry, and extended state control over the nomadic tribes of the Iranian desert. To many in the outside world, he seemed to be a man like Turkey's Kemal Ataturk, dragging a backward Islamic county into the twentieth century.

"The Shah, who believes in the modern world, will not admit camels into Tehran," wrote John Gunther, recounting an observation made by his driver. "In fact, he almost refuses to concede that camels still exist. So the caravans have to sleep outside the city gates." Gunther's Iranian chauffeur asked him: "Have you got rid of the camels yet in Paris and New York?"

As a capital, Tehran had one foot in the twentieth century and one in antiquity. "The city is one of the most beautiful I have ever seen," Gunther wrote. "The new boulevards are spacious, the trees are nicely planted. But between street and sidewalk are the ditches, full of dogs, cats, and the drinking water. Tehran does things by sudden jumps. It is a mixture of primitiveness and sophistication. Splendid boulevards and dial telephones—but no sewage system!"

While Tehran might lack a modern sewer system, Reza had his own grandiose public works projects, including a massive, German-engineered railway station. It opened in 1930 before there were rail lines to use it.

When the British nagged him to build an east-west railway across Iran that would link British-influenced Iraq to British India, Reza defiantly spent $2.5 billion (in today's dollars) to build a north-south railway from the Caspian Sea to the Persian Gulf, with a small connector route to Basra. The route of the Trans-Iranian Railway, like the rail station, seemed frivolous at the time, but the times would be changing.

Like so many other twentieth-century Middle Eastern potentates, Reza Shah's political power was fueled by oil revenue. The British had struck the first oil deal with Iran in 1901. When Reza took the throne, the British-controlled Anglo-Iranian Oil Company (originally Anglo-Persian) was a major player on the world market, and essentially the only player in the third largest oil-producing nation in the world. The Soviets, meanwhile, had inherited oil-rich Azerbaijan, on Iran's northwest frontier, from the Russian Empire.

Iran's oil gave it money and a place on the strategic map, but it also tied Reza's kingdom to the British, for whom the Iranian government had harbored an institutional disdain since the nineteenth century.

It would have been easy to have turned to the British technocrats who were active throughout the Middle East, but to assert Iran's independence, Reza and his predecessors looked elsewhere for Western technical advisors. Reza pragmatically retained as finance minister a Johns Hopkins–educated American named Arthur Chester Millspaugh, late of the U.S.

State Department's Office of the Foreign Trade. Millspaugh arrived at the end of 1922, found the Iranian treasury as dry as the drifting pumice of its deserts and rolled up his sleeves. He stayed on for more than four years, balancing the budget, managing oil revenue, reforming taxation and saving Reza's government from its spendthrift ways. He might have stayed longer had he not gotten into a squabble with Reza over the military budget in 1927, but he would be back.

Meanwhile, however, the foreign power to which Reza had turned most eagerly was Germany, which had been very much involved in the Middle East since the nineteenth century.

After his well-received tour of the Middle East in 1898, there were even rumors that Kaiser Wilhelm II had converted to Islam. Though unfounded, the rumors played into German ambitions in the region. The Berlin-to-Baghdad Railway, a favorite conceptual project of the Kaiser before World War I, was seen as a contributing cause of that war by intruding into a British sphere of influence with a continuous corridor from the heart of Germany to the Persian Gulf, with a line to Tehran. In 1907, the British had also complained loudly when the Hamburg-Amerika Line challenged their seagoing monopoly by initiating regular freight and passenger service from Germany to the Persian Gulf.

George Lenczowski, who was on the staff of the Polish Embassy in Tehran during World War II, writes that "the resentment against British and Russian imperialism was exploited by German diplomacy. Consequently, a large part of the Majlis [the Majlis-i Shaura-yi Milli, Iran's parliament], including its President, became pro-German. The same had been true of a number of important ministers in the cabinets that preceded the First World War. A German school was founded in Tehran, offering excellent education to the sons of the most prominent Iranian families, who not infrequently continued their higher studies at German universities."

For his exploits as a saboteur and guerilla leader during the Great War, the world remembers T. E. Lawrence as "Lawrence of Arabia." However, for many years after World War I, he was no better known throughout the Middle East—nor more highly regarded among many Iranian factions—than Wilhelm Wassmuss, known as "Wassmuss of Persia."

Posted as vice-consul in Bushehr, Wassmuss had thoroughly immersed himself in Iranian language and culture to the extent that he was ideally suited for covert operations against British interests after 1914. He was at least as successful as Lawrence in fomenting tribal insurrections, and he ran a network of agents that extended into Afghanistan and India.

Lenczowski recalls that "by extraordinary feats of energy and shrewdness he managed to provoke a rebellion of Tangistani tribes in the south, to enter into alliance with the powerful tribe of Qashqais in Fars, and to win over a number of traditionally pro-British Bakhtiari chieftains.... Wassmuss, leading a force of tribal warriors, attacked Bushehr and immobilized in this port British Resident Sir Percy Cox and a force of eight hundred Indian troops.... The British, in order to protect their oilfields and pipe lines in Khuzestan, were compelled to dispatch forces to southern Iran. The result was a considerable weakening of their offensive in Mesopotamia, and in April, 1916, General Townshend and his 12,000 troops had to surrender to the Turks at Kut el-Amara."

After World War I, the Germans returned to Iran. As the historian T. H. Vail Motter writes, "On they came, first under the Weimar Republic, then under Hitler, advising in education, lending technical skill, building docks, roads, and parts of the railway ... lecturing, giving parties, organizing Boy Scouts, and generally spreading the Germanic gospel as Kaiser Wilhelm had done in the nineties."

Thanks to Reza's fondness for Germany, the Reich became Iran's leading international trading partner in the 1930s. Lenczowski reports that Germany's share of Iranian foreign trade increased from 8 percent in 1932 to 45.5 percent by 1940. Iran imported 80 percent of its industrial machinery from Germany and exported 60 percent of its cotton and 90 percent of its exported wool to Germany. Most of the imported aniline dye that was used in the making of Persian carpets came from Germany, especially from the great I. G. Farben, the largest chemical company in the world.

German engineers had played an important role in Reza's railway, and provided much of its rolling stock. Many of the automobiles on Iranian streets were German. The German airline Junkers Luftverkehr AG was active in Iran in the 1920s, and in 1937 Deutsche Luft Hansa (predecessor of today's Lufthansa) inaugurated flights from Tehran to Berlin via Baghdad, Damascus, and Athens.

Like many prominent Iranians, Reza shared Hitler's obsessive fascination with being ethnically Aryan. Reza exchanged autographed photos and good wishes with Adolf Hitler, whose minions actively reminded the Iranians that both the German and Iranian ethnicities were Aryans in a world of inferior races. Indeed, the term "Iran" has its roots in the Sanskrit "*arya*," and in turn the old Indo-Iranian "*Airyanem Vaejah*," which is roughly translated as "Home of the Aryans." The ethnic Iranian people were proud to consider themselves ethnically Aryan, and distinct from their Semitic neighbors, the Arabs and Jews. Reza went so far as to inform the League of Nations and all countries with embassies in Tehran that herewith Persia should be called "Iran" as it was internally.

In 1935, Nazi Germany enacted the Nürnberger Gesetze (Nuremberg Laws) formally integrating institutional anti-Semitism into the German legal code. A year later, additional laws were enacted which formally recognized Iranians as Aryans under the Nazi definition. The German chancellor was referred to respectfully in Iran as "Hitler Shah" or "Emperor Hitler."

In 1954, *Name-ye Iran-e Bastan* (*The International Journal of Ancient Iranian Studies*) observed that in the 1930s, Hitler had been considered "one of the greatest men in the world ... the sign of Aryan triumph (swastika) is everywhere Aryan and respectable, be it on ceramics of Isfahan's Masjid-e Shah or on the column of Darvazeh Dovlat in Tehran; or be it placed on the flag of Germany or embellishing the arm of Hitler. From ancient times the Black dress has been an exclusive property of the Iranic race."

George Lenczowski, who was in Iran at the time, writes that "great use was made of the Aryan legend to encourage friendship between both nations. The adoption of the swastika as a symbol of the Nazi Party was interpreted as pointing to the spiritual unity between the Aryans of the north and the nation of Zoroaster. The German architects who constructed the railway station in Tehran adorned its ceiling with a discreet yet clearly recognized pattern of swastikas. After the visit to Tehran in 1937 [of] Professor Fritz Hoger, of the Nordic Academy of Arts in Berlin, Iranian architecture fell under considerable German influence."

Lenczowski adds that Alfred Rosenberg, the chief ideological overseer and official racial theorist of the Third Reich sent Reza "a collection of books called the German Scientific Library, composed of 7,500 volumes. These carefully selected books were destined to convince Iranian readers of the cultural mission of Germany in the East and of the kinship between the National Socialist Reich and the 'Aryan culture' of Iran."

In the pragmatic spirit of backing a winner, it was easy for Reza Shah to fall in with the Third Reich. In 1940, the Germans conquered most of Western Europe in a couple of months, and it was generally perceived that Great Britain had only narrowly survived defeat by the Germans.

If there was any European power whose star was rising across the Middle East, it was certainly Germany. Through its domination of Vichy France, the Reich had de facto control of Morocco, Algeria, Tunisia, Lebanon, and Syria. The French had given the German Luftwaffe the use of a string of air bases across Syria. In early 1941 the German Afrika Korps intervened in Libya, an Italian colony, and was pressing the British hard in a drive on Cairo and the Suez Canal. Encouraged by Germany's successes in North Africa and the defeat of the British in Greece in April 1941, there was a tide of pro-German sentiment throughout the Middle East. Iraq, a British mandate after the fall of the Ottoman Empire in World War I and an independent monarchy since 1932, experienced a coup in April

1941, led by the pro-German Rashid Ali al-Gaylani and supported by German airpower based in Syria. Rashid Ali took control of Baghdad and the RAF base at nearby Habbaniya, while German paratroopers seized the oilfields and refineries at Mosul in northern Iraq. Had the Germans attacked with even part of the force they had just used to swallow Greece, Iraq would have been theirs. The British intervened in force with troops from India and Jordan, and it was quickly too late for Germany to gain the upper hand; but pro-German sentiment in Iraq remained strong.

Germany's friends across the region knew that as soon as the panzers of the Afrika Korps reached Suez, the Middle East would be part of the war. However, as they anxiously watched the battles in the desert west of Cairo, unexpected events occurred elswhere.

The end of Iran's isolation from the world at war came on June 22, 1941, with the great German invasion of the Soviet Union. Suddenly, the British and the Russians could no longer be played against one another. They were now on the same side in battles for their own existence.

The immense scale and swift success of the German operation, which swallowed an area the size of prewar Germany in two months, combined with the apparent ineffectiveness of the Soviet forces, led to thoughts previously unimaginable. The Soviets imagined that the German armed forces, the Wehrmacht, could potentially capture or destroy the oilfields of Azerbaijan, while the British pictured German agents using subversion to take control of the Anglo-Iranian Oil Company refinery at Abadan in Khuzestan that had pumped eight million tons of refined petroleum into the British war economy in 1940.

These factors, combined with the perceived influence of an active German espionage apparatus within Iran, meant that the land of Reza Shah was now neither remote nor a fastness. It was very relevant and very vulnerable.

Reza was tardy in recognizing the shifting sands of geopolitics after the German invasion of the Soviet Union on June 22. In diplomatic notes issued in August, the Soviets and the British insisted on an expulsion of German advisors and secret agents, but Reza ignored their demands, thinking it was the familiar diplomatic game of jostling for influence.

On the morning of August 25, Reza awoke to find that Iran's armed forces had been surprised by simultaneous air and ground attacks from the British and the Soviets. By the end of the day, the Abadan oil refinery was no longer "Anglo-Iranian"; British troops, crossing into Iran from Iraq, were in *full* control.

Reza had hoped for air support from his German friends, but the airfields in Vichy Syria that had been used by the Luftwaffe were now in British hands, and the nearest German airpower was in Crete.

Reza had built a 200,000-man military force, complete with Czech-made light tanks received from the Germans. However, just as he had built an impressive rail station without a rail line, he had built armed forces without a combat capability. As often happens with armies designed for parades and to address domestic disturbances, the nine Iranian divisions were incapable of meeting an invasion. Within four days, the Iranian navy had been sunk and the Iranian army was in complete collapse. On August 29, Reza Shah ordered his retreating army to stand down.

"When his parade army collapsed he made no effort to prevent disintegration," British Ambassador Sir Reader Bullard communicated to Foreign Secretary Anthony Eden. "Moreover he showed no consciousness of responsibility for the collapse of his pretentious military facade, or of recognition of the urgent need for reform: even after the occupation he one day beat the Minister of War and the Chief of Staff with his sword for putting up a scheme of which he disapproved, and then threw them into prison, and he would probably have had them executed if he had not had to abdicate."

His abdication did not come immediately. Reza spent three weeks trying to hold on to power, bringing in the widely respected elder statesman and former prime minister Mohammed Ali Furughi to be his new prime minister. It was not until September 16, when the Soviet army reached Tehran, that Reza finally abdicated. He escaped the capital along with a large number of upper crust residents who feared a Bolshevik bloodbath. Before he could leave the country, he was picked up by the British, who exiled him to house arrest in South Africa, where he died three years later.

The historian Ryszard Kapuscinski reports that the British handed Reza an ultimatum, asking, "Would His Highness kindly abdicate in favor of his son, the heir to the throne? We have a high opinion of him and will ensure his position. But His Highness should not think there is any other solution."

There was not, and Reza knew it.

As Reza's successor, the British—with the acquiescence of the Iranian Majlis—did install his twenty-two-year-old, Swiss-educated son, Crown Prince Mohammed Reza Pahlavi, who would reign until deposed by the Islamic revolution in 1979. Iranian historian Fakhreddin Azimi notes that the new Shah "enjoyed neither the backing of the Allies nor any sustained domestic support. There was, however, no viable alternative … Furughi had refused a reported Allied offer of heading a new regime in Iran, opting instead to avoid complications and subscribe to the letter of the constitution" and thus keep the monarchy in place.

Realizing that a new rule book had been issued for the game he had watched his father play, young Reza Mohammed immediately pledged his full support to the Allies, and they promised to withdraw their troops after the war. At the time, few in Iran believed that they would actually pull out.

An appropriate epitaph for the reign of Reza Shah was penned by Muhsin Sadr, his socialist one-time Justice Minister, who observed that "Reza Shah was forced out of the country neither by the threats of the Russians nor by the tricks of the British; it was his unbounded arrogance and the unbridgeable rift between him and the nation which resulted in his exile. His links with the nation had been severed to such an extent that when foreign troops took him away as a captive, the people not only showed no sorrow but rejoiced in his departure and congratulated each other."

The German-Iranian Nexus

The new young Shah Mohammed Reza Pahlavi would later gain the reputation of a tyrannical despot, but in 1941 he was more intimidated that intimidating. The Iranian Parliament, the Majlis, long marginalized by Reza Shah, relegated the new shah to a role more suited to a European constitutional monarch.

The first prime minister was Mohammed Ali Furughi, but he was succeeded six months later by Ali Soheili (a.k.a. Suhaili), who ruled through March 1944, except for the six-month term of the pro-American Ahmad Qavam between August 1942 and February 1943.

Iranian politics came to resemble a multi-headed hydra. It was difficult for the politically weak Shah Mohammad Reza Pahlavi, with a revolving door of politicians and the squabbling Majlis, to maintain the kind of control that Reza Shah had exerted over the country. In a series of 1942 memos to the Foreign Office and to Anthony Eden, British Ambassador Reader Bullard complained of Soheili's eagerness to take bribes, but admitted that he was "as good a prime minister as [we] could hope to get." Bullard once observed that the idealistic Furughi "believes in the power of reason, a commodity in small demand among the Deputies of the Majlis."

While Furughi sought reason, Soheili pocketed cash, Qavam bickered with the deputies, and they all grappled with periodic riots over the lack of bread—but the *real* power centers in Iran for the duration of the war were *not Iranian.*

The face of the British occupation, Sir Reader William Bullard, was the son of a dock worker in suburban London, spent two years at Queen's College, and entered the Consular Service in 1906 when he was twenty-one. He went abroad in 1920 as the British military governor of Iraq, and served as a consul in Saudi Arabia, Greece, and Ethiopia before going to the Soviet Union in 1930. He was transferred to Morocco in 1934, and in 1936 returned to Saudi Arabia as the British minister. He arrived in Tehran in 1939 as the British minister (the post was upgraded to ambassador in 1943). He knew the Middle East well and his years in Moscow and Leningrad would prove useful.

His opposite number at the Soviet Embassy across town was Andrei Andreyevich Smirnov. Like Bullard, he was a career diplomat, though his career had barely begun. Two decades younger than Bullard, Smirnov joined the Commissariat of Foreign Affairs in 1936. He had been posted as a junior diplomat to the Soviet Embassy in Berlin for a year when the Germans attacked the Soviet Union in June 1941, and was part of the trainload of diplomats allowed to leave the Reich under the cloak of diplomatic immunity. A week later, he was appointed as ambassador to Iran, where he was able to welcome the arrival of Soviet troops in September.

During the Soviet occupation, Ambassador Smirnov was aided by the Soviet-influenced Tudeh Party, the "Party of the Masses," which was formed in September 1941, two weeks after Reza Shah left the stage. Styling itself as a "liberal rather than a radical party," it was formed by many of the same people who had been involved in the Iranian Communist

Party, repressed and forbidden by Reza Shah, who were now being released from the prisons.

The American ambassador, Louis Goethe Dreyfus, had been born in Santa Barbara County, California, in 1889. The early years of his Foreign Service career were spent mainly in South America. During World War I, however, he had been a consular official in Berlin, Budapest, and Sofia. Iran was his first assignment in the Middle East. In 1940, the position of non-resident minister to Afghanistan was added to his portfolio.

When the British and the Soviets rolled into Tehran in September 1941, Dreyfus watched events as a neutral bystander, but after three months and the Japanese surprise attacks on Hawaii and the Philippines, he found himself representing a third occupying power. Within a very short time, the United States would become the largest single foreign influence in Iran, a circumstance that would prevail for nearly four decades.

Before the United States officially went to war against the Axis Powers in December, the Americans had already chosen sides. Under the Lend-Lease Act of March 1941, the United States was supplying Britain with war materiel on a deferred payment basis under the theory that supporting the British containment of Hitler's ambitions was preferable to actually entering the war.

When Germany invaded the Soviet Union, the Lend-Lease pipeline was extended to the Soviets, who were officially brought into the program in October 1941, though there were logistical challenges. Shipments of Lend-Lease supplies via cold-water ports such as Murmansk and Arkhangelsk on the Arctic Sea would be problematic as winter ice began to form.

The United States, however, was already preparing to ship Lend-Lease supplies to the British forces in the Middle East via the Persian Gulf; so why not add a supply line into the Soviet Union via the Persian Gulf as well? The Trans-Iranian Railway, now part of Iranian State Railways, which had seemed pointless when Reza Shah had built it, was suddenly of great strategic importance—albeit not to Iran. It ran from the warm water port of Bandar Shaphur to near the Soviet border.

While the Soviets and British had invaded Iran with combat troops, the U.S. Army invaded Iran with engineers. The Military Iranian Mission was formed in September and redesignated as the Persian Gulf Service Command (PGSC) the following summer. In October 1942, under the PGSC umbrella, a U.S. Army Military Railway Service contingent commanded by Colonel Paul Yount took over operations of the Trans-Iranian Railway from the British who had seized Iranian State Railways in 1941.

Meanwhile, the PGSC (later shortened to Persian Gulf Command) proceeded with a massive bridge, highway and rail line construction and improvement program that oversaw the development of what became known as the Persian Corridor. In November-December 1941, a monthly average of 6,000 tons of supplies was delivered to the Soviets, but by the spring the monthly average had grown ten-fold.

Major General Donald Connolly assumed command of the operations in October 1942, taking over from Colonel Raymond Wheeler, former head engineer of the Panama Canal and an expert in rail and highway operations. From his headquarters at Tehran, Connolly commanded an organization comprised of 30,000 American troops and nearly that many Iranian workers.

It was a logistical challenge for Connolly not only to do his job but also to take care of his troops. Lieutenant William Rigdon, who later traveled to Iran with President Roosevelt, noted that "our forces here bring in all of their foodstuffs. Nothing is bought locally. This is done because of the extreme scarcity of foodstuffs in Iran and consequently, in order not to deprive the Iranians of what little there is."

The American invasion of Iran, of which the U.S. Army Corps of Engineers was the most visible manifestation, included a stream of technical and bureaucratic advisors who flooded into Mohammed Reza Pahlavi's government. Arthur Chester Millspaugh, who had balanced Reza Shah's bank balance as his minister of finance in the 1920s, was invited back.

Historian Vail Motter recalled that the Majlis "empowered Millspaugh to establish or work toward rigid governmental regulation of grain collection, prices, transport, and distribution; and to recommend enactment of a high, graduated income tax to spread the tax burden more fairly and to combat inflation and other war-born evils. The Majlis also authorized employment of up to sixty American specialists, and gave Millspaugh the power to direct the government's entire financial program."

Granted the title of "Administrator General of Finances of Iran," Millspaugh took to his task with single-minded determination, but with the weary resignation of a pessimist. In his 1946 book *Americans in Persia*, Millspaugh wrote that even after the war "Persia cannot be left to herself, even if the Russians were to keep their hands off politically.... Persia has never yet proved its capacity for independent self-government."

Other American experts were brought in as advisors to the petroleum industry, or to improve agricultural education, and Yanks in the Ministry of Public Health helped to beat a typhus epidemic. And then there were the cops.

The Persian Corridor cut through Iranian territory that was essentially lawless since the fall of Reza Shah. The Iranian gendarmerie, the national police force that traditionally held things together, was a rudderless crew, rapidly unraveling and in urgent need of someone who could ravel it up again. The job of taking charge of the gendarmerie and taming this wild frontier was given to U.S. Army Major General Herbert Norman Schwarzkopf. He arrived in Tehran on August 29, 1942, one day after his forty-seventh birthday, surrounded by a handpicked team that included Lieutenant Colonel Philip Boone and Captain William Preston.

A West Point-educated veteran of the First World War and the first chief of the New Jersey State Police, Schwarzkopf had made his reputation in the Roaring Twenties by launching a full-scale war on Al Capone wannabes in the Garden State, and became a national icon in 1932 when he arrested Bruno Hauptmann for the kidnapping of Charles Lindbergh's twenty-month-old son.

Even after a squabble with New Jersey Governor Harold Hoffman returned him to the private sector, Schwarzkopf landed on his feet as the narrator of the *Gang Busters* radio show on CBS. As his son General Norman Schwarzkopf Jr., the future hero of Desert Storm, later recalled, his father earned enough from doing the show to buy the Green House, a small mansion in Lawrenceville, New Jersey, hire a maid, and send the kids to private school.

In the summer of 1942, the chief of staff of the U.S. Army summoned the Crime Buster. "From my point of view as a seven-year-old, all I knew was that my dad had gone to Washington to meet with a guy named George Marshall," Norman Jr. recalled in his memoirs. "After he'd been gone a couple of days the telephone rang and he told Mom the news. [She] called us together and announced Pop was going to Tehran. We had no idea where that was, so she got out the globe and we started searching. It seemed as if we spun it a great distance. Suddenly Ruth Ann jabbed her finger down and said, 'Here.' It was halfway around the world! Mom turned to me and explained that Pop was about to travel to an exotic, magical, faraway place, the land of the Thousand-and-One Nights, where people wore long robes and carried knives in their belts and rode camels across the desert. I'm sure she knew all too well what could happen if the Wehrmacht attacked across the Caucasus, but she didn't talk about that. I still hadn't made the connection that this was war and that my father might get killed. So his leaving was no big tragedy. He was going off for a long time. Well, what was a long time? He was gone all week long anyhow. That was already a long time. Nobody expressed it to me in terms of months and years."

It *would* be years.

Secretary of State Cordell Hull cabled Ambassador Dreyfus on August 18, 1942, that having a high-profile crime fighter like Schwarzkopf running the Iranian gendarmerie "would be most helpful in strengthening our position in Iran at the present time and in building a firm foundation for future relations.... It would also place us in a position to observe and control any movement within the [Iranian] Army tending toward its use as a fifth column in the event of threatened Axis invasion."

A German invasion of Iran was a very real possibility.

As Vail Motter points out, "In August the British informed Iran that, should the Germans reach Astrakhan on the Caspian delta of the Volga below Stalingrad, Tehran would probably be bombed. The Iranian Government, aware of the rising restlessness of the people, applied to the Allies to declare Tehran an open city. In Washington, conferees of the State and War Departments agreed to face the possibility that within three or four months, possibly less, a large part of the Middle East, specifically Iran, Iraq, and Palestine, would be under enemy occupation. It was further agreed that every effort should be made to save the Persian Corridor supply route, as an alternative to Murmansk and Archangel and as providing access to the Caucasus for military action and a base for air operations against the Balkans and German-occupied southern Russia."

At the start of the Second World War, the German ambassador to Iran was Erwin Ettel. A preacher's son, born in Cologne, he had served in the Imperial German Navy before World War I and in the Army during the war. He was an early devotee of Hitler, joining the Nazi Party in 1924. In 1925, Ettel worked in Iran as head of air cargo operations for the airline Junkers Luftverkehr AG—later part of Deutsche Luft Hansa. He eventually worked in South America for the airline Sociedad Colombo Alemana de Transporte Aéreo (SCADTA), the Colombian-German Air Transport Society, while spending his spare time as the Nazi Party boss within the German expat community in Colombia. He joined the Foreign Service in 1936, and served as secretary of the German Embassy in Rome before moving to Tehran in 1939.

In the words of Bernhardt Schulze-Holthus, an Abwehr officer who operated in Iran under the cover of being the German vice-consul in

Tabriz, Ettel was "a small, sinewy man with sharp features that spoke of energy and a certain amount of brutality [who] worked in a vast pompously furnished room, from whose window was a park planted with firs.... In the Foreign Office he was looked upon as a hard and dangerous man, a sort of fighting cockroach which attacks even stronger opponents quite ruthlessly and defeats them by the vehemence of its attacks."

Reza Shah and the German diplomat shared a disdain for the world's Jewry, and Reza gave Ettel a forum to speak his mind against the Jews and the British.

Matthias Küntzel, in "From Goebbels to Ahmadinejad," a 2010 article in *Tribune zum Verständnis des Judentums*, quotes a radio broadcast that Ettel made in which he said "a clear way of working out of Mohammed's struggle against the Jews in this age would be ... connecting the British and the Jews, this would be extraordinarily effective anti-Semitic propaganda among the Shiite Iranian people."

Until October 1941, Ettel reigned as the prince of the Tehran diplomatic corps. When the Allied tanks arrived and Reza Shah departed, however, he became persona non grata. An order was issued for the round-up and internment of the German men living in Iran; women, children and embassy personnel with diplomatic passports, such as Ettel and his staff, would be allowed to leave Iran via neutral Turkey.

There are varying estimates of the number of Germans in Iran in the fall of 1941. The two most widely cited sources are the still-extant Tehran daily newspaper *Ettelaat*, which gave the number as being no more than 690 in its July 4, 1941, issue, and an estimate of 2,000, found in a May 1, 1940, memo to Reader Bullard from A. K. S. Lambton, the Persian-speaking press attaché at the British legation in Tehran. At the time, Lambton reckoned there were 2,590 British nationals in Iran.

Germans surrendering to the British were luckier than those snagged in the Soviet dragnet, ending up in Australia rather than Siberia. An unknown number of German agents went underground, aided by numerous pro-German factions within Iran, including those loyal to Majlis

Deputy Habibullah Nobakht and to the Melliyun-I-Iran, the nationalist underground that opposed the Allied occupation and looked forward to the eventual arrival of the German armies that were expected to sweep through the Soviet Union to the oilfields of Azerbaijan and then into Iran. In these efforts, the Melliyun had the support of General Fazlollah Zahedi, an Iranian Army corps commander who was an old friend of Reza Shah and had once led his secret police.

As the German agents scrambled to make themselves scarce, Erwin Ettel departed Iran in style, shielded by his diplomatic passport and confident that he would soon return. Joachim von Ribbentrop, Germany's foreign minister and Ettel's boss, had already hinted that he would serve as military governor—when Germany occupied the Middle East.

Spy vs. Spy

To defend its interests in the shadowy global war of spy versus spy, the United Kingdom operated a complex web of intelligence services centering on the Secret Intelligence Service (SIS), an entity dating back to 1909, but not officially acknowledged until 1994, which contains and is often considered synonymous with the Directorate of Military Intelligence Section 6 (MI6). The latter is distinguished from the Security Service, or MI5, which deals with domestic counter-intelligence operations.

Distinct from the SIS was the super-secret Special Operations Executive (SOE), organized under the Ministry of Economic Warfare in 1940 and active during World War II. The SOE's agents called themselves "Baker Street Irregulars" because SOE's headquarters was at Norgeby House on Baker Street in London. The "professionals" in the SIS and MI6 had a different handle for the SOE. They called it the "Ministry of Ungentlemanly Warfare" because the SOE mandate included not only espionage but also sabotage and assassination.

British military *counter*intelligence was the bailiwick of MI5, which extended its reach overseas during World War II, with numerous subagencies, including the Security Intelligence Middle East (SIME), which was led by Brigadier General Raymond Munsell and headquartered at the Middle East Command in Cairo, with branch operations in Baghdad and Tehran.

With their sphere of influence stretching across the Middle East from Egypt to India for more than a century, British intelligence operatives had always kept an ear to the ground in Iran. But after the defeat and occupation of Iran in September 1941, the principal British strategic interest in occupied Iran was in the oil that flowed from the wells and refineries of the Anglo-Iranian Oil Company. Otherwise, it was still seen as a backwater compared to pressing military engagements in the Mediterranean where German armies were on the move. The principal British strategic interest in occupied Iran was in the oil that flowed from the wells and refineries of the Anglo-Iranian Oil Company. In September 1942, with this in mind, the British created a new Persia and Iraq Command, split off from their Middle East Command and led by General Sir Maitland "Jumbo" Wilson. Its headquarters were in Baghdad, though Wilson's chief of staff, Major General Joseph Baillon, spent part of his time in Tehran.

In the United States, the intelligence apparatus, such as it was, came into World War II still operating under the principle articulated in 1929 by Secretary of State Henry L. Stimson, who famously said that "gentlemen don't read other gentlemen's mail." Fast forward to 1941, Stimson was back in government as Secretary of War, and American military and diplomatic intelligence was still an oxymoron.

The U.S. Army and U.S. Navy, serious rivals under the best of circumstances, each operated their own completely separate intelligence services and considered it a matter of pride *not* to cooperate. The Military Intelligence Division (MID) and the Office of Naval Intelligence (ONI) were both underbudgeted, understaffed—the MID had fewer than twenty officers— and concerned mainly with compiling statistics on rival armies and navies. Meanwhile, the U.S. Army's Corps of Intelligence Police had only twenty total personnel—*none* of them officers—when it was optimistically reorganized a week after Pearl Harbor as the Counter Intelligence Corps (CIC).

Though the CIC had personnel attached to the U.S. Army Persian Gulf Command, the CIC's own official history notes that "The British were technically in control of the Middle East but had more to do than they could handle and were willing to have the assistance of the CIC. All information gained by the CIC was usually turned over to the British Intelligence for action. The CIC maintained a liaison officer with the British SIME at all times where he had access to all files."

It was not until the creation of the Office of Strategic Services (OSS) in June 1942 that the United States had an espionage organization that could undertake significant covert operations behind enemy lines. Frustrated by the bureaucracy and inefficiency within his own War and Navy Departments, President Franklin Roosevelt had called on William J. "Wild Bill" Donovan to form an outfit based on the British MI6. A New York attorney and retired infantry colonel—he earned a Medal of Honor in World War I—Donovan was a political rival of Roosevelt's but the president admired his no-nonsense approach to getting a job done.

Brought back into uniform as a general, Donovan recruited people— both men and women—from a broad spectrum of society, including Ivy League graduates and immigrants with special language skills, as well as both professional and amateur adventurers. As such, the OSS was similar in its image and activities to the British SOE. Indeed, despite the presence of "gentlemen" of the Ivy League upper crust, the OSS was as devoted to "ungentlemanly warfare" as their SOE equivalents.

The Soviet Union maintained an entirely different sort of intelligence apparatus, whose role was intimidation more than intelligence gathering; beating up suspects rather than opening their mail. The Narodny Kommissariat Vnutrennikh Del (People's Commissariat for Internal Affairs or NKVD) was a successor to a series of Soviet state security organizations going back to the revolution-era Cheka, and a predecessor of the Komitet Gosudarstvennoy Bezopasnosti (Committee for State Security or KGB).

Though the Red Army and the Kommisariat of Foreign Affairs each had their own intelligence organizations, the NKVD was the big dog of Soviet intelligence, respected and feared by all. The NKVD was headed by the sinister Lavrenty Pavlovich Beria. According to historian Simon Montefiore, Stalin once introduced Beria to Franklin Roosevelt as "our Himmler," which well summarizes his role and that of the NKVD. Not only did the NKVD concern itself with foreign and domestic intelligence, but it had also long been tasked by Stalin and Beria with carrying out targeted assassinations, mass executions of enemies of the state, reigns of terror, and it was the proprietor of the infamous gulag archipelago.

The NKVD carried on Russia's historic rivalry with the British in Iran, but with the ideological mandate of the Comintern (the Communist International), which Vladimir Lenin had created to foment worldwide revolution, to overthrow "the international bourgeoisie," and to create "an international Soviet republic." The capitalist and imperialist British were considered, ideologically, enemy number one of the Soviet Union. Though the Comintern was "officially" suspended in May 1943, its aims were still in place; and within Iran, the Communist Tudeh Party remained an agent of Soviet policy.

Rivaling the NKVD for brutality and the British services for complexity were the German clandestine services. Gradually, most of these were being consolidated under the black umbrella of the Schutzstaffel (SS), which was ruled by the ice-blooded Reichsführer Heinrich Himmler, who owns a place on every short list of the most sinister public figures of the twentieth century. Within his SS chain of command were the Geheime Staatspolizei (Secret State Police or Gestapo), which was a component of the Reichssicherheitshauptamt (Reich Main Security Office or RSHA).

In turn, the Gestapo was comprised of the Ordnungspolizei (Regular Police), Kriminalpolizei (Criminal Police), and Sicherheitspolizei (Security Police), which were known respectively as Orpo, Kripo, and Sipo. Though these sound almost comical, like a gaggle of missing Marx Brothers, there was nothing amusing about *any* part of the Gestapo.

Parallel to the RSHA within the SS, and later part of it, was the Sicherheitsdienst (Security Service or SD), commanded originally by the notorious Reinhard Heydrich, and later by Ernst Kaltenbrunner. Often characterized as an "SS inside the SS," the SD was responsible for both domestic and foreign intelligence, with the latter being handled through SD-Ausland, also known as Abteilung VI (Section VI) of the SD. The man in charge was young Oberführer (later Brigadeführer) Walther Friedrich Schellenberg, who had been a deputy to Himmler at the RSHA and a special SD covert operations man under Heydrich before taking command of SD-Ausland in 1942.

The principal rival of the SD was the Abwehr, the German *military* intelligence apparatus, which was part of the Wehrmacht and headed by Admiral Wilhelm Canaris. The Abwehr equivalents to SD-Ausland were its Amtsgruppe Ausland, the foreign espionage group, and its Abteilung I (Section I), which was tasked with intelligence collection, but functioned more as a counterintelligence organization.

Despite a cordial personal relationship between Canaris and Schellenberg—they often went riding together—the relationship of the Abwehr to the SD was characterized by intense competition and distrust. In contrast to the ardent Nazi leadership of the SD who kept an eye on internal subversion, Canaris was ambivalent to the Nazi Party—he later actively opposed Hitler—and concentrated exclusively on Germany's *external* enemies.

Heinz Höhne, a Canaris biographer and author of a postwar history of the SS, wrote that "there was, of course, no mistaking the steady self-aggrandizement of Himmler's complex organization. The Reichs-führer SS was welding his policemen, secret servicemen, bureaucrats, and soldiers into a separate state, a species of counterforce with a growing tendency towards independence of the party and government. Himmler controlled the police and security services, he was supreme arbiter of the regime's cultural and racial policy, his representatives were ensconced in industry and diplomacy, occupation authorities and administrative departments, his Waffen SS was developing into a serious rival of the Wehrmacht."

Both the Abwehr and SD-Ausland created their own separate "ministries of ungentlemanly warfare" that were roughly analogous to the British SOE and the American OSS. Their elite special operations units created for secret activities behind enemy lines were organized and based near one another in suburban Berlin.

The Abwehr's organization originated in Brandenburg in 1939 as the Lehr und Bau Kompanie zbV (zur besonderen Verwendung) 800, which translates as "Training and Construction Company for special use, number 800." It was soon redesignated as the Brandenburg Battalion, and grew into the Brandenburg Division by early 1943. Still headquartered at Brandenburg, the division's facilities incorporated the Quenzgut sabotage school, where most of operatives who later went into Iran had their training.

The parallel SD organization originated in 1942 in nearby Oranienburg as a subsidiary of SD-Ausland's Abteilung VI. It was known as Sonderlehrgang zbV Oranienburg, and became SS Sonderlehrgang zbV Friedenthal in 1943 when it moved a short distance to Friedenthal. The Sonderlehrgang, which translates literally as "Special Unit" or "Special Course," is effectively the equivalent of modern special forces.

In the Tehran of 1941, the rival German intelligence services were represented by Franz Mayr of the SD and Major Julius Bernhardt Schulze-Holthus of the Abwehr.

Mayr's handler in Berlin was a Bavarian attorney named Winifred Oberg, one of Schellenberg's "special" special agents. His role within the SS was to serve surreptitiously as that staple of espionage organizations, the spy who spies on fellow spies.

Oberg had joined the Nazi Party even before Hitler had brought it to power in 1933. He had worn the brown shirt of Ernst Röhm's Sturmabteilung (SA) during its ultimately failed internal power struggle with the black shirts of Heinrich Himmler's SS. He also shared the beefy SA leader's sexual preferences, and possibly his bed, though he was not nearly as openly homosexual as Röhm. When the SS prevailed decisively in the Night of the Long Knives in June 1934 and Röhm was executed, Oberg promptly switched his allegiance to the SS. Photographs of him with Röhm that resided in Schellenberg's personal safe *assured* Oberg's continued and ardent loyalty.

As a handler of agents in Iran, Sturmbannführer Oberg was tasked with becoming an expert on the Middle East, although he never learned Farsi, and, until Operation Long Jump, had come no closer to Iran than Turkey.

Mayr and fellow SD man Roman Gamotha arrived in Tehran in 1940, where Erwin Ettel arranged for them to be employed by the freight forwarder, Nouvelle Iran Express. Over the ensuing months, they gathered useful intelligence on airfields, roads, and the British-controlled oil industry in Khuzestan Province.

Schulze-Holthus came in February 1941, traveling across the still-neutral Soviet Union pretending to be Dr. Bruno Schulze from the Interior Ministry, en route to Iran to look at German technical schools. On his way, he stopped off in Baku, the heart of Soviet oil country, where he was escorted by an NKVD operative pretending to be an Intourist guide: a "fair-haired woman—to me she looked like a character from a nineteenth century novel in modern dress."

In Tehran, Schulze-Holthus made his way to the German Embassy, where he introduced himself to Ettel, the "ruthless fighting cockroach." Schulze-Holthus needed a cover job, and asked to be named German consul in Tabriz. The ambassador offered him a glass of schnapps and made him *vice* consul, insisting that he return to Germany and come back with his wife before taking up the post.

Having reported to Canaris in Berlin with a summary of the airfields, oilfields, and open fields suitable for mechanized warfare, the "vice consul" returned to Tabriz with Frau Schulze-Holthus in mid-May.

Schulze-Holthus's first local contact in Iran was with a wealthy Armenian industrialist named Ahmad Asadi, who represented a German firm, and who provided the German newcomer with an overview of the Iranian perspective on meddling outsiders.

"You must understand the situation in this land properly," Asadi explained. "For decades we have been living in a high-tension field of international politics between Russia and England. The Russians have exploited our earlier weaknesses and taken the Caucasus from us. Azerbaijan on the other side of the frontier, for a Nationalist Persian, corresponds to Alsace-Lorraine for a German. The British! Have you ever watched how they strut about here in their khaki uniforms? And even when they're in mufti, in their pith helmets. . . . The sahibs, the white lords who look upon us as colonials and treat us with unbearable arrogance. What remains to us then, except to play the one off against the other? The Russians against the British and vice versa. But today we are expecting a great deal from a third power, which can be either Germany or the United States. In any case, a power which is ready to treat us fairly on a basis of equality."

Another contact was the Tabriz police chief, Major Wasiri, who would play a key role in Schulze-Holthus's coming adventures, and whose son was a leader within the Melliyun-I-Iran underground. For a few weeks, it was a pleasant routine, with the Schulze-Holthuses hosting dinner parties for German expats and friendly locals, while gathering intelligence from Asadi and Wasiri, and sending it via coded wireless transmissions to Berlin.

On June 22, 1941, everything changed with Operation Barbarossa, the German invasion of the Soviet Union. Suddenly the Soviets were on the same side as the British, who were putting pressure on Iran to distance itself from the Germans. Schulze-Holthus's network of informers brought him warnings of Soviet preparations for an incursion into Iran, which Schulze-Holthus did not take as seriously as he should have. When this actually happened in August, it came as a surprise, as did the swiftness of the collapse of Reza Shah's defenses.

German nationals—including Mayr and Gamotha, the two SD men—began converging on the Tehran embassy, seeking diplomatic protection. As they watched the bombing raids from the roof of the building, Ettel was furiously burning sensitive documents, knowing they would soon have to abandon the city.

When Ettel announced he was going to use his diplomatic passport to escape with his staff via Turkey, Gamotha, who didn't speak Farsi, decided to go with him. Mayr announced that he would go underground in Tehran. Through an Armenian contact named Musa, he got a job as a gravedigger, where he was unlikely to be noticed.

Schulze-Holthus, meanwhile, decided that he and his wife would escape to Afghanistan, where they would continue their espionage activities. Wasiri, who thought this to be a good idea, provided them with a car and advice for the best route to the border.

Traffic, however, was blocked by a large convoy of vehicles, racing from the gates of the royal palace. Neither Reza Shah nor the Schulze-Holthuses escaped; both were arrested in Kerman, slipped away from their captors temporarily and then were nabbed again in Birjand. The Schulze-Holthuses' diplomatic passports were seized and they were interned at the former German summer embassy at Shimran, now under Swedish management. Wasiri helped them escape to a series of safe houses in Tehran.

Though their first inclination had been to operate separately, Mayr and Schulze-Holthus made contact early in 1942 on a darkened street corner, disguised as Iranians. They had promising news to share. Schulze-Holthus had learned from Wasiri that the Melliyun might back a coup putting the pro-German Habibullah Nobakht in the place of Prime Minister Mohammed Ali Furughi. There was little chance of this succeeding, under the Allied occupation, but it indicated how pro-German much of Iran was.

According to Schulze-Holthus, Mayr told him that he had met secretly with General Fazlollah Zahedi. Zahedi had said that "a great percentage of the Persian Army is ready to rise at a signal from us. At my audience I had the impression that Zahedi was not only speaking for himself, but that even higher authorities stood behind him. Probably the Minister of War and maybe the new Shah."

In his memoirs, Schulze-Holthus recalls that "Mayr paused as though to give me time to think over the importance of this news. It was really sensational, possibly one of the greatest successes that the secret diplomacy of the Third Reich had ever pulled off."

"I congratulate you," Schulze-Holthus told Mayr, as he tried to "stifle a trace of envy."

"Thank you," Mayr replied. "The difficulty is to bring this news safely to Berlin. I tried to broadcast a coded message to [the overseas wireless communications center near Berlin at] Gatow through the Japanese Embassy, but we could not get through. Nor did a courier succeed via Ankara, for the Russians have hermetically sealed the Western Frontier."

George Lenczowski, who was at the Polish embassy in Tehran at the same time, wrote in 1949 that Mayr found a "valuable ally" in the Japanese minister in Tehran, who "gave him five wireless transmitter sets, [but they] were of no use as long as he had no operators to handle them. Hence his efforts were centered on establishing liaison with Germany through Ankara. For this purpose he sent several couriers to Turkey. For a long time, however, none of them were able to reach their destination. One was even arrested by the British."

Lenczowski does not mention that one of the couriers was Frau Schulze-Holthus. She departed Tehran in March 1942 on a two month horseback journey to the Turkish border, disguised as an Iranian woman and accompanied by pro-German Iranians.

Mayr and Schulze-Holthus now saw their role in Iran as coordinating the disparate factions of the Iranian "resistance movement," into position to exploit the anticipated arrival of the German army. By all accounts, the pro-German elements assumed that it was only a matter of time before the Germans would slice through the Soviet Union and come in force to liberate Iran from the Allies. The first half of 1942 was a time of many victories for the Axis across the globe, and the German offensive against the Soviet Union was pushing ever closer to the Baku oilfields and the Iranian border.

Mayr worked directly with General Zahedi's forces, and as Lenczowski recalled, his "plans were modeled on the German invasion of Norway," in which the way for the German takeover was paved by the efforts of the Norwegian traitor Vidkun Quisling in 1940.

Ambassador Bullard found out about Zahedi's intrigue with the Germans, and reported it to Jumbo Wilson's headquarters in Baghdad. Wilson's team brought in Fitzroy Maclean to deal with the situation.

No narrative of World War II covert operations is complete without mention of Sir Fitzroy, though he made but one—albeit very dramatic—cameo appearance in Iran. One of the many alleged inspirations for Ian Fleming's James Bond, the aristocratic Fitzroy Maclean was a Cambridge-educated diplomat who resigned from the Diplomatic Service, enlisted in the British Army as a private, and retired with the rank of major general. Before the war, he had traveled extensively in Central Asia, from China's Xinjiang to Afghanistan and across the breadth of Soviet Central Asia. During the war, he specialized in leading covert operations behind enemy lines in North Africa and Yugoslavia.

When given the assignment to quietly neutralize the troublesome Iranian general, Maclean simply walked into Zahedi's office in Isfahan in a British general's uniform on the pretext of making a courtesy call and took him into custody at gunpoint. One of the biggest potential threats among the pro-German elements in Iran was defused without a shot being fired. It was one of the great early British victories in the sometimes deadly game of spy versus spy.

Tehran, the Nest of Intrigue

One of the best descriptions of wartime Tehran was penned by Bernhardt Schulze-Holthus who wrote in his memoirs that at its heart, the city was an "old town with a network of narrow alleys and the covered-in passages of the bazaars in whose magical twilight the riches of the land seem to be piled, as in an Aladdin's cave—barbaric carpets, miniature paintings, wonderful tarsia work of precious woods and the sparkling splendor of the silversmiths' craft. The life in this old town seems like the circulation of the blood in an old body at high pressure. It flows faster than in the smart streets of the government quarter with the palaces of the shahs and the ministers, more actively too than in the broad avenues of the new town which dates from 1900, with their broad two-storied houses set back from the road and shady alleys reminiscent of a Russian provincial town."

The "remote fastness" that John Gunther had seen in prewar Iran still described wartime Iran. British agent Sydney William "Bill" Morrell addressed this point most eloquently when he wrote of his time in-country that "ten months in Iran gave you a feeling of complete isolation from the world. No other capital was so completely cut off from the war, except perhaps Lhasa in Tibet."

Born in Lancashire, Morrell had started his career in 1930 as a reporter for the *Manchester Daily Herald*, and went on to work as a foreign correspondent for London's *Daily Mirror* and *Daily Express* in Vienna, Prague, and Budapest. He had been recruited into the Secret Intelligence Service by his boss, the high-profile media tycoon—and friend and ally of Winston Churchill—Lord Beaverbrook. Morrell was married to Beaverbrook's secretary. Before Morrell's "exile" to Tehran, he had worked with the British Security Coordination (BSC) organization, which conducted counterespionage and propaganda activities for the British Empire in North and South America. Britain's Secret Intelligence Service had set up the BSC in New York City in 1940 with the knowledge of the United States government. He was sent to Tehran ostensibly to edit a newspaper for British personnel.

Tehran was a definite change of pace. Morrell described it as a people "living partly on memories of a civilization of four thousand years ago and partly on participation in modern commerce, with a shrewdness that would set the West agape: envying, imitating, inwardly despising Western standards of culture." It was a long, long way from New York or London, and a long way from the teeming centers of intelligence service excitement. And it was a long way from Cairo—where Morrell's handlers at Security Intelligence Middle East were based. Yet as isolated as Tehran might seem, it was a hub of international intrigue with an underworld of double and even triple agents.

One such double agent was Ernst Merser, whose house on fashionable Kakh Street became a safe house that would be used by members of all sides during Operation Long Jump. An accountant and financial advisor by trade, Merser was born in Switzerland, attended the Institut Le Rosey, the famous Swiss boarding school in Vaud, and began his career in a country where banking and intricate financial matters are the national industry.

Fluent in French, Italian, and English, as well as German, Merser was much in demand during the 1930s as a consultant to international companies. International espionage services also had him in high demand, and he had provided information to the Italians, the Austrians, and Switzerland's own intelligence service, the Schweizer Nachrichtendienst (ND), which was then little more than an underfunded newspaper clipping service.

In 1938, while Merser was on a business trip to Berlin, he was contacted by Martin Mohnke, the director of an aniline dye company called Freudenreich & Sohn. It turned out that director Mohnke was actually Hauptman Mohnke, and Freuedenreich & Sohn was actually an Abwehr front organization. Since Germany had absorbed Austria into the Reich a few months earlier, Merser's Austrian file had been among the mountain of documents turned over to the Abwehr. Merser was told that the agencies for whom he had freelanced were amateurish operations compared to the Abwehr, and was asked to start working for a *serious* service of a great power. Merser agreed, with his consulting work continuing to serve as a cover for his work in espionage. After a year in Hungary, Merser returned to Switzerland.

The Abwehr apparently did not know that Merser had already been recruited by the British. Merser was an Anglophile, both of his grandmothers were British, and he had long had an interest in working with British intelligence. He joined the SOE, the "Baker Street Irregulars," after a meeting with W. Somerset Maugham at the home of mutual friends on Lake Geneva. Maugham, the international best-selling author of such works as *The Razor's Edge* and *Of Human Bondage*, had worked intermittently as an agent of British intelligence since 1915. After this auspicious beginning of his career as a double agent, Merser relocated to Tehran late in 1940, where he acted as a representative of several European firms.

After the Anglo-Soviet occupation and the expulsion of German nationals, the Abwehr regarded Merser, a Swiss citizen, as a prize asset. A prosperous businessman, he gave to charity and turned up at all the right parties; everyone loved the neutral Swiss, and women too seemed to love Merser, though he was short and stocky.

While Schulze-Holthus and other Abwehr men went underground, Merser's cover as a neutral businessman allowed him to move about in the sunshine, and to be seen regularly at the places frequented by the elite of Iranian society and the upper crust of the international community. One such place was the Cafe Continental, where Merser dined regularly with a young British intelligence officer named Percy Downward. Downward served in the SOE's covert propaganda section, originally called SO.1 and associated with the Political Warfare Executive of the Foreign Office, whose agents operated under journalistic cover. Percy is not to be confused with Jim Downward, who worked for the U.S. Office of War Information in Tehran at the same time.

Hungarian journalist Laslo Havas interviewed Percy Downward and Ernst Merser in the 1960s and had access to Merser's unpublished writings about his time in Iran. He recalled that "Percy Downward trusted Ernst Merser absolutely. He knew that Merser's connection with the intelligence services of various countries, including the Abwehr, had been established on direct orders from British Intelligence. It happened sometimes that a double agent was 'turned around' by the organization in which his original employers had planted him, but in Merser's case there was not the slightest cause for suspicion."

In an August 13, 1943, memo to Walther Schellenberg, Oberst Georg Alexander Hansen, the chief of Abwehr's Abteilung I counterintelligence component, wrote that Merser "carried on the most effective work that could be carried on in the given, and extremely difficult, situation, and the activities of his group can serve as an example to other, much larger groups working under much more favorable conditions."

The astute and cosmopolitan double agent was highly regarded by both of his masters.

The Tehran of Merser and Downward, and of Mayr and Schulze-Holthus, was a crowded place. Before the war, it had been a city of a quarter million, but with the influx of refugees, the population had more than doubled by 1943. Inflation was rampant. A pound of butter cost more than $25 in today's dollars and a modest apartment rented for more than $10,000 a month. Among the refugees pouring into Iran were Poles. This is important to mention here, because two of these Polish refugees were later to play roles in the Operation Long Jump saga.

After the Soviet occupation of eastern Poland in 1939, at least 320,000 Polish citizens, according to the estimates of Poland's Institute of National Remembrance, were deported to the Soviet gulag archipelago. The Red Army and the NKVD interned at least another 100,000 Polish prisoners of war. Of these, 14,000 were murdered in the spring of 1940 by the NKVD in the infamous Katyn Massacre.

In March 1942, under pressure from the German invasion, the Soviets released about 120,000 Poles from the gulags and deported them to Iran.

Many of the released Polish POWs were later organized by General Wladyslaw Anders into the II Polish Corps, which was attached to the British Eighth Army. About 70,000 deported Polish civilians remained in Tehran or in internment camps set up by the British elsewhere in Iran. Among these was Wanda Pollack, a young woman who would find herself as an unwitting pawn in the back alley intrigues of Tehran—and an unexpected part of Ernst Merser's life.

Wanda's own life was molded by unspeakable cruelty, a hell on earth that began on her seventeenth birthday in the fall of 1939. It was a week into the German occupation of Warsaw and Wanda had gotten hold of a bottle of vodka. When she awoke, the bottle was half empty and a kind, young German officer was stroking her long blonde hair. They drank together, finishing the vodka. He promised to marry her and take her to Switzerland. She told him that she was Jewish, and blacked out. When she awoke, the room was filled with Germans taking turns with her. She was eventually discarded. She fled to Pinsk where she was captured by Soviet troops who raped her as well. By the time she reached Siberia, she was starved and battered into a grotesque caricature of the girl she had once been.

A year later, she was in a refugee camp outside Tehran. Though she had escaped the gulags, her day-to-day existence was not a happy one. As Sydney Morrell wrote of what he witnessed, "in the best of surroundings, life in a refugee camp is degrading. The restrictive atmosphere, the deadly boredom of day following day in routine monotony, the restraints on movement outside the camp, the feeling of utter helplessness—all these factors combine to induce in the refugees a feeling of lassitude and despondency, a state of mind which is aided and abetted by conditions of life in the Middle East."

It was in the midst of this situation that someone from the Polish Red Cross asked Wanda if she would like to take a job as a housekeeper in the home of a Swiss businessman who wanted to help with the Polish refugee situation. He had two Iranian houseboys and a Russian cook, but he had room for a housekeeper. In March 1943, half a year short of turning twenty-one, Wanda found herself in an unimaginable world of expat elegance.

Ironically, it was through Wanda, who seemed—and very probably was—merely naive and unassuming, that Merser became entwined in several relationships that would become integral to his role in Operation Long Jump later in the year.

Franz Mayr was keeping a low profile in 1943, but he remained active. He divided his time between Isfahan and Tehran, though after Fitzroy Maclean abducted General Fazlollah Zahedi in Isfahan in late 1942, Mayr spent most of his time in the capital, using couriers to smuggle information out through Turkey. He continued to work with his contacts within the pro-German Melliyun-I-Iran underground and with pro-German politicians like Habibullah Nobakht. By most accounts, Mayr lived a nocturnal existence, always traveling in disguise and packing two automatic pistols.

It was not long after she came to live with Merser that Wanda Pollack met Franz Mayr. It was a casual meeting at a cafe. Wanda was the sort of woman, attractive but unpretentious, with whom men like to make small talk in cafes. They saw one another from time to time, but it is uncertain whether the German took a professional interest in her because he knew of her connection with Merser, or whether she was just a pretty smile and a little casual flirtation.

In May, when he found out about Wanda's connection to Mayr, Merser became nervous. Was Mayr using her to get to him, or was Wanda somehow involved with the German security police, the SD, and using Merser? He was, after all, a stringer for the Abwehr, who were rivals of the SD. Percy Downward had similar reservations about Wanda and told Merser that she had been observed taking money from Mayr. Downward insisted that Merser nudge his little Polish waif out of her comfortable nest on Kakh Street.

It was then that Merser realized that he cared for Wanda. It was not his intention at first that she should be anything more than just a member of his household staff. Indeed, he had been, and was, involved with any number of more sophisticated women. He thought of himself as her protector or older brother, and not, at least not *yet*, as a potential lover. Nevertheless, he succumbed to his feelings for Wanda. He ignored Downward and his own better judgment.

He knew, however, that he needed to confront her about Mayr and about their relationship. When he did so, she was more bewildered than evasive, and she told Merser everything. It was, Merser deduced, that she was genuinely naive. She had known men physically, hundreds of them, but she had virtually no experience in relationships with men. She still had the naïveté of an innocent teenager. She readily admitted that Mayr had given her money—to buy clothes, because he felt sorry for her—and in front of Merser she ripped up the bank notes. As the torn paper fluttered to the floor, she tearfully hugged her benefactor and pleaded with him not to kick her out.

He did not, and Wanda stopped seeing Mayr, but she continued to frequent the cafes, and to talk to strangers. One Iranian with whom she talked was Misbah Ebtehaj, not a stranger exactly because she had met him through Mayr. He was a practitioner of Pahlevani, an ancient Iranian mixed martial art, and was popular in the ring—or *zurkhaneh*—as well as with the Germans who saw successful Palavans as physically fit young Aryans. Ebtehaj was also part of Percy Downward's network of agents and informers, and he seemed to know everyone worth knowing.

One of the men Ebtehaj knew, and Downward knew about, was Mervyn Wollheim, an American expat who dabbled in archeology, wrote articles for obscure scientific journals, and was a fixture of the international set, turning up at the right parties and at serious card games. Among his friends was Khalil Chapat, who was on the faculty of the Lycée Française (French High School). The son of a French father and an Iranian mother who had lived most of his life in Beirut, Chapat was fluent in French, English, and Farsi.

In 1942, a Polish refugee appeared at the Lycée Française to ask Chapat for a job. Her real name is lost to history, though Laslo Havas, who interviewed her after the war under conditions of strict anonymity, called her Ida Kovalska, and so shall we. She was fluent in French and English and had studied, she claimed, at the Sorbonne in Paris. There were no job openings at the school, but Chapat invited her to leave the refugee camp and move into his house. He had imagined, as men do, an amorous liaison, but she emphatically refused such an arrangement. Eventually, they settled on a truce and became close friends.

Wanda Pollack met Ida Kovalska in the middle of July 1943. Wanda was shopping in the bazaar and having a difficult time making herself understood to a shopkeeper. Ida overheard, recognized Wanda's Polish accent, and intervened on her behalf. With this, the two gradually became good friends, and met occasionally for lunch at those cafes patronized by the international set.

Wanda told Ida about Merser, which was not unusual. She told everyone about everything, as though she had nothing to hide. Being a trusting person, she had no secrets but one—and she shared it with Ida. Wanda told her new friend that she was in love with Ernst Merser. She admitted that she wanted to be in a loving relationship with a man, something that she had never experienced—but that her host was too much of a gentleman. Wanda explained that because Merser had failed to respond to her clumsy attempts at seduction, she feared that he did not like her.

Gradually, Ida brought Wanda into her own circle of friends, which included Chapat, Wollheim, and their American friend, Peter Ferguson.

Peter Ferguson was an American agent. The OSS sent him to Iran in 1943 to set up an intelligence network. The circumstances of his being there were almost incomprehensibly straight-forward by European standards. He had gotten his assignment simply because he had been to Tehran before—in 1942, as a footloose adventurer—and wanted to go back; and his job with the OSS had come the old fashioned way: his father had gone to school with Bill Donovan, and they were fellow Wall Street attorneys.

Ferguson had known Wollheim before the war, and through him, in 1942, he had met Khalil Chapat, and through him he met Ida Kovalska, with whom he fell in love. When he was rebuffed, he announced that he was returning to the United States and joining the army. He did make it home, no easy task in a world at war, and joined the OSS.

He returned to Tehran at the end of March 1943 on a USAAF C-47, flying out of Cairo on a routine Air Transport Command flight. He was every bit the stereotype of the OSS agent in the early days—an extroverted amateur, his pockets brimming with cash and his manner brimming with confidence. Lured into a card game on the eve of going overseas, he had lost most of the money which the OSS had given him to start building a network of agents, but as soon as he reached Tehran, he found another card game and won it all back—and more.

Ferguson defined and shaped his role as a secret agent as he had seen it done in the movies—up all night at clubs and card games with a glass of whiskey in his hand and a gun beneath his jacket. Ida Kovalska rounded out the picture as the unattainable *femme fatale* with whom Ferguson was still infatuated.

As part of his network of "agents," Ferguson recruited Wollheim and Chapat. Ida showed little enthusiasm, but to humor her would-be suitor, she agreed to be part of Ferguson's fledgling cabal.

"The British, Germans, and Russians considered it natural that the Americans, too, should have their own organization," Laslo Havas observed. Ferguson did nothing to hide the fact that the OSS was in town. "It did seem somewhat quaint, because it was vastly different from what one usually encountered in the espionage arena, but the general opinion was that the Americans obviously knew what they were doing when they employed such eccentric agents. They must have some good reason for it. Perhaps the Americans were deliberately acting [like] bohemians, were only pretending to be permanently drunk in order to lull the enemy's vigilance."

Time would show whether Ferguson was a worthy agent.

A Free Island in Occupied Persia

hile Ernst Mayr remained in urban environs, Bernhardt Schulze-Holthus had gone to live among the nomadic, pro-German Qashqai people, who lived in Iran's western provinces, especially in Fars and Khuzestan, where the oilfields were.

"A free island like this in occupied Persia could be of greatest strategic importance in the event of a German invasion," Schulze-Holthus wrote in his memoirs of the vast tract that was controlled by the Qashqai. "In politics it is always the realities that count and 20,000 armed nomads on the periphery of the oilfields was a reality."

Schulze-Holthus had been a houseguest at the sprawling Tehran compound of the pro-German politician Habibullah Nobakht when he received an invitation from Nasr Khan, the powerful leader of the Qashqai. Schulze-Holthus recalled that the unruly warlord, who had long been a thorn in the side of the Tehran government and the British, wanted the German as his "military adviser for the duration of the war."

And so the Abwehr man retired into the remote hinterlands, out of communication with Berlin, to organize the Qashqai for the arrival of the German armies that were expected to eventually liberate Iran—and its oilfields—from the Anglo-Soviet occupation. In the meantime, the Qashqai skirmished with British troops, Iranian government troops, and Norman Schwarzkopf's gendarmes.

Nasr Khan saw Schulze-Holthus as a potential latter-day "Wassmuss of Persia." Khan had actually met Wilhelm Wassmuss, when Khan's father had allowed the "German Lawrence" to stay in the family's tent for a time. Khan still had a Mauser rifle that Wassmuss had given him. The Qashqai remembered Wassmuss fondly, welcomed Schulze-Holthus as his spiritual successor, and fully expected that *this time* the war would end differently.

Gradually, though, Nasr Khan had grown impatient. By 1943, he and his German advisor had spent nearly two years together, and though the great German invasion of the Soviet Union was well into its second year, there were no signs of panzers thundering into Iran. The warlord took Schulze-Holthus aside.

"I must now ask you a question, and I must ask you to give me an absolutely honest answer," he said in a low voice, without looking at the man whom he had taken on as his German military advisor. "Do you think, that the outbreak of an armed rebellion in the Qashqai zone could hasten the German invasion? Or, to put it better, that such a rebellion could be the spark to set off the decision of the German Army Command to invade Persia at once?"

"I felt the weight of the decision which stood behind this question," Schulze-Holthus reflected in his memoirs. "It was a question of war or peace and like a *fata morgana* loomed before me the possibility of perhaps once more repeating Wassmuss' experiment, but in greater style. It was an intoxicating possibility and in the background gleamed temptingly the fame of Lawrence, the unique fame of a romantic adventurer in the cold, sober world of sly, political calculations.... It was a different matter if one accepted the premise that Nasr Khan's war would immediately call the

Germans into the country. But could I, one man alone, completely out of touch with Berlin, give such a promise with a clear conscience?"

"Your Highness," Schulze-Holthus replied, "I do not think that a local event such as the revolt of the Qashqais would alter the basic plans of the German General Staff."

This was *not* the answer which Nasr Khan wanted to hear, but it was the best that the "German Lawrence" had to offer. Schulze-Holthus was under deep cover and out of touch with Berlin, but he did realize that after the disastrous defeat and capture of the entire German Sixth Army at Stalingrad a few months earlier in January 1943, it was extremely unlikely that anyone would ever see panzers in Iran.

What Nasr Khan and his German military advisor did not know, but would soon learn, was that Walther Schellenberg and Ernst Kaltenbrunner *had* embraced the notion that the "free island in occupied Persia could be of greatest strategic importance," and SD-Ausland was taking steps to exploit the same sort of operations that Schulze-Holthus had undertaken essentially on his own initiative.

Schulze-Holthus did not know that Schellenberg's SD-Ausland had formed the Sonderlehrgang zbV Friedenthal special forces teams to undertake covert operations, nor that Schellenberg's imagination had been seduced by the notion of sustained operations by small teams operating behind enemy lines. His Unternehmen Franz (Operation Franz, also called Operation François) involved such special ops teams within Iran, and was built on the foundation of the earlier efforts of Franz Mayr and Roman Gamotha. It differed from Schulze-Holthus's activities insofar as it was to be organized and managed by Berlin, with ongoing communications between headquarters and the field, rather than having operatives completely on their own and out of touch with any form of command and control; there would be no going underground for months at a time.

Though Iran was the immediate target of Operation Franz, Schellenberg imagined similar operations under the noses of the Allies elsewhere in the Middle East, such as in Iraq and Syria. He envisaged, for instance, covert operations in British-administered Palestine, where Britain was already wrestling with rival Muslim and Zionist insurrectionists. The former had as their spiritual leader Mohammed Effendi Amin el-Husseini, the anti-British, anti-Jewish Grand Mufti of Jerusalem, who had met personally with Hitler to lobby for German support for a postwar all-Muslim Palestine.

Operation Franz was also loosely based on Schellenberg's ongoing Unternehmen Zeppelin in the Soviet Union. The idea behind Operation Zeppelin was to enlist captured Soviet troops who opposed Stalin, and put them into action behind enemy lines in Russia and against Soviet partisans who harried the occupying Germans. Among the hundreds of thousands of Soviet prisoners who had been taken by the Germans during two years of war were tens of thousands who despised the Man of Steel and communist rule and were willing to make common cause now with the Nazis.

Zeppelin had been initiated in 1942 with one unit assigned to each of the three Wehrmacht army groups, South, Center, and North, operating in the Soviet Union. As Schellenberg wrote in his memoirs, "these units, whose tasks were sabotage, political subversion, and the collection of information, were to be flown over the lines by special squadrons of the Luftwaffe along the entire length of the eastern front. A courier system across the front lines and secret wireless transmissions were to be their main means of communication. Most of the agents were dropped in places where they were able to shelter with friends. Some were equipped with bicycles with wireless batteries and transmitters built into the pedal mechanism, so that regular pedaling would ensure inconspicuous and smooth transmission. On one occasion an agent succeeded in reaching Vladivostok: with a Russian troop transport. There he observed and sent back full details of certain troop movements."

As Schellenberg noted, Operation Zeppelin used the advantage of the Soviet Union's vast scale against it. "The enormous size of Russia's territory enabled our agents to move about without hindrance," he wrote, "sometimes for months on end, although finally most of them were caught by the NKVD who, when the need arose, would mobilize a whole division near the front line, or detachments of guerilla fighters in the rear, in order to track our agents down."

Much to Schellenberg's chagrin, though, neither Himmler nor Hitler showed much enthusiasm for these covert operations or for expanding them as Schellenberg wanted. In his memoirs, he complained that his discussions with Himmler "were always met by the stereotyped answer: 'That's all very interesting—but your assignment is still as before—to furnish the Führer with information.'"

Meanwhile, there was an anti-communist former Red Army general who was trying to form an entire anti-Soviet Russian *army* under the auspices of the Wehrmacht. Lieutenant General Andrei Andreyevich Vlasov had heroically commanded the Soviet 37th Army near Kiev in the summer of 1941 and the 20th Army in a major counterattack in the defense of Moscow during the ensuing winter. He later led the 2nd Shock Army in a failed attempt to lift the siege of Leningrad, and had been captured in July 1942.

While in captivity, he met the Latvian-born German officer Hauptman Wilfried Strik-Strikfeldt, who was trying to form a whole legion of former Soviet troops to fight against Stalin. In Vlasov, Strik-Strikfeldt found the ideal leader for his anti-Bolshevik Russkaya Osvoboditel'naya Armiya (Russian Liberation Army).

"This form of co-operation suited me admirably," Schellenberg later recalled. "Certainly our Russian colleagues worked with an entirely different spirit now that they were fighting for their freedom and for a new Russia."

Again, Himmler and Hitler were skeptical. They expressed not only a lack of enthusiasm for Vlasov, but a nervous distrust. Schellenberg called it "a fundamental error that sprang from the arrogant determination not to give autonomy even to the smallest group, and from an unholy fear that

Vlasov might not be entirely sincere and might open an important sector of the front to a Russian breakthrough. There was also the fear of organized resistance in Germany, for with such a tremendous number of foreign workers, especially the millions of Soviet Russians employed in the Reich.... The best thing would have been to mount all these gentlemen on Cossack ponies and send them into battle ahead of Vlasov's army. This would have solved the problem once and for all."

Hitler and Himmler ultimately sanctioned the creation of such an entity with Vlasov as its leader—but for propaganda purposes, *not* as a combat organization.

While the tens of thousands who signed up for Vlasov's army never went into battle as a unit, they did provide a pool from which Schellenberg could choose a hundred men here or there to support Operation Zeppelin—and ultimately, Operation Long Jump as well. Zeppelin provided the logistical and operational template that would be invaluable in Operation Franz and Operation Long Jump.

A key figure in both of these would be the man whose name was to become synonymous with German covert special operations during World War II.

Hauptsturmführer Otto Skorzeny had, like Ernst Kaltenbrunner and Adolf Hitler himself, been born in Austria and had always believed in its merger into the same entity as Germany. In fact, Skorzeny and Kaltenbrunner had known one another years earlier as students in Graz. When the war started in 1939, Skorzeny, now an engineer, enlisted in the Luftwaffe, and was assigned to a communications unit when he was deemed—at age thirty-one—too old for flying.

In December 1939, he was selected as an officer candidate in the Waffen SS, the part of the SS organized for field combat operations. During the German invasions of France in 1940 and of the Soviet Union in 1941, he served with the unit which evolved into the 2nd SS Panzer Division, known as "Das Reich."

In April 1943, Skorzeny's Waffen SS career took him into the world of special operations and into the Sonderlehrgang special forces command, which was then making the move from Oranienburg to new, expanded facilities at Friedenthal. His first assignment was to take over Operation Franz, which was, as he explained in his memoirs, designed to "interrupt the supply lines far behind the enemy front and for that purpose foment revolts among the restless mountain tribes in Iran. Comparatively small parties of Germans were to supply them with arms and above all give them the necessary training and instruction. The orders of the German High Command would be transmitted to the instructors and the most important targets indicated."

Besides running an insurgency against the British, the priority was to disrupt the flow of Lend-Lease supplies into the Soviet Union via the Persian Corridor. "American war material had made a vital contribution to the stiffening of the eastern front," Skorzeny wrote. "I had never realized its immense importance until I was given the relevant figures. In the fire and fury of the crisis at the front we had not appreciated the full significance of America's entry into the war."

The Sonderlehrgang teams would be well trained and well prepared. As Skorzeny noted, "for several months 20 men of the Sonderlehrgang had been learning Persian from a native. To each group was attached a Persian, who was to take part in the operation."

The Sonderlehrgang commando teams would be inserted by air, brought in aboard big four-engine Junkers Ju 290 transports flown by the Luftwaffe's Kampfgeschwader 200, a wing that had been specifically created for long-range reconnaissance and special operations. Based on the Ju 90 commercial transport, the Ju 290 was a huge aircraft, ninety-four feet long, with a wingspan of nearly 138 feet and a range of more than 3,800 miles. For Operation Franz, they were operated out of bases in German-occupied Crimea.

Teams of five or six men, plus their equipment, were air-dropped by parachute. Daryacheh-ye Namak, a mainly dry salt lake about sixty miles northeast of the City of Qom, became a chief landing site. According to George Lenczowski, the first Operation Franz mission took place on

March 30, 1943, shortly before Skorzeny was involved, and was coordinated by Franz Mayr.

Though the Ju 290 had adequate range to reach Iran from neutral Turkey or German-occupied Crimea, this had to be balanced against payload capacity. "The weight of the equipment and petrol to be carried had to be calculated most accurately," Skorzeny recalled. "Only those who have actually planned such an expedition can appreciate how often we had to reconsider and revise the list of equipment, from weapons to food, clothes to ammunition, from explosives to presents for the tribal chiefs. I remember all the trouble we had to procure sporting rifles with silver inlay and Walther pistols decorated in gold, much coveted gifts" for tribal leaders with which the Germans wished to curry favor.

In an August 1943 wireless message to SD headquarters (quoted in the *Tehran Daily News* of March 16, 1945), Ernst Mayr explained optimistically that "Our aim would thus be the creation of an independent and neighboring war zone with the object of interrupting supplies and keeping the occupying troops busy."

Unlike Schulze-Holthus, who went among the tribal warlord as an advance man for panzer armies, the Franz teams came not to liberate Iran from the British and the Soviets, but merely to foment an insurgency that would tie down Allied troops. Even so, Operation Franz was too little, too late by at least a year.

In Spring 1943, British and Iranian troops made another attempt to quell the Qashqai uprising. But the Qashqai, who knew the lay of the land and who were skilled with small arms, kept their enemies at bay.

"Now that the plan to drive us into the desert has failed, the British are trying to achieve their object by different means," Nasr Khan told Schulze-Holthus at a tribal meeting. "I have news that the British agents are buying corn and rice from the peasants throughout the region. They pay the highest prices and if the peasants will not sell, they simply requisition them against a delivery note. The aim of this action is clear. What they cannot achieve with arms, they will try to achieve with the silver bullets of the Bank of England."

That wasn't the only bad news. Nasr Khan noted German reversals across many battlefronts, from North Africa to Stalingrad, which prompted Schulze-Holthus to respond.

"Your Highness has surprised me so much by his pessimistic outlook on Germany's position that I find it difficult to find words in reply," Schulze-Holthus said. "When he mentions Rommel's retreat in Africa, I must counter with another question. What was the object of the African campaign? Did not the German General Staff intend to tie down their enemies' forces on the African field until the European defense system was built up? And has this plan not succeeded? Didn't Rommel inflict grievous losses on the enemy.... Your Highness has dwelt on the events in Russia [including German defeat at Stalingrad]. Today Kharkov and Rostov are once more in German hands and we are on the eve of a new great offensive. Why should we surmise that this new German attack will have less chance than the former one?"

The tribes were doubtful.

In July, Nasr Khan had surprising news for Schulze-Holthus: "Four Germans were dropped in our region by parachute. They have brought gold and dynamite, together with a message from Hitler Shah to Nasr Khan."

"Where are they now?" Schulze-Holthus replied, noting in his memoirs that the unexpected news "was like an electric shock." He was still unaware of Operation Franz, and had never heard of Otto Skorzeny.

Nasr Khan said the Germans had landed on July 15 between Shiraz and Semirom in southern Isfahan Province, and had brought "funny poles." These sounded like radio antennas. They knew about Schulze-Holthus and wanted to make contact with the Abwehr man. Schulze-Holthus mounted his horse immediately, and rode to make contact with them.

He found his countrymen in a camouflaged encampment atop a steep cliff. He was greeted by SS Hauptsturmführer Martin Kurmis, whom Schulze-Holthus later described as "the first German I had seen for years—at least the first who had come directly from Germany wearing a German uniform."

Kurmis told him, "You should muscle me in as quickly as possible to your relationship with this Nasr Khan. I must get a good hold on the fellow when you've gone."

"Gone?"

"Well, you're to be fetched by the next plane. They want you back at headquarters as expert on the whole Middle East. Quite a step up the ladder for you."

"Thank you," the Abwehr man said hesitantly. "What about you?"

"We're going to 'hot this place up a bit.' Commandos like us have been dropped everywhere—in Iraq, Palestine and Syria. A brand new magnificent eastern program."

Kurmis introduced the other members of his team, two German radio operators named Piwonka and Harbers, and an Iranian named Farsad. They told Schulze-Holthus that "we've had special training with Skorzeny in Oranienburg, in Zistersdorf and Wiener Neustadt. We've been very well trained in blowing up oil pipes and pumping stations."

Schulze-Holthus now fully realized there would be no German invasion. He later wrote, "I was disappointed and depressed. So this was my meeting with the home country which I had been looking forward to for so long. Retired, thrown on the scrap heap.... The young men from SD would from now onwards 'hot things up' and they would do this with dynamite and acts of sabotage. Very well, let them play it their way. My job was over. The dice had fallen in the big gamble between Abwehr and SD in Berlin."

High Value Targets

In World War II, there were several notable covert actions against "high value targets."

One of the SOE's most famous missions was the targeted killing of SS-Obergruppenführer Reinhard Heydrich. In addition to his having been the founder of the SD and the chief of the RSHA (the Reich's main security office), he was also the director of the occupation of the Reich Protectorate of Bohemia and Moravia (part of Czechoslovakia until being absorbed into the Greater German Reich in 1939). Heydrich was targeted by two former Czech soldiers recruited by the British, Jan Kubis and Jozef Gabcik. Parachuted into the country by the Royal Air Force, they attacked Heydrichs's car in Prague on May 27, 1942, severely wounding him. He died eight days later. His assassins were tracked down by the SS and committed suicide to avoid capture.

In Washington, Franklin Roosevelt approved the targeted killing of Admiral Isoroku Yamamoto, commander of the Imperial Japanese Navy

Combined Fleet and the architect of the Pearl Harbor attack. Having broken Japanese naval codes, the U.S. Navy was keeping track of Yamamoto's movements in the Pacific. On April 14, 1943, it was discovered that he would be flying near Bougainville in the Solomon Islands on April 18. Sixteen P-38 Lightnings were sent to intercept him and shot down the Japanese G4M bomber on which Yamamoto was a passenger.

In Moscow, the special operations department (Inostranny Otdel) of Lavrenty Beria's NKVD had the targeted assassination of Stalin's political rivals as part of its mandate. Well known at the time was the dramatic killing of the exiled Leon Trotsky—once one of the most powerful figures in the Soviet Union—in Mexico City in 1940. Not so much a targeted killing as Soviet business as usual was the Katyn Massacre, in which more than 14,000 Polish POWs, including 3,000 officers, an admiral, two generals, twenty-four colonels, and a prince were murdered by the Soviets.

Adolf Hitler was sure that the British planned to kill him, and indeed, the SOE *did* have an elaborate contingency plan called Operation Foxley, though it was apparently never activated. The real conspiracies to target Hitler came not from the British, but from officers of the German Army, including the nearly successful July 20, 1944, attempt on Hitler's life by Oberst Claus von Stauffenberg.

Winston Churchill suspected that Hitler had plans to assassinate him. The full extent of these plots will probably never be known, but occasional snippets have become public, including that the Germans had planned to place *exploding chocolate*—bombs disguised as Peters brand candy bars—into the dining room used by Churchill's War Cabinet.

In 2009, a letter was discovered by journalist Jean Bray in the effects of her late husband, the illustrator Laurence Fish. Dated May 4, 1943, it was written by Baron Nathaniel Victor Rothschild, the wartime head of MI5's Section B1C, the explosives and sabotage section.

In his memo, Rothschild explained the whole plot, writing that "we have received information that the enemy are using pound slabs of chocolate which are made of steel with a very thin covering of real chocolate.

Inside there is high explosive and some form of delay mechanism.... When you break off a piece of chocolate at one end in the normal way, instead of it falling away, a piece of canvas is revealed stuck into the middle of the piece which has been broken off and sticking into the middle of the remainder of the slab. When the piece of chocolate is pulled sharply, the canvas is also pulled and this initiates the mechanism ... after a delay of seven seconds the bomb goes off." He was telling this to Fish so that he could draw up a poster warning about the exploding chocolates.

There is no evidence of anyone having been hurt by these dangerous sweets, but this was not the end of the supposed schemes that targeted the prime minister.

On June 1, 1943, thirteen passengers and four crewmembers boarded British Overseas Airways Flight 777 at Portela Airport in Lisbon, Portugal, for a regularly scheduled flight to Bristol, England. Among the passengers was a particular portly gentleman smoking a cigar.

Throughout the war, commercial flights regularly used the air corridor over the Bay of Biscay off the west coast of occupied France. These flights were detected and observed—but usually unmolested—by Luftwaffe interceptors because of Portugal's neutrality. This was not the case on June 1. Shortly before 11:00 a.m., about three hours into the flight, communications with the Douglas DC-3 were lost. At about the same time, eight Ju 88 fighters of the Luftwaffe's Kampfgeschwader 40 ran across the airliner, while returning from a patrol. Visibility in the air was poor and the German fighters, for whatever reason, shot down the airplane.

One possibility: the man with the cigar had been mistaken by German agents for Winston Churchill. The Abwehr and SD-Ausland had many agents in Lisbon, and the Germans knew Churchill had traveled to North Africa to meet with General Eisenhower in late May.

In fact, the man was Alfred Chenfalls, accountant to the British movie star Leslie Howard, best known for his role as Ashley Wilkes in *Gone with the Wind* (1939). When Flight 777 went down, both men perished along with fifteen others aboard. Howard's notoriety kept the incident in the media spotlight. Howard, a veteran of the First World War, was deeply involved in pro-British propaganda efforts and there was speculation that he had worked for British intelligence.

Churchill saw himself as the target in the shot down plane, and mentioned the incident in *Hinge of Fate*, the fourth volume of his history of the war.

"The brutality of the Germans was only matched by the stupidity of their agents," Churchill wrote. "It is difficult to understand how anyone could imagine that with all the resources of Great Britain at my disposal I should have booked a passage in an unarmed and unescorted plane from Lisbon and flown home in broad daylight.... It was a painful shock to me to learn what had happened to others in the inscrutable workings of fate."

Whatever the truth about Flight 777, SD-Ausland *did* make Lisbon the epicenter of Operation Willi, a conspiracy hatched by Walther Schellenberg to abduct the Duke of Windsor. The Duke was Britain's former King Edward VIII, who had abdicated in 1936 in order to marry his divorced American girlfriend. On the eve of the war, the duke had proved to be somewhat of an embarrassment to the British government for his pro-German pronouncements and for traveling to Germany to meet Hitler, and there was even talk that in the event of a German victory, Hitler might reinstate Edward as a puppet king.

Estranged from the royal family and the British government, the duke and his wife were in France when it fell to Germany. They escaped via Spain to Portugal, where both the SD and Britain's SIS converged on the former, and potentially future, monarch. Not fully trusting the duke, and dreading what his pro-German sympathies might lead him to do or say—he had publicly criticized Churchill since the start of the war—the British wanted him under their control. In order to get him as far from Europe as reasonably possible, the British government appointed him as the governor of the Bahamas and ordered him to report there immediately.

Meanwhile, Hitler and Foreign Minister Joachim von Ribbentrop decided that the duke should be lured into officially neutral but pro-German

Spain on the pretext of a hunting trip. Here, Schellenberg's men would convince him that the SIS was out to kill him, and bribe him to remain in Spain under German "protection." When it was learned that the Windsors were preparing to leave for the Bahamas, Hitler ordered Schellenberg to simply kidnap them. However, the best that Schellenberg—who traveled to Lisbon personally—was able to do was delay the arrival of the Duke's luggage at the ship bound for the Bahamas.

Josef Stalin feared assassination, but most of the plots against the Man of Steel came from within the Soviet Union. German SD-Ausland did develop a plan to use a lone Arado Ar 232 transport aircraft to land a hit team near Moscow, but the operation was never put into motion—so far as we know.

Operation Long Jump was easily the most ambitious targeted killing plot of the war.

Ever since Roosevelt and Churchill had met in Casablanca in 1943, German intelligence had yearned for another meeting of Allied leaders close to the war zone, where they might be vulnerable to a German covert operation. It was at Casablanca that President Roosevelt announced that the Allies sought Germany's and Japan's "unconditional surrender"—and this too fired German ambitions to remove the Allied leadership.

A conference of "the Big Three"—Roosevelt, Churchill, and Stalin—had long been assumed and rumored, but it was publicly confirmed on May 19, 1943. The Big Two were in Washington, D.C., for the Trident Conference, their first face-to-face meeting since Casablanca, and Churchill was invited to address a joint session of Congress. During his remarks, Churchill explained that he and Roosevelt "earnestly hope that at no distant date we may be able to achieve what we have so long sought—namely, a meeting with Marshal Stalin and if possible with Generalissimo Chiang Kai-shek. But how, when, and where this is to be accomplished is not a matter upon which I am able to shed any clear ray of light at the present time, and if I were I should certainly not shed it."

Himmler began discussions about a targeted attack on the Big Three with SS Obergruppenführer Ernst Kaltenbrunner, head of the RSHA since Heydrich's assassination, and directly with Schellenberg at SD-Ausland, who reported to Kaltenbrunner. The code name for the operation, assigned by the SD, would be Unternehmen Weitsprung. Admiral Wilhelm Canaris's Abwehr drew up its own parallel scheme to take out the Big Three, and codenamed it Unternehmen 3x3, or Operation 3x3. There was also talk of including Charles De Gaulle, the leader of the Free French, on the hit list, because he had been present at the Casablanca Conference, but the focus was on the Big Three.

On July 26, Schellenberg and Kaltenbrunner sat down with Canaris and Oberst Georg Hansen, the chief of Abwehr's Abteilung I, at the bar of the Eden Hotel in Berlin, one of the most popular watering holes in the German capital—and a strange place to sift through pages of contradictory intelligence reports about the Allied meeting.

The four men met again on August 14 at the headquarters of the RSHA at Number 8 Prinz Albrechtstrasse. Hitler had by now suggested that perhaps the objective ought to be to *capture and kidnap* the Big Three rather than kill them, a much more challenging logistical task, and one apparently quietly dismissed by his intelligence chiefs.

The rival German services decided to continue planning separate operations, Schellenberg acting as point man at the SD and Wessel von Freytag-Loringhoven at the Abwehr. The latter served under, and soon succeeded, Generalmajor Erwin von Lahousen as head of Abwehr's Abteilung II, which dealt with sabotage. The two German agencies did, however, agree to keep one another informed on their respective progress and on the particulars of the weapons and tactics they planned to use. They also needed to share agents and safe houses inside Iran. While the SD had Franz Mayr in-country, Bernhardt Schulze-Holthus and Ernst Merser were Abwehr assets.

As the August 14 meeting was adjourned, however, they parted company without any idea of "how, when, and where" the three high value targets would meet their demise.

How, When, and Where

If the Germans were unclear as to date and venue, they were not alone. The Big Three themselves had yet to decide when, where, or even *if* they would meet.

There was even the thought in Franklin Roosevelt's mind of meeting Stalin one-on-one, as Churchill had met with Stalin in Moscow in August 1942. On May 5, 1943, a week before Churchill arrived in Washington, Roosevelt put pen to paper and wrote to the Man of Steel, telling him, "I am sending this personal note to you by the hands of my old friend, Joseph E. Davies. It relates solely to one subject which I think it is easier for us to talk over through a mutual friend. Mr. Litvinov is the only other person with whom I have talked about it. I want to get away from the difficulties of large Staff conferences or the red tape of diplomatic conversations. Therefore, the simplest and most practical method that I can think of would be an informal and completely simple visit for a few days between you and me.... it is my belief that you and I ought to meet this summer."

Roosevelt went so far as to suggest a venue, proposing that "we could meet either on your side or my side of Bering Straits.... It is my thought that neither of us would want to bring any Staff. I would be accompanied by Harry Hopkins, an interpreter and a stenographer and that you and I would talk very informally and get what we call 'a meeting of the minds.' I do not believe that any official agreements or declarations are in the least bit necessary. You and I would, of course, talk over the military and naval situation, but I think we can both do that without Staffs being present."

Having told Stalin that he was doing "a grand job," Roosevelt added that they might also invite Churchill to the Bering Strait summit, and wished the Soviet leader luck.

In those days, communications between Roosevelt and Churchill passed mainly through coded naval wireless transmissions, while communications between Washington and Moscow were by way of emissaries. Roosevelt favored using roving troubleshooters such as Joseph Davies, a former ambassador to Moscow, and Averell Harriman, a businessman and Wall Street attorney turned diplomat who had been Roosevelt's Lend-Lease coordinator and who made several trips to Moscow before being named as ambassador to the Soviet Union in October 1943. Stalin used his ambassadors to Washington: Maxim Litvinov until October 1943 and Andrei Gromyko thereafter.

On May 27, Davies wrote from Moscow that he had met Stalin and "there is complete agreement in principle."

In Stalin's reply, hand delivered by Davies, he explained that "I agree with you that such a meeting is necessary and that it should be not be postponed. But I ask you to appreciate duly the importance of the circumstances set forth just because the summer months will be extremely serious for our Soviet armies. As I do not know how the events will develop at the Soviet-German front in June I shall not be able to leave Moscow during this month. Therefore I would suggest that our meeting should be arranged in July or in August."

Though there is no written record on file at the State Department, William Franklin, the deputy director of the department's Historical Office, who later compiled the papers, reported that Stalin suggested verbally to Davies that the meeting take place in Fairbanks, and Roosevelt mentioned this in later correspondence.

In turn, Roosevelt dispatched Harriman to London to brief Churchill, who insisted that a Big *Three* meeting should be a multi-level conference, not a mere conversation. He wrote Roosevelt on June 25 to say that "Averell told me last night of your wish for a meeting with U.J. [Roosevelt and Churchill consistently referred to Stalin as "Uncle Joe"] in Alaska *à deux*. The whole world is expecting and all our side are desiring a meeting of the three great powers at which, not only the political chiefs, but the military staffs would be present in order to plan the future war moves and, of course, search for the foundations of post war settlement. It would seem a pity to draw U.J. 7,000 miles from Moscow for anything less than this."

The prime minister added that the meeting should be "not only of us three but also of the [military chiefs of staff], who will come together for the first time, would be one of the milestones of history. If this is lost, much is lost."

The Big Three meeting took place in neither July nor August, which was understandable given the scale of the fighting across the Soviet Union, but Roosevelt and Churchill met again in mid-August in Quebec for their Quadrant Conference. Looking ahead to future meetings, the American and British leaders discussed a three-way meeting with China's Chiang Kai-shek for some time in the autumn of 1943. As a venue for their summit with Chiang, Roosevelt and Churchill chose Cairo. Both the British and Americans had a substantial headquarters infrastructure there, and the Allies had uncontested control of the airspace across southern Asia from India to Egypt.

Given that much of the communication between Washington and London was carried via naval wireless, German naval codebreakers were able to listen in and pass what they learned to Admiral Canaris at the Abwehr. The Allies, meanwhile, had access to Ultra, the high value intelligence data that flowed from decryptions of the German Enigma Code that were being made—unbeknownst to the Germans— inside the beyond-top-secret halls of the Government Code and Cypher School at Bletchley Park near London.

By late August, there were news reports in the media of an upcoming Roosevelt-Churchill summit in Cairo, and naturally, there was speculation that Stalin might attend. Egypt's Prime Minister, Mustafa el-Nahas Pasha, told a reporter from London's *News Chronicle* that he looked forward to welcoming Roosevelt, Churchill, *and* Stalin to Cairo.

However, for the Soviet leader to be in the same location as Chiang would be politically problematic. Chiang was fighting the Japanese—not the Germans—and Stalin had refused to violate the April 1941 Soviet-Japanese Neutrality Pact. Adding to the awkwardness of such a meeting was that Stalin was actively working to overthrow the Chinese leader. He had been nurturing the Chinese Communist insurgency of Mao Zedong for the better part of a decade and wanted to see him eventually topple Chiang and assume control of China.

It was Roosevelt who suggested the idea of meeting somewhere else in North Africa. On September 4, he told the Man of Steel that "I personally could arrange to meet in a place as far as North Africa between November 15 and December 15."

Stalin replied four days later that he agreed they should aim for late November, but added that "it would be expedient to choose as the place of the meeting the country where there are the representations of all three countries, for instance, Iran.... taking into consideration the situation on the Soviet-German front where more than 500 divisions are engaged in the fighting in all, and where the control on the part of the High Command of the USSR is needed almost daily."

Roosevelt balked at the suggestion of Iran. As he told Stalin on September 9, "the time about the end of November is all right. I fully understand that military events might alter the situation for you or for

Mr. Churchill or myself. Meanwhile, we can go ahead on that basis. Personally, my only hesitation is the place but only because it is a bit further away from Washington than I had counted on. My Congress will be in session at that time and, under our Constitution, I must act on legislation within ten days. In other words, I must receive documents and return them to the Congress within ten days and Tehran makes this rather a grave risk if the flying weather is bad.... I hope that you will consider some part of Egypt, which is also a neutral state and where every arrangement can be made for our convenience."

Churchill wrote to Stalin, telling him that with regard to timing, "I will of course conform to whatever arrangements are convenient to you two. There appears to be a very real constitutional difficulty in the President going so far as Tehran and I still hope you will consider Egypt or perhaps a Syrian port like Beirut."

"Stalin was a 'homebody,'" wrote his biographer Dmitri Volkogonov. "While he was willing to meet the Allied leaders he was reluctant to travel either far or for long periods from the USSR. Churchill and Roosevelt suggested locations such as Cairo, Asmara, Baghdad, Basra and other points south. Churchill even thought Stalin would agree to meet in the desert where three tented encampments would be set up and where they would be able to talk in safety and seclusion. Stalin insisted on Tehran because he would, in his words, be able to continue 'the day-to-day running of the Staff.'"

The colorful reference to the tents in the desert came from an October 14 memo, in which Churchill made reference to Chapter 6 of the Bible's Book of Mark. He used biblical references frequently in his messages, and this one came from Mark 9:5, in which the prophets Elijah and Moses had just appeared to Jesus and His disciples, and Peter said to Jesus, "Master, it is good for us to be here: and let us make three tabernacles; one for thee, and one for Moses, and one for Elias."

As Churchill told Roosevelt, "St. Peter sometimes had real inspirations. I like the idea of three tabernacles. We can add one later for your old friend Chiang [Kai-shek]."

Much as he liked the idea of three tabernacles, Churchill realized that Stalin was stuck on Tehran, and so he tried to nudge Roosevelt in that direction. Indeed, in his October 5 memo, this decision seemed a *fait accompli*, when he wrote that "good arrangements must be made for security in this somewhat loosely controlled area. Accordingly, I suggest for your consideration that I make preparations at Cairo in regard to accommodation, security, etc., which are bound to be noticed in spite of all praiseworthy efforts to keep them secret. Then perhaps only two or three days before our meeting, we should throw a British and a Russian brigade around a suitable area in Tehran including the airfield and keep an absolute cordon till we have finished our talks."

Cautiously intuiting the intrigue already being plotted in Berlin, the prime minister told Roosevelt—as he had told Stalin on September 25—that "We should of course have to control absolutely all out-going messages. Thus we shall have an effective blind for the world press and also for any unpleasant people who might not be as fond of us as they ought."

For the sake of security, Churchill proposed that they use the term "Cairo Three" when referring to "Tehran," and the codename "Eureka" for the conference itself. In practice, though, both terms were used only sporadically in communications between the Big Three.

Stalin thought the idea of sending brigades into Tehran "inexpedient as it would cause an unnecessary sensation and would decamouflage the preparations. I suggest that each of us should take with him a sufficient police guard. In my opinion, this would be enough to secure our safety."

Throughout October, Roosevelt continued to resist the idea of coming to Tehran. He wanted to meet in the *actual* Cairo—to which both he and Churchill already planned to travel—over Cairo *Three* as a venue, while offering as a compromise Baghdad, Basra, Beirut, or Asmara.

On October 21, Roosevelt told Secretary of State Cordell Hull, who was then on his way to Moscow for a foreign ministers' conference, to explain to Stalin that, just as the Soviet leader needed to be close to his nation at war, Roosevelt needed not to stray far from being in touch with his own government. Roosevelt asked Hull to remind Stalin that he would already be more than meeting Stalin half way. Cairo is 6,200 miles from Washington, but only 1,800 miles from Moscow.

In the memo to Stalin that was hand-delivered by Hull, the president articulated his concern about the remoteness of Iran, writing that "the trouble with Tehran is the simple fact that the approaches to that city over the mountain often make flying an impossibility for several days at a time. This is a double risk; first, for the plane delivering documents from Washington and, second, for the plane returning these documents to the Congress. I regret to say that as head of the Nation, it is impossible for me to go to a place where I cannot fulfill my constitutional obligations.... Therefore, with much regret I must tell you that I cannot go to Tehran and in this my Cabinet members and the Legislative Leaders are in complete agreement."

He continued, referencing Mark 9:5, "I can make one last practical suggestion. That is that all three of us should go to Basra where we shall be perfectly protected in three camps, to be established and guarded by our respective national troops."

Roosevelt added that "it would be regarded as a tragedy by future generations if you and I and Mr. Churchill failed today because of a few hundred miles."

Stalin was unmoved.

It was not until November that the venue was finally set in stone. In a November 5 memo, hand delivered to Roosevelt by Hull, the Man of Steel said tersely that "the decision of w[h]ether you are able to travel to Tehran remains entirely with yourself. On my part, I have to say that I do not see any other more suitable place for a meeting.... [A]s Supreme Commander, the possibility of traveling farther than Tehran is excluded."

As Volkogonov later pointed out, "Stalin had not revealed that he was somewhat afraid of flying. This would be his first flight ever, and his last. Never one to take risks, he saw no good reason why he should start now.

He was at the peak of his glory and even the possibility of unpleasantness, however slight, troubled him."

On November 8, Roosevelt finally agreed, writing to Stalin that "You will be glad to know that I have worked out a method so that if I get word that a bill requiring my veto has been passed by the Congress and forwarded to me, I will fly to Tunis to meet it and then return to the Conference. Therefore, I have decided to go to Tehran and this makes me especially happy. As I have told you, I regard it as of vital importance that you and Mr. Churchill and I should meet. The psychology of the present excellent feeling really demands it even if our meeting last only two days."

On November 11, Stalin confirmed that he would be at Tehran to meet the Big Two, whom Roosevelt estimated would arrive from Cairo on November 26. At 9:30 p.m. on the evening of November 11, a few hours after receiving Stalin's message, Roosevelt departed the White House secretly and quietly for what would be a month-long Middle East sojourn. Accompanied by Harry Hopkins, his closest advisor, and Admiral William Leahy, his military advisor and the Chairman of the Joint Chiefs of Staff, he was driven to the Marine Corps Base at Quantico, Virginia, where he boarded the presidential yacht USS *Potomac* under cover of darkness. At 9:16 a.m. on the rainy, cloudy morning of the following day, they transferred to one of the newest and mightiest ships in the fleet, the 45,000-ton, 887-foot fast battleship USS *Iowa*, which had been commissioned only nine months earlier, and which had been with the Atlantic Fleet only since August.

Roosevelt, who had *flown* across the Atlantic to the Casablanca Conference, would be crossing the ocean by sea this time. He and his companions were now joined aboard by the rest of the Joint Chiefs of Staff, General George Marshall of the U.S. Army, Admiral Ernest King, and General Hap Arnold of the USAAF. After fueling in Hampton Roads, the battleship and her screen of escorting destroyers reached the heavy seas and open water of the Atlantic Ocean shortly after midnight on November 13.

The following morning, as the generals and admirals were placing bets on the Army-Navy game, the Navy arranged a gunnery demonstration for the highest concentration of VIPs at sea anywhere in the world at that moment. The huge 16-inch guns of the battleship remained silent, but the smaller-caliber guns from the whole flotilla thundered and pounded.

Suddenly, someone noticed a torpedo wake in the water.

It was headed *straight* for the *Iowa* and its all-star guest list.

Lieutenant Bill Rigdon, Roosevelt's personal secretary, who penned the official record of the voyage, later wrote with understated aplomb that "a moment of extreme tension was brought on by an unexpected explosion, of an underwater nature, in the vicinity of the ship.... All hands wondered, had we been attacked? This doubt was soon cleared when the USS *William D. Porter*, our antisubmarine screen to starboard, reported by visual dispatch that she had accidentally fired a torpedo in our direction. Fortunately the wake of the torpedo had been detected and reported by the *Iowa*'s lookouts in time for the *Iowa* to maneuver and to avoid being hit.... The *William D. Porter*'s ship's company presumably did not know who rode the *Iowa*."

Bill Rigdon added "had that torpedo hit the *Iowa* in the right spot with her passenger list of distinguished statesmen, military, naval and aerial strategists and planners, it could have had untold effect on the outcome of the war and the destiny of our country."

"This is *not* a practice," Hap Arnold recalled hearing in an announcement over the ship's public address system.

But it was a very inauspicious beginning for Franklin Roosevelt's perilous journey to distant Tehran.

Hit Men

By August, Walther Schellenberg and Wilhelm Canaris knew that the long-rumored Big Three Allied summit conference would probably take place somewhere in the Middle East. Indeed the newspapers were filled with rumors that placed the officially unannounced conference in Cairo. By September, the German spymasters knew that Stalin had put his foot down on traveling no further than Tehran. They also correctly predicted that Roosevelt and Churchill would not let their own reservations about coming to Tehran stand in the way of a chance to sit down with the Soviet leader.

While Schellenberg and Canaris were now in a position to be able to make an educated guess as to *where* the Eureka Conference would take place, the only thing that they could surmise about the timetable was that it would be *soon*. Time was now of the essence in the planning and execution of Operation Long Jump.

When it came to seriously implementing Operation Long Jump, there was one name on everyone's mind: Hauptsturmführer Otto Skorzeny.

In July 1943, the twenty-one-year rule of Benito Mussolini came to an embarrassing end when he was dismissed from power by King Victor Emmanuel and was arrested. He was imprisoned high in the Apennines at the isolated Campo Imperatore Hotel, a ski resort about eighty miles from Rome. When Hitler ordered that his former Axis partner be plucked from his alpine dungeon, Ernst Kaltenbrunner selected Skorzeny to lead the joint operation, which involved a contingent of SD Sonderlehrgang special forces, as well as a Luftwaffe Fallschirmjäger (paratrooper) detachment. The troops landed by glider, overwhelming the Italian defenders. Skorzeny spirited Mussolini off the mountain in a Fieseler Fi 156 short take-off and landing aircraft and escorted him to Berlin and Hitler's welcoming arms. Known as Unternehmen Eiche (Operation Oak), it was a tremendous public relations coup for German special operations forces, and it earned Skorzeny both a Knight's Cross of the Iron Cross, a promotion to Sturmbannführer, and an indelible reputation.

With Eiche behind him and with his Sonderlehrgang teams already operating inside Iran, it was only reasonable that Skorzeny would be tasked with leading Operation Long Jump. Technically, the insertion of the hit men into Iran would follow the pattern that Skorzeny had pioneered during Operation Franz. The Luftwaffe's Kampfgeschwader 200 special operations unit would drop multiple hit teams and their equipment by air; the teams would then make their way into Tehran and a network of safe houses.

The Operation Long Jump hit teams would be led by members of Skorzeny's Sonderlehrgang, but in their ranks were Soviet defectors in Red Army uniforms. It was hoped that these men, handpicked from those previously used in Operation Zeppelin and from among the thousands who had volunteered for General Vlasov's anti-Soviet Russian Liberation Army, would help the teams infiltrate Soviet security in Tehran.

One of the Sonderlehrgang team leaders would be Sturmbannführer Rudolf von Holten-Pflug, an aggressive and ambitious officer who, according to the historian Joseph Persico, "hoped to be the next Skorzeny." Von Holten-Pflug, unlike Skorzeny, had the advantage of having been inside Iran with Operation Franz, so he knew the lay of the land and had at least some idea of how to navigate the back streets of Tehran.

Winifred Oberg, meanwhile, had been recalled by Schellenberg from Turkey, where he had been since March 1943, serving as Schellenberg's covert go-between for Ernst Mayr and other SD agents in Iran. Though he had never actually gotten across the dangerous passes into the Shah's kingdom, his experience of having studied Iran and having been in contact with agents in-country was deemed useful in planning Operation Franz missions. He had now been assigned on the training staff at the sabotage school at Quenzgut, near Oranienburg.

Ultimately, Oberg, not von Holten-Pflug, was assigned as the advance man for Operation Long Jump. The reason was probably that Walther Schellenberg knew he could trust Oberg. He did, after all, have those compromising photographs of Oberg and Ernst Röhm in his safe. The mere mention of Röhm still made Himmler apoplectic, even nine years after he had had him executed. Oberg's main job was to have the safe houses ready in Tehran for the hit teams.

Among the teams was Untersturmführer Josef Schnabel, a young and energetic SS man who had never been out of Europe. During his briefings for Operation Long Jump, as he told Laslo Havas many years later, his superior officers "taught us to hate. We had to know the *curriculum vitae* of the enemy leaders—the way [Propaganda Minister Josef] Goebbels' propaganda had transformed them. Thus, when asked who Roosevelt's advisors were we had to enumerate a dozen names, adding after each, 'the Jew.'"

Schnabel did not, however, like Winifred Oberg, whose sexual advances annoyed him. When he confided in von Holten-Pflug of Oberg's overtures, the Sturmbannführer shrugged that it was "only the stinking

Jewish bourgeoisie and those hypocrites at the Vatican who imposed the so-called 'morality' that even now is accepted quite blindly by too many of our countrymen."

Schnabel replied that he still did not "care for that sort of thing."

Another Oberg protégé—professional, not personal—was Sturm-bannführer Hans Ulrich von Ortel. After the war, Oberg told Laslo Havas that von Ortel was "one of the boldest, cleverest, and most aggressive men I ever knew. Unfortunately, he was also one of the most talkative, most incalculable, and a drinker. It was impossible to leave him for long in a foreign country on any mission, because sooner or later a scandal would become unavoidable. However, on a short-term commando action he was invaluable."

Oberg knew of von Ortel's boldness and cleverness before he called him into his office to talk about Long Jump. Oberg learned the hard way about von Ortel's liquor-lubricated loose lips, however.

Until the summer of 1943, von Ortel had been assigned to occupied Ukraine—recently redesignated as the German Reichskommissariat Ukraine—where the Gestapo was charged with administering this new German protectorate. This involved removing Jews and Slavs, repopulating Ukraine with ethnic Germans, and turning it into the great Lebensraum, or "Living Space" in the east about which Hitler had been emoting since he penned *Mein Kampf* two decades earlier.

Assigned to a desk job in the small city of Rivne (then called Rovno) in western Ukraine, von Ortel's only breaks from paper-pushing were occasional visits to Berlin. It was on one of these trips that Oberg took him to meet Schellenberg. Oberg insisted that von Ortel would be perfect for an upcoming project and Schellenberg seemed to agree. All that von Ortel was able to glean about this unspecified covert action was that it was probably going to take place in Iran. Skorzeny's name was mentioned, and von Ortel was sworn to silence.

Seeing this as a welcome change from his current monotonous drudgery, von Ortel returned to Rivne excited about the prospects. He was so delighted that he could not help but mention it to one of his card-playing friends. Lieutenant Paul Wilhelm Siebert was a wounded combat veteran who now worked for the Wirtschaftsorganisation Ost (Economic Organization East), which was the massive bureaucracy tasked with taking over and exploiting the economy of the Ukraine for the benefit of the Reich. Von Ortel also mentioned it to Lydiya Lissovskaya, a young Russian woman who worked in the Gestapo office, and who was Siebert's off-and-on girlfriend.

Unfortunately for von Ortel, Paul Wilhelm Siebert was *not* Paul Wilhelm Siebert. The real Siebert was dead. He had been killed in action, but his mortal remains had been discovered without identification and buried as "unknown." His papers were not lost, however. They had been recovered by the NKVD and had found their way into the possession of Nikolai Ivanovich Kuznetsov (a.k.a. Kuznecov). An NKVD double agent specializing in covert operations behind German lines in Ukraine, Kuznetsov remained a shadowy figure described mainly through innuendo until details of his activities began to dribble out of Russian archives in the 1990s.

A gifted linguist, Kuznetsov had grown up in a German-speaking area of the Perm Governorate in the Ural Mountains, and was able to flawlessly impersonate German officers. According to the legends that have grown up around his memory, he worked himself into German command centers sufficiently well as to have personally killed several generals. The smiling young NKVD man made friends easily, and one of the friends whom he made was Hans Ulrich von Ortel.

In his description of the "something big" in which he was to be involved, von Ortel bragged to Siebert/Kuznetsov that he would be working with the illustrious Skorzeny, but even after the Russian had gotten him talkatively drunk, the Gestapo officer did not tell Kuznetsov *where* the operation was to take place. However, when he told Lydiya that he was soon going away on a special mission, he promised that he would bring her a nice Persian rug.

It was through Kuznetsov that the NKVD first learned that the Germans were planning something big in Iran, Though von Ortel still did not know what, nor when, Lavrenty Beria *did*. Von Ortel had confirmed that the Germans knew about the upcoming summit, and they had plans for a disrupting it.

By September, the Abwehr's Operation 3x3 had been subsumed into the SD's Operation Long Jump, but the military intelligence service was still contributing manpower to the enterprise, including Lothar Schoellhorn, handpicked by Admiral Wilhelm Canaris on the recommendation of Artur Nebe, the head of the Gestapo's Kripo (Criminal Police) where Schoellhorn had frequently figured in homicide investigations—usually as the *suspect*. A former prizefighter turned dashing man-about-town, he had a way of "coincidentally" crossing paths with people who later died in unexplained accidents or who went missing and turned up deceased. Schoellhorn had never been charged. Canaris appreciated Schoellhorn's skill and discretion.

During the summer of 1943, while Canaris was working *with* Schellenberg and SD-Ausland in plans for Operation Long Jump, it is possible that Canaris and his Abwehr operatives might have been working *against* SD-Ausland in another high profile targeted operation.

According to SS General Karl Wolff, and corroborated by testimony during the Nuremberg trials, Wolff was ordered by Hitler and Himmler to kidnap Pope Pius XII, shortly after Skorzeny snatched Mussolini. Wolff thought the operation would be a colossal mistake and worked with the Abwehr to covertly leak the plan to the Italians. When the SD realized that the scheme was no longer secret, the mission was cancelled. Even without kidnapping the pope, the Germans would be in control of Rome for the better part of another year.

Inside Iran, the schism between the Abwehr and the SD was manifest on the mountaintop where Bernhardt Schulze-Holthus of the former agency was camped with the Operation Franz SD Sonderlehrgang team of Martin Kurmis.

Schulze-Holthus later claimed that by the summer of 1943, he could see that "The Third Reich was lost and, [the SS and SD only] wanted to prolong the disaster by dragging others down in their own catastrophe. What else could the acts of sabotage in Persia, Iraq and Palestine mean, except the beginning of a war in the Middle East, a war which would be disastrous for the Eastern peoples? In the vulgar jargon of the SD, they wanted to 'hot up' the people in order to give the power maniacs of the Third Reich a little breathing space. I had served this power and served it with a good conscience. I knew that there were dark spots in the picture, as did many others. How dark they actually were, very few of us realized. Besides, weren't there the same dark spots everywhere? Was not the history of British colonization a tapestry of the sweat, blood and tears of oppressed peoples?"

On the night of September 9, Nasr Khan invited Schulze-Holthus and the SD men to dine with the Qashqai. He had bad news: the Tehran government was now officially at war with the Reich. In the big picture this made little difference; Iran was already an occupied country. But it could make things much more difficult for Operation Long Jump and securing safe houses for the German and Russian hit men. Moreover, a key SD asset, Franz Mayr, had been arrested by the British three weeks earlier. It was not an auspicious beginning to the execution of a dangerous and difficult plan.

Behind the Most Elaborate of Curtains

In Iran, the Americans and the Soviets were a study in contrasts. The Americans were men with straightforward jobs. Major General Donald Connolly was there to run supplies up the Persian Corridor. Major General Norman Schwarzkopf was there to protect the Corridor. Connolly was more interested in rolling stock, importing American-built locomotives, and meeting schedules than he was about alleyway intrigues in Tehran. Arthur Chester Millspaugh, Iran's Administrator General of Finances, the technocrat's technocrat, was in Tehran only to keep Mohammed Reza Pahlavi's imperial checkbook balanced.

The Soviets were just the opposite, erecting the most elaborate of curtains to obscure the surreptitious activities of the NKVD. Tehran was within the British area of occupation, but the NKVD was there anyway—indeed, after a century of rivalry in Iran, the Soviets regarded the British almost as warily as they did the Germans.

Andrei Andreyevich Smirnov, the Soviet ambassador who had welcomed Soviet forces into Iran in September 1941, was replaced by Mikhail Maximov on September 1, 1943. But the most important Soviet diplomat in Iran was Daniel Komissarov. A Farsi-speaking translator of prewar Persian literature—including the works of the internationally fashionable modernist Sadegh Hedayat—he served as the embassy press attaché and as the chief Soviet propagandist in Tehran.

George Lenczowski, the press attaché at the Polish embassy, who knew him, recalled that Komissarov "maintained direct and constant contact with a host of newspapers in Tehran, and his frequent receptions and press conferences were destined to bring the Soviet Embassy and the press ever closer. One of the major tasks of the Press Office was to secure in the Iranian press as much space as possible for Tass Agency items."

Lenczowski pointed out that the heavy hand of Soviet intimidation was seen in the propaganda war between Tass and the British Reuters news agency for dominance of news space in the Iranian press.

"The one-sided policy of outright Communist papers published in the Persian language was, of course, pronounced," Lenczowski observed. "Non-Communist papers, which did not dare to refuse, also printed the Tass material in abundance. In the *Journal de Tehran*, for example, three-quarters of the news items published were often Tass dispatches ... the servility of the Iranian newspapers toward Russia was extreme. Even the papers that indulged in open polemics with the Communist Tudeh party were careful not to say a word against the Soviet Union. Instead they competed with each other in praising the 'great and generous Northern Neighbor.' ... Apart from exerting various pressures and inducements, the Soviet Embassy had one very important weapon: it supplied newsprint to some newspapers. The general consensus was that the Journal de Tehran was among the recipients."

In one example, which appeared on February 23, 1944, the editors of *Journal de Tehran* gushed that "for us Iranians who from the first day have been the sincere friends of the Soviet peoples and for us who are at present active allies, it is a joy to assist in the triumphs of this Red Army without which very certainly the freedom-loving nations would have succumbed long ago under the boots of the fascist hordes."

In the autumn of 1943, Maximov and Komissarov opened the Irano-Soviet Society for Cultural Relations, a subsidiary of the All-Union Society for Cultural Relations (Vsesoiuznoe Obshchestvo Kul'turnoi Sviazi or VOKS) at what Lenczowski described as a "pompous ceremony of inauguration [initiating] innumerable lectures, concerts, receptions, art exhibitions, and sponsored shows," adding that "hardly a day passed without the press giving notice of some cultural or artistic event at the society."

Part of the role of VOKS was to invite Iranian "students and younger intellectuals" to study in the Soviet Union free of charge, where, of course, they could be indoctrinated in communism.

Lenczowski later observed that it was an open secret that the Soviet Hospital in the city was an important center of propaganda and espionage. He wrote that these activities were "conducted by Dr. Baroyan, an Armenian, who was believed to hold an important position in the Foreign Section of the NKVD, and whose travels to Cairo were undoubtedly a riddle to many an intelligence agent of the Western powers. Since medical services were greatly needed, the hospital possessed an excellent reputation. Iranians were permitted to use this hospital, and many prominent members of Iranian society took advantage of it."

While Baroyan befriended his patients and plied them for their secrets, and the smiling Komissarov seduced the press and worked the room at embassy receptions, the barracudas of the NKVD swam in the inky waters beneath the surface, where their activities in wartime Tehran were, and remain, little known. Laslo Havas mentioned Colonel Andrei Mikhalovits Vertinski, who arrived in June 1943 as the NKVD "resident agent" in Tehran. Also known on the streets of Tehran was the "most hated" Mikhail Moisseevich Melamed, a Ukrainian-Jewish NKVD man who came to Iran to iron out discipline problems within the Red Army occupation forces.

In addition, Havas mentions the mysterious and multilingual "Fabien Martiensen." No one in Iran knew his real name, or his nationality, but he was regarded as the NKVD equivalent of Winifred Oberg of the SS, a spy who spied on his fellow spies.

Even more obscure—until he created an international media buzz early in the twenty-first century with his revelations of his own undercover activities with the NKVD in Tehran in 1943—was Gevork Andreevich Vartanian. Awarded the Hero of the Soviet Union for his later espionage work, Vartanian was born in 1924 in Nor Nakhichevan in suburban Rostov-on-Don. In 1930, when he was two, his ethnic-Armenian father moved the family to Tehran, where he operated as a merchant, while doubling as an NKVD informant or agent. Young Gevork began working with the NKVD when he was sixteen, and was a veteran operative by the time that he turned nineteen in February 1943.

While Vartanian came in from the cold decades later, NKVD Colonel Andrei Mikhalovits Vertinski, mentioned by Havas, remains a mystery. Irapuan Costa, writing in the September 15, 2012, issue of *Jornal Opção* of Goiânia, Brazil, asserted that Vartanian and Vertinski were actually the *same person*. It seems improbable—though not impossible—that this teenager could have been the NKVD "resident agent" in Tehran.

Vertinski—if that was his real name—played an important role in the events in Tehran in 1943. Much of what is known about him comes from a Belgian swimming instructor named Paul Pourbaix, who was interviewed by Laslo Havas after the war. Pourbaix was part of the Tehran expat community, and had been recruited as a paid informant by the NKVD. Like many Europeans of his generation, Pourbaix was a coffee-house intellectual who held a romantic fascination with the *idea* of socialism, so working with the NKVD had seemed to him an exciting adventure.

Pourbaix—who used the pseudonym Pierre Petit when dealing with the NKVD—gradually grew bored, if not disillusioned, with Vertinski and his men. He was put off by their clumsiness, and how poorly they were able to utilize or understand their assets. He considered it wasteful that they devoted more resources to working with the Tudeh Party against the Shah's government than ferreting out German agents.

In order to continue getting his Soviet paycheck, Pourbaix began to make things up. Apparently the Soviets never figured this out, because the Belgian survived the war.

"It needed so much imagination to invent my stories that with the same effort I could have written novels," Pourbaix later told Havas. "The attention of my employers extended to the smallest detail. They never told me whether or not they believed me, but as they maintained our contact for six months and paid me, I don't think they suspected me. I always knew the people about whom I spoke and kept an eye on them. From the questions the Russians asked about them it was easy to guess their intentions. When I noticed that a critical point had been reached, I recanted. There was never anything concrete in my reports, anyway, only that X was spending a suspicious amount of money, or that he showed conspicuous interest in some things, or that he did not like the occupiers. This could be said more or less about everyone."

While he later insisted that "I never said that someone was a German spy or was preparing to commit sabotage actions," Pourbaix did tell Vertinski about Ernst Merser and the "Polish girl"—Wanda Pollack—who lived at his house.

It could be said that until September 1943, the foreign intelligence-gathering operations of the NKVD in Iran were inferior to those of the British and the Germans, and that much of what they thought they knew was either wrong—thanks to Paul Pourbaix—or seriously incomplete. By October, though, with the realization that Stalin was probably coming to Tehran—and that the Germans were planning a special operation—the NKVD flooded Tehran with men and began to scramble to make up for lost time.

A Maiden in Distress

anda Pollack was probably the most misunderstood westerner in Tehran in the autumn of 1943. It is deeply ironic that the most innocent and clueless woman anywhere near the espionage circles was also the most distrusted.

Ernst Merser, her beloved benefactor and benevolent "older brother," did not fully trust her. Percy Downward regarded her as a dangerous problem for both Merser and himself. When he discovered Wanda, and saw how she seemed to move from circle to circle with ease, Andrei Vertinski got the idea that she was some sort of double agent, and that she might be the diabolical thread winding circuitously between the Germans and the British. As his NKVD men shadowed her, Vertinski saw the young Polish woman as a spy who knew too much, when in fact she knew virtually nothing.

Wanda stumbled unwittingly into the opening moment in Operation Long Jump, dragging Ernst Merser and all of the others down the rabbit hole behind her.

One day, Wanda and Ida Kovalska went with Khalil Chapat and Mervyn Wollheim for an outing to a park on the edge of town. Late in the afternoon, Wanda went off by herself. A couple of hours later, when she had not returned, her friends went to look for her. She was nowhere to be found.

As night fell, their frantic search turned up a man who had seen a woman matching Wanda's description being pulled into a car by three men. They contacted Peter Ferguson, who guessed that she had been abducted. If that was indeed the case, none of them had the first idea of who might have wanted to take her, or where they might have gone.

Finally, they decided to go to the house on Kakh Street—Ernst Merser's home—where Wanda lived. Maybe the woman being pulled into the car wasn't Wanda, and she had simply walked home.

One can imagine Merser's surprise when Ida Kovalska showed up on his doorstep shortly before midnight with the two Americans and Khalil Chapat. Though he knew about them, he had never met any of these men, and he had met Ida only a couple of times.

When they learned that Wanda had not returned to Kakh Street, they suspected the worst. Ida told the story of Wanda's supposed abduction as Merser insisted that they remain calm, and tried to remain calm himself.

Excusing himself from the room, he phoned Percy Downward, who had used every mention of Wanda's name to scold Merser for not ridding himself of his problem child. Sensing Merser's worry, the British agent finally promised him that he would make some calls to the Tehran Police and Schwarzkopf's gendarmes, and try to figure out where Wanda might have been taken, and by whom.

Somewhere during the wee hours and the second bottle of whiskey, it became Ida's turn to scold Ernst Merser. With her loosened tongue, she told Merser that he was just as Wanda had described him: austere and imperious—and unlikable.

"What have I done to her?" Merser asked when Ida told him that Wanda complained about him. "Have I ever hurt her?"

"Why did you bring her here?" Ida replied. "Why did you keep her here if you felt nothing for her?"

"Why do you dislike me?"

"You know very well that Wanda is in love with you! And if you know it, why do you torment her? Hasn't the poor girl suffered enough already?"

Merser was stunned.

"What you have told me is very important to me," he said at last in his careful, unemotional manner. "Very important. I think I should even thank you for it. Perhaps I am stupid but, believe me, I am not insensitive. Where Wanda is concerned, I am not insensitive at all."

By the time that dawn broke and Merser started to make coffee, the conversation had trailed had off, but no one had slept very much.

Downward phoned in the early morning to say that he had yet to learn anything, but that he was still working his sources. The next time he called, just before noon, what he had to say made Merser visibly anxious.

He explained that the NKVD had cast a dragnet across Tehran and that people were being pulled off the street all over town, and that Wanda might have been caught up in such a sweep. He did not add the phrase "by accident," because he still believed that Wanda, rightly or wrongly, had a target on her back.

As he thought about Wanda and about what Ida had said through the haze of whiskey the night before, Merser's anxiety turned to panic. He begged Downward to do something, to tell him something. Could he please contact the Soviets?

Downward was reticent. For a long litany of political and practical reasons, he could not get himself entangled in an NKVD operation.

Finally, though, after listening to Merser beg—even though he knew the whole thing cold blow up in his face—Downward relented. Against his better judgment, he told Merser that he knew a man who knew the Russians, a man who even worked as an informant for the NKVD.

That man was Paul Pourbaix.

Later in the afternoon, the swimming instructor opened his door to the same foursome who had come calling at Ernst Merser's home in the middle of the night before. It was now Pourbaix's turn to be pushed into a car.

Against his better judgment, Merser agreed that they could bring the Belgian back to Kakh Street. Ferguson, who was excitable to begin with, and now hung over and sleep deprived, decided that the best way to get information out of Pourbaix was to threaten to kill him. This was, after all, the way it was done in the movies, and Hollywood spies were Ferguson's role models. Pourbaix initially held firm to the notion that it did not matter whether Ferguson shot him, because if he talked, death at the hands of the NKVD would be much worse.

Merser later explained to Laslo Havas that "Ferguson and Chapat waved their guns under his nose so vigorously that even I was afraid one might go off. They described to the man in such detail how they were going to torture him that I could almost see the puddles of blood on my carpet. However, before they even touched him, the Belgian declared that he would tell us everything."

In his own postwar conversation with Havas, Pourbaix insisted that he was not—however it may have seemed at the time—intimidated.

"Not for a moment did I take their threats seriously," he maintained. "I wanted them to understand that I had about as much sympathy for communism as the Pope. I thought I was serving the interests of the Allies and also making a little money on the side. Besides, except in this one instance, my reports had never led to any trouble."

According to Pourbaix, it was not Ferguson's "bad cop," but Ida Kovalska's "good cop" that finally loosened his tongue.

"If it hadn't been for the girl, they could never have convinced me," he insisted. "But when I remained alone with her for a moment, she spoke to me so kindly, told me so movingly how pretty, young, and unhappy the other girl was that I couldn't say no ... I began to feel pretty uncomfortable. I recalled that in my reports I had mentioned Merser and the girl. I had but one desire, to make up for the harm I had done."

Because the NKVD could not very well operate their torture chamber out of the embassy where Maximov and Komissarov wined and dined the media and the diplomatic corps, their base of operations was at a secret undisclosed location. Pourbaix did not know the address to the safe house, but he had his contact's phone number. Merser paid off one of his own contacts, who could extract the address from the number.

While Ferguson and his gang had the enthusiasm for a direct assault on the NKVD facility—more of an impervious bunker than a safe house—they were pitifully short of both manpower and firepower.

Who better to call than Misbah Ebtehaj, the martial arts master who knew everyone in town? How hard could it be for him to put together a sizable assault team?

When they met later that evening, more than twenty-four hours after Wanda had gone missing, Ebtehaj said that it could not be done, and certainly not on short notice. That was his final answer, so they turned to haggling over what a "hypothetical" assault on NKVD might cost. When Ferguson finally reached an astronomical sum which Ebtehaj could not refuse, he admitted that it could be done after all, and right away.

To tip the odds a bit further in their favor, they decided to stage a diversion to draw as many NKVD operatives as far as possible away from their base. The idea was to plant German-made weapons and German-language documents—Merser had both—in a location on the opposite side of town from the NKVD bunker where Wanda was imprisoned. Pourbaix would then phone his NKVD contact and tell him that he had learned of a German hideout at the decoy location. Some of Ebtehaj's men would even hide nearby and fire a few shots to add realism to the faux safe house before they sped across town to the real target.

Using his cover name, "Pierre Petit," Pourbaix phoned his NKVD contact around 2:00 a.m., gave him the prearranged code words, and told him that there were thirty Germans at the phony safe house.

Three hours later, two dozen heavily armed Soviet agents, led personally by Andrei Vertinski, departed to attack the Germans. As soon as the Soviets left their building, Merser, along with Ferguson, Wollheim, Chapat, Ebtehaj and a half dozen of his men went to call on the NKVD jailhouse. Ferguson suggested that they break in through a barred window, but Chapat, rolling his eyes, simply rang the doorbell.

Amazingly, this worked. The three Soviets in the doorway as the heavy door swung open were quickly overpowered, and four more who were inside surrendered immediately without even going for their guns.

It took about ten minutes to find Wanda, who was unconscious in a cell in the basement where the Soviets had beaten, drugged, and threatened to rape her. When Merser reached her and took her into his arms, she could barely speak.

In the meantime, the others set about releasing all the other prisoners. By releasing everyone, they intended to draw attention away from Wanda having been their sole objective. This was easier said than done. Because the other prisoners had such a dread of NKVD reprisals, it took a great deal of cajoling and even physical dragging to get them to leave their cells.

In the confusion, the liberators had not immediately noticed that one of these prisoners was a light-complected man who moved with an assured military bearing. As Merser was heading for the door with Wanda, this man addressed him in German. He said that he had heard Merser speaking German, and wanted to know if he was a German.

When Merser asked him who he was, the man quickly introduced himself as Sturmbannführer Winifred Oberg of the SS.

Oberg noticed Merser's Swiss accent, but he knew that the Abwehr had a Swiss agent in Tehran. He explained to Merser that he had been in Iran for a week and needed a hiding place. Merser had no choice. He agreed, and Wanda's rescuers left with an unexpected companion.

When they reached Kakh Street, Merser tucked the groggy Wanda into her bed and sat down to hear Oberg's tale. He had parachuted into Iran the week before, made contact with a Melliyun agent at Dary-acheh-ye Namak, the dry lake near Qom, and been taken to a safe house in Tehran. When the NKVD had broken in on him a couple of days later, he thought his cover had been blown, but in fact, the NKVD was merely casting their net to round up anyone with German sympathies, and this safe house was on a list supplied by Franz Mayr. The NKVD had not known beforehand about Oberg's presence, nor did Vertinski realize that Oberg had just arrived or why. He was, so far as Vertinski knew, just another German in Iran who needed to be rounded up.

The following morning, Merser phoned a doctor friend to make a house call to check on Wanda. The doctor recommended another day of bed rest, and she rolled over to doze off. Merser then locked the door to the guest suite, where both she and Oberg slept, and slipped out to meet with Percy Downward for coffee. Merser apparently knew of Oberg's sexual preferences, and had no qualms about leaving Wanda alone with the sturmbannführer. There would be no unwanted advances.

Even before their meeting that morning, Downward had nearly had enough of his Swiss asset. He had complicated Downward's life and virtually neutralized his usefulness to British intelligence. Downward was appalled when he learned that during the course of the past few hours, Merser had broken into an NKVD safe house at gunpoint, and that he now had an SS sturmbannführer in his *own* safe house.

Aside from Merser himself, there was only one person to blame for Merser's dangerous carelessness—poor misunderstood Wanda.

"I believe that our lives would be much easier without you," Downward said firmly. "I stopped trying to understand you long ago. But if you have a spare hour, think of the complications you have caused everyone by taking Wanda Pollack into your house."

As he later recalled in conversations with Laslo Havas, Merser offered to leave Tehran immediately if Downward could arrange for transportation for Wanda and him to London.

Downward said that he would get back to him by the end of the day. When he did, it was not what Merser had expected. The British secret services had decided that Merser's having Oberg was not a complication after all, but rather a major intelligence coup. Far from ordering him to leave town, Downward now told Merser to stay put and to nurture the sturmbannführer in his home like he would a rare flowering plant.

When Oberg finally awoke, it was after dark. He had slept the whole day. Merser gave him something to eat and to keep him off guard, asked rhetorically whether he could truly be certain that Oberg was who he said he was, and not a double agent. He explained that, while he did not want to be rude to his new houseguest, unless he could establish Oberg's credibility, he would have to ask him to leave.

"I could mention a dozen people who could vouch for me, and not unimportant people," Oberg insisted. "However, this can only be done if and when you find an opportunity to contact Berlin and get a reply."

Merser explained that he had a wireless transmitter and could, in fact, contact Berlin.

"Name the person in Berlin who can give me the required information about you."

"Walther Schellenberg or Ernst Kaltenbrunner," Oberg answered smugly. "Is that satisfactory?"

With this, Merser made contact with the Abwehr, identifying Oberg as a man that had turned up in a raid on a Soviet facility in Tehran.

It took three hours, but a message came back from Abwehr to the effect of their having contacted the SD, and that Oberg was, indeed, one of theirs, and that he should be given "every assistance."

When Merser told him that his identity was confirmed, Oberg guessed correctly that Merser was on the Abwehr payroll.

"Don't worry," Oberg laughed, alluding to the rivalry between the Abwehr and the SD. "There will be no conflict between us. In this action the Abwehr and the Sicherheitsdienst work side by side. This has been decided in the highest quarters."

Merser replied that cooperation between the two agencies was highly irregular.

"They are bureaucrats in Berlin," Oberg said dismissively. "I am not supposed to tell you anything yet, but in a few days you will learn it from them anyway. As I see the situation here, we shall greatly need each other's help. Give me your word as an officer that you will not inform Berlin of what I tell you now until they themselves enlighten you."

Merser did. With bait like that, how could he not?

"In two or three months the most important enemy statesmen are to meet, probably in Tehran, but at any rate in the Near East," Oberg whispered when Wanda was out of earshot. "We shall soon know exactly when and where. On the Führer's orders they are to be liquidated."

11

Cicero, the Million-Dollar Master Key

Turkey during World War II—as so often before and since—was an exasperating puzzle. The Turks were wary of Germany and Britain, and fearful of the Soviet Union, yet readily courting all sides. Indeed, President Ismet Inonu was adept at reading the winds of change, playing cozy with the Germans as the Wehrmacht was marching relentlessly into Soviet territory, but cooling the warmth of Hitler's embrace whenever the German offensives faltered.

The Turks remembered their disastrous alliance with Germany in World War I, yet, more than anything, they dreaded Russia's longstanding coveting of Turkey's access to the Aegean and Mediterranean Seas, most especially through the Bosphorus Straits.

A secular state that arose from the implosion of the decaying Ottoman Empire after World War I, Turkey was on the cusp of the ancient and the new. As with Tehran, the boulevards of Ankara and Istanbul sparkled with the bright face of European modernity, but their narrow back streets were filled with spies of all nations. This, and official Turkish neutrality, had made the country the conduit for German agents slipping—beneath the noses of the British—in and out of Iran, Syria, and Iraq before and during the war. Frau Schulze-Holthus had used the country as an escape route from Iran, as had Roman Gamotha of the SD, Franz Mayr's colleague. Gamotha had remained based in Turkey, commuting in and out of Tehran to set up safe houses for the Operation Franz operatives.

In 1942, because of their traditional distaste for the Russians and the apparent success of the Wehrmacht against the Soviet Union, the Turks readily cooperated with Walther Schellenberg and his SD in Operation Zeppelin covert activities.

"Specially trained Georgians, Caucasians, Azerbaijanis and Turks had been sent in from Turkey to southern Russia and the Urals," Schellenberg wrote in his memoirs. "This infiltration had shown surprising results. Whenever we got information that concerned Turkey, it was passed on to the Turkish Secret Service."

Schellenberg's "principal agent" in Turkey was Ludwig Carl Moyzisch, an attaché working for Franz von Papen, the German ambassador in Ankara—who had himself been heavily involved in espionage activities as the German ambassador to the United States before the Americans entered World War I. Schellenberg also maintained other operatives in-country, including Gamotha and Winifred Oberg—as well as an entire parallel espionage organization that was unknown to all the others.

"In almost every country I had a second organization working quite separately from the main one and unknown to the latter," the always-paranoid Schellenberg confided in his memoirs. "I considered this necessary in order to be able to check and control the information and material received from my regular service. Often the chiefs of my evaluating sections were surprised at the questions I was able to ask on points of detail, until they slowly began to realize that I had other sources of information. My No. 2 organization in Turkey [based in Istanbul] was directed by a Turk, an Egyptian, and an Arab, whom I left free to select their own assistants. They had set up a commercial firm which dealt chiefly in carpets and old gold and silver. Over the years they had organized their own extensive network in the Near East. Normally they communicated with me through a cover firm in Berlin, but in case of emergencies sent wireless messages which I received independently from the SD."

It was through Moyzisch, however, that Schellenberg achieved his greatest intelligence coup in Turkey, and the one that proved the most useful to Operation Long Jump.

On October 28, 1943, Schellenberg learned that a man had just approached Moyzisch with an offer that Schellenberg later described as "quite staggering." The man, who called himself "Pierre," was actually a Kosovo-born ethnic Albanian named Elyesa Bazna, who worked as the valet for Sir Hughe Knatchbull-Hugessen, the British ambassador in Ankara. The offer was that he had access to the "most secret documents in the British Embassy," which he handled freely while his employer, who routinely took sleeping pills, was out for the night. He was offering to photograph these and provide them to Moyzisch—for a very high price.

Like the documents themselves, the price was staggering. The first batch would cost £20,000—more than a million dollars in current valuation—with subsequent installments being £15,000 for each roll of film that he was able to shoot and supply to Schellenberg's agent.

As Schellenberg recalled, the mystery man impressed Moyzisch "as being a ruthless and very able man; his answers to all Moyzisch's questions were definite and precise. After a rather dramatic conversation with this strange character, Moyzisch found himself in a difficult situation. As an SD agent he was, of course, tremendously tempted to accept. On the other hand, the sum demanded was extremely high and the business itself very risky.... To complicate matters, Pierre set a time limit of three days for Moyzisch's decision and indicated with an unequivocal gesture towards the Soviet Embassy that he had other customers lined up.... After weighing up the considerations involved, I suggested that the offer should be accepted."

While the initial payment was being flown to Ankara by courier, Pierre agreed that he would shoot two rolls and allow Moyzisch to look at them before the cash was transferred. As Schellenberg described them, the pictures were "breathtaking.... highly secret correspondence between the British Embassy in Ankara and the Foreign Office in London. There were also private notes in the Ambassador's own hand, dealing with developments between Britain and Turkey, and Britain and Russia. Of special importance was a complete list of the materials shipped from the United States to the USSR under Lease-Lend during the years 1942 and 1943; and there was a provisional report from the Foreign Office on the results of the Conference of Foreign Ministers."

The latter was the secret meeting between Cordell Hull, Anthony Eden, and Vyacheslav Molotov that had just taken place in Moscow in early October.

Indeed, when he saw the material, von Papen nicknamed the brilliant new spy "Cicero," after Marcus Tullius Cicero, the famous Roman orator, because the documents he handed over spoke so eloquently. Schellenberg quickly ordered a presentation for Hitler by way of Himmler.

Summoned to Berlin by the foreign office, Moyzisch was also debriefed by Schellenberg and Kaltenbrunner, who promised that they would send photographic technicians and an entire photo lab to Ankara to assist in processing the film. During their meeting, Moyzisch explained that Bazna had made his offer because he despised the British for killing his father. How exactly this happened was never clear. In one story, he had been shot in Istanbul during a fight over Bazna's sister. In another version, he had been killed on a hunting trip in Albania.

As Schellenberg later reflected, the "discrepancy between these two stories gave rise to some doubts about Cicero's truthfulness, but the documents spoke for themselves. He also claimed not to speak a word of English, although later this was found to be completely untrue. I considered all this of incidental importance, but it did raise considerable difficulties in my proving to Hitler and Himmler the validity of Cicero's material."

In fact, it was later shown that Elyesa Bazna had fabricated *both* stories. His father had died peacefully of natural causes. The subjects of his photographs were apparently genuine, though.

The Cicero documents provided—albeit at astonishing cost—a clear and detailed inside look at the plans and preparations for the summit conference of Roosevelt, Churchill, and Stalin that was soon to take place in Tehran. With this, Schellenberg, Skorzeny, and the planners of Operation Long Jump had the master key with which to plan the precise methods and timing for the assassination conspiracy of the century.

Danger at Every Turn

"**S**talin don't want to do much travelin' of any kind, but I got him to go far as Tehran to meet with the President," the old man in the car told Michael Francis Reilly of the Secret Service. Cordell Hull was speaking ironically. He knew that Tehran had been Josef Stalin's idea and Franklin Roosevelt was being dragged off to the ends of the earth against his better judgment.

The location of the summit was still so secret that the president's bodyguard had to be told by the secretary of state at a nearly deserted airport in an otherwise empty car.

"I met most of the politicians, statesmen, diplomats, and leading warriors of my generation while I was attached to the White House, and none appealed to me more than the squeaky-voiced, courtly, yet adamant, hillbilly Judge from Tennessee," the president's bodyguard wrote of Hull in his memoirs. "From what I read I take it the old judge was a great Secretary of State; from what I saw, I know the old gentleman was a great man."

Reilly had taken leave from the U.S. Navy in 1934 to join the Secret Service, and became chief of the White House Detail after Pearl Harbor. It was Reilly who had the idea that the White House Detail should use Al Capone's five-ton bulletproof Cadillac, which had earlier been seized by the Treasury Department, to protect the president.

Reilly had traveled to North Africa ahead of Roosevelt, who was still at sea, and met with Hull, who was returning from the top secret foreign ministers conference in Moscow, where he had just met with Vyacheslav Molotov and Britain's Anthony Eden to plan the upcoming summit at Tehran.

Reilly's security problem was immense. The president was at sea, en route to not one, but three high-level conferences that would convene in places where security was a bodyguard's nightmare. Roosevelt and Winston Churchill would meet in Cairo on November 22 for the Sextant Conference with China's Chiang Kai-shek, before traveling on to Tehran to meet Stalin five days later for the conference designated as Eureka. They would then return to Cairo on December 2 for another five days of Sextant.

The dates and locations of these conferences had not been officially announced, nor had anything about Roosevelt's itinerary. Postwar summits would be media events, but the wartime conferences were closely guarded secrets. It was not until November 20 that Soviet Ambassador Mikhail Maximov phoned Iranian Prime Minister Ali Soheili to officially alert him that the Man of Steel was coming to Tehran.

Official secrecy notwithstanding, a potential Big Three meeting had, of course, been the subject of occasional unsubstantiated speculation in the press since the summer, and all sorts of things were being whispered on the streets in neutral capitals from Lisbon to Ankara to Cairo itself. The Germans had a better idea of the president's progress and his ports of call than the press, and though Reilly did not know this, he knew enough to fear this.

From the moment that errant torpedo almost hit the USS *Iowa*, Reilly felt he was guiding the president through a figurative minefield.

Reilly continued on to Algeria immediately after he met with Hull, where he spent a few hours conferring with American military authorities about the security arrangements for the president's arrival at Mers el Kabir, the port adjacent to Oran. He then flew on to inspect the site of the Sextant Conference.

"Cairo was filled with Axis spies and the price of a life was even cheaper than at Casablanca," Reilly wrote, describing his impressions of the situation in the Egyptian capital that month. "A sixty-dollar fine was the general punishment meted out by the courts for killing a native. For ten dollars one could hire a professional agitator who would provide one thousand natives to create a frenzied demonstration for or against anything or anybody. The price increased in exact proportion to the number of demonstrators wanted.... When I arrived in Cairo, native heads were being bashed in by the hundreds in front of the British and French Embassies in the riots associated with the Axis-agitated uprisings in Lebanon. The city was seething with unrest."

Roosevelt and Churchill would never see the head-bashing. The Allies had requisitioned the Mena House luxury hotel—located west of the city in the shadow of the pyramids—as well as several surrounding villas. The latter included that of American Ambassador Alexander Kirk, which is where Roosevelt would be staying. When Reilly arrived, they were already stringing the barbed wire around the area, and the kitchen workers at all the villas had been replaced by Allied culinary staff. Roosevelt would bring his own cooks and stewards from the White House. At least Reilly could check poison off the list of dangers that potentially awaited his boss.

Reilly then flew secretly to Tehran to make a quick inspection of the airfield at Qaleh Morgi (a.k.a. Ghale Morghi) that would be used by Roosevelt and his entourage when they flew in on November 27.

"It was cursory because I didn't want to contact the Russians or the British until I had seen the President on his arrival at Oran," Reilly recalled.

He was wary of the SIS as well as of the NKVD. Today, the Secret Service would communicate with "friendly" security agencies in advance of a presidential visit, but this was wartime, and it was an era when even the friendly services kept secrets from one another. "I knew I would have ample time while he was at Cairo to effect arrangements at Tehran."

As Reilly returned to Algeria to meet Roosevelt, the Allies had Ultra decryptions of Enigma traffic indicating that Canaris and Schellenberg knew of Roosevelt's impending arrival by sea. That raised the prospect of a Germany U-boat attack, though the *Iowa's* foot-thick belt armor would have provided a challenge for German torpedoes. Another threat mentioned by Reilly in his memoirs was the new air-launched Ruhrstall SD 1400X (a.k.a. "Fritz-X") glide bombs. Two of these had been used by the Luftwaffe just a few weeks earlier to sink the Italian battleship *Roma*. The erstwhile pride of the Italian fleet was nearly 90 percent the size of the *Iowa* in both length and displacement. Thinking back in recent memory to Pearl Harbor, American planners were only too aware that airpower had been very unkind to battleships during World War II.

Allied air and naval power was ordered to launch a full court press against the U-boat threat around the Straits of Gibraltar, and sank at least one German submarine, while Allied aircraft provided air cover to keep the Luftwaffe at bay as the *Iowa* and her flotilla approached and slipped through the straits by night. Nevertheless, the Spanish, friendly to the Germans, though not a declared belligerent, annoyed the Americans by illuminating the president's ship with searchlights—for the benefit of any German vessel in the area.

Roosevelt reached Oran at daybreak on November 20, where he and his party were greeted by General Dwight Eisenhower, then the senior American commander in the Mediterranean, and soon to be appointed as Supreme Allied Commander in Europe.

On November 22, after spending two nights at Eisenhower's headquarters in Tunisia and a day touring nearby battlefields, they boarded a USAAF C-54 Skymaster piloted by Major Otis Bryan that had been set aside for the president's use, and flew on to Cairo. At that time, there was no permanent presidential aircraft. As noted in official U.S. Air Force records, the first such aircraft, specially fitted out for Roosevelt with a stateroom and a wheelchair elevator, designated as VC-54C and nicknamed "Sacred Cow," was not used by him until February 1945. The call sign "Air Force One" was not used until 1953.

By the time that he headed for Cairo with the president, Reilly had been joined by his second in command, Guy Spaman, and by Agent Charley Fredericks. Roosevelt, meanwhile, had been joined by his sons, Elliott and Franklin, who were officers, respectively, in the USAAF and the U.S. Navy.

"We had a fighter escort from takeoff to landing, which wasn't surprising in view of our passenger list," Mike Reilly recalled of the continuing security measures. "Any Luftwaffe pilot who knocked off that plane would have very little trouble getting himself a weekend pass to Berlin."

Counterintuitively, Reilly was soon complicit in a serious breach of security, although he did do so under orders.

"After we were airborne and out of contact with the ground because of radio silence, the Boss told me he wanted to fly along the Nile and over the Pyramids. He asked me to awaken him when we reached the southernmost Pyramids. I called the President shortly after 7:00 a.m. He was thrilled by the monuments, the Sphinx, and the Nile. Major Bryan circled the plane constantly to give the Boss a good view."

"Man's desire to be remembered is colossal," Roosevelt remarked, shaking his head as he pondered the pyramids.

Meanwhile, the dread of possible Luftwaffe action was at fever pitch at the Cairo West airfield, where the presidential C-54 was now overdue. As Reilly later noted, "Our unreportable sightseeing jaunt set the Cairo air headquarters on its ear. A fighter escort had been dispatched to meet us at dawn south of Cairo, and when we pulled into that city, sans escort and two hours late, you could hear ulcers popping and the brass sizzling all over headquarters."

Through it all, the president was unfazed, and everyone who had been pacing the tarmac breathed a sigh of relief when the presidential party finally arrived.

The following day, Roosevelt and his chiefs of staff sat down with Prime Minister Churchill and Chiang Kai-shek for the first full day of meetings.

Also present was Andrei Yanuarevich Vyshinsky, the Soviet deputy foreign minister, who nudged close to the president and invited him to stay at the Soviet embassy compound when he flew up to Tehran. It was, Vyshinsky pointed out, located in the heart of the city, while the American compound was on the edge of town. He added that because most of the actual conference meetings were to take place at the Soviet compound, this arrangement would be more convenient for the president than having to drive across town every day.

Roosevelt flashed his famous toothy grin and told the Soviet diplomat "Thanks, but no thanks."

When Vyshinsky had moved on, the president whispered to Reilly that both Churchill and the Shah of Iran had extended similar invitations, but that he planned to stay under an American roof because he wanted to remain "more independent than a guest could hope to be."

There would be more to be said on that subject after the Big Three had reached the Iranian capital.

Early in the afternoon, Mike Reilly departed from the Egyptian capital aboard the president's C-54 on his second visit to distant Tehran, accompanied by agent James Joseph Rowley. A five-year veteran of the Secret Service at the time, Rowley would become its director in 1961. In this role, he was destined to figure in several of the conspiracy theories about the assassination of John F. Kennedy—which occurred on his watch, although he was not present in Dallas at the time that shots were fired.

Reilly and Rowley were headed to Tehran specifically to inspect security arrangements in advance of the president's arrival. The 29,589 American personnel in Iran at that time were concentrated mainly in the

Persian Corridor, but at his headquarters in Tehran, General Donald Connolly maintained a force of about a thousand men at two U.S. Army posts, Camp Amirabad and Camp Atterbury.

Each of the Allied powers maintained its own security force in Tehran, and did not rely on the Tehran city police, most of whom were not favorably disposed to the occupying powers, and many of whom were nationalists who had supported the notion of the now improbable German "liberation" of Iran from the Allies. Norman Schwarzkopf's gendarmes, meanwhile, were situated mainly on lines of communication, including the rail line through the Persian Corridor.

Reilly's advance team planned the route that Roosevelt's aircraft would take, and inspected the airfields en route. At the time, it had yet to be determined whether the president would fly all the way into Tehran, or fly only to Basra in Iraq and travel the rest of the way by train. Back home, he typically traveled by train, and if he traveled by rail between Basra and Tehran, he would essentially be traveling on an American railroad. By this time, the locomotives and rolling stock were American-made, and they were crewed by U.S. Army Military Railway Service personnel who answered to Connolly's Persian Gulf Service Command.

On the other hand, Reilly found the route itself to be daunting in the extreme, with the "tracks reaching an elevation of 8,000 feet at some points as they wind crazily along the crest of the mountains. The ferocious Bedouin mountain tribes living along the railroad periodically made raids, killed the American MPs assigned to protect the railroad, removed sections of the rails, and wrecked the trains."

He inspected the Shah's four-car royal train, which would be used by Roosevelt if he went by rail, noting that the "fittings in the cars were gold plated, and the dining car table service was made of solid gold. The interior of the cars was beautifully constructed. The train was certainly the finest typhus-laden piece of traveling equipment in the world."

The only reason that the rail option was even being considered was the concern expressed by Admiral Ross McIntire, the president's personal physician, who had accompanied him on the trip. It was the doctor's understanding that Tehran was surrounded by mountains, and he feared the adverse effects on Roosevelt's heart that might come from his having to fly as high as 16,000 feet in the unpressurized C-54.

Otis Bryan, the president's pilot, had studied the charts and claimed that he could fly the entire route from Cairo to Tehran at an altitude no greater than 6,000 feet and he proceeded to prove it that day. Reilly could now cross a 600-mile train trip, typhus-laden traveling equipment, and ferocious mountain tribes—such as Nasr Khan's Qashqai, of course—off of his list of potential uncertainties.

As they circled the Qaleh Morgi airfield—elevation 3,600 feet—they noted the enormous red star painted across the runway now that the field had been commandeered by the Soviets. As soon as Reilly emerged from the aircraft, he was greeted by General Dmitri Vasilevich Arkadiev of the NKVD. Reilly later called him "Artikov," and described him as "my opposite number and head of the NKVD." While the official United States State Department record of the Cairo and Tehran conferences does list him as the Soviet Commissar of State Security, Gary Kern of the CIA points out that Arkadiev was in charge only of the "NKVD department of transportation," adding that "Reilly never saw the real head of the NKVD [and of Soviet state security], Lavrenty Beria, who was present [in Tehran] but kept to the shadows."

In any case, Arkadiev had become the face of Soviet security operations in the city, which effectively *did* make him Reilly's opposite number. He showed the Secret Service team around Qaleh Morgi and answered their questions. When Reilly wanted to know whether there was a radio navigation beacon at the airport that the presidential aircraft could use for its approach and landing, Arkadiev just laughed.

He explained that "using radio beams for navigation [was] for girls and old women."

Arkadiev then proceeded to tell Reilly a story about a Russian pilot who was flying an American Lend-Lease B-25 bomber from Qaleh Morgi to Moscow. En route, he wanted to check his position, so he buzzed a rail station to read the sign. In so doing, he hit a passing train and crashed. Though the pilot survived, destroying a precious Lend-Lease aircraft was a capital crime. At his court-martial, the pilot asserted that the train was early, and it was the engineer's fault that it was in the way. When the judge verified the story, the engineer, not the pilot, was executed.

"You know," Arkadiev told the bewildered Reilly with a chuckle, "pilots are scarce in my country, but engineers are plentiful."

Reilly later observed that the "Russians are nothing I care to dismiss in a sentence, but I found them suspicious, yet completely without guile; grim, yet devoted to parties and gaiety; frank beyond the point of rudeness, yet as sensitive as so many prima donnas. In other words, I understand them no better than most Americans do."

13

Boots on the Ground

"Cairo was filled with Axis spies," Mike Reilly had observed, and he was right. Walther Schellenberg's complex network of agents, including those of his mysterious "No. 2 organization" in Istanbul, with its vast network across the entire region, knew of Franklin Roosevelt's arrival within an hour of his touching down at Cairo West on the morning of November 22. Schellenberg, in Berlin, had the information four hours later and shared it with Keltenbrunner of the SS and Canaris of the Abwehr.

The Germans had calculated that the Allied leaders would spend no less than two days and no more than a week in the Egyptian capital, so their arrival in Cairo was set as the operational trigger for Long Jump. Reichsführer SS Heinrich Himmler and Generalfeldmarschall Wilhelm Keitel of the Oberkommando der Wehrmacht signed off on the operation, and the go-code was issued. SD Sonderlehrgang hit teams, along with Lothar Schoellhorn's Abwehr team, were already on the ground at the

Luftwaffe bases in Crimea and ready to roll. Much of their equipment had been air dropped earlier, and was already on the ground inside Iran.

That night, the powerful BMW 801 engines of the Ju 290s roared to life and the big transports of Kampfgeschwader 200 headed south across the Black Sea toward Iran. There were two contingents to Operation Long Jump, each tasked with a separate aspect of the mission. Landing first were those dropped on November 22 near Qazvin, about a hundred miles northwest of Tehran, directly under the noses of the NKVD in the Soviet occupation zone. Coincidentally, Qazvin was the northern end of the American-controlled Persian Corridor, the point where Lend-Lease supplies were turned over to the Soviets.

The second group was inserted two nights later at Daryacheh-ye Namak, sixty miles east of Qom, where most of the Operation Franz teams had arrived. Laslo Havas reports that four Sonderlehrgang men, along with more than fifty anti-Soviet Russian troops, were part of the first wave, while six Sonderlehrgang hit teams—each with an Iranian interpreter assigned—comprised the second.

The teams jumped into the darkness of the desert night, assuming that they would be met by fellow Germans and Melliyun-I-Iran agents, and that safe houses awaited them.

In fact, the British—thanks to Ernst Merser—now knew about the site near Qom, although they had not yet shared this information with the Soviets.

Not only had Oberg told Merser about the air drops at Daryacheh-ye Namak, two weeks earlier he had actually invited him to *go there*.

Using Merser's wireless transmitter, Oberg had been carrying on a dialogue with his handlers in Berlin, and had been informed of an Operation Long Jump supply drop scheduled for November 7. Oberg had turned to Merser for help. How could he transport crates of weapons and ammunition from the desert dry lake to Melliyun-I-Iran safe houses in Tehran?

No problem. The well connected Swiss double agent made a few calls and found an Iranian gendarmerie officer who had a weakness for being

The autographed photo that Adolf Hitler personalized for Reza Shah, seen here in its original frame on display at the Sahebgharanie Palace in Tehran. Hitler signed it "With the Best Wishes, Berlin, 12 March 1936." (Wikimedia Commons)

Reza Shah ruled Iran from 1925 to 1941. To counter the British and Soviets he encouraged the Germans to invest heavily in Iran, but he hired an American to balance his checkbook. Born a commoner, he called himself a "simple soldier," but ruled with an iron fist and developed lavish tastes. (Author's collection)

A young Polish refugee answering the description of Wanda Pollack, the accidental heroine of Operation Long Jump, as photographed by Nick Parrino of the U.S. Office of War Information in Tehran in early 1943. (Library of Congress)

Brigadeführer Walther Friedrich Schellenberg headed Germany's Sicherheitsdienst (Security Service), the elaborate espionage and covert operations component of the dreaded SS. (Author's collection)

Admiral Wilhelm Franz Canaris was the chief of the Abwehr, the military intelligence service of the Wehrmacht, Germany's armed forces high command. (Author's collection)

A smiling Mrs. Louis Dreyfus, the wife of the United States ambassador to Iran, is seen here out and about on a photo op in Tehran in 1943. She and the grim faced Iranian gendarme escorting her were photographed while chatting with some local people by Nick Parrino. (Library of Congress)

Major General Donald Connolly commanded the U.S. Army Gulf Service Command (PGSC). He and his men ran the Persian Corridor, a massive road and rail supply line through Iran that delivered Lend Lease supplies to the Soviet Union. (Library of Congress)

Herbert Norman Schwarzkopf (right) was Iran's "top cop" during World War II (seen here with Charles Lindbergh). As superintendent of the New Jersey State Police, he earned a reputation as a "crime buster" and garnered national attention during his investigation of the kidnapping of Lindbergh's son. In 1942 as a U.S. Army major general, Schwarzkopf went to Iran to take command of Iran's 20,000 gendarmes, who handled security in the Persian Corridor. (Library of Congress)

A U.S. Army Persian Gulf Service Command train surrounded by Schwarzkopf's Iranian gendarmes, photographed at a stop in the Persian Corridor by Nick Parrino. (Library of Congress)

Nikolai Ivanovich Kuznetsov was an NKVD double agent specializing in covert operations behind German lines in Ukraine. A gifted linguist, he was able to easily impersonate German officers. He befriended Sturmbannführer Hans Ulrich von Ortel of the SS, learning from him some of the important elements of the planned Operation Long Jump. (Author's collection)

Standartenführer Otto Skorzeny, the legendary Waffen SS master of special operations who became known as "the most dangerous man in Europe." (Author's collection)

Otto Skorzeny with Benito Mussolini after Skorzeny personally led the mission that successfully liberated the Italian dictator from captivity atop Gran Sasso in the Apennines on September 12, 1943, two months before final preparations were under way for Operation Long Jump. (Author's collection)

U.S. Secret Service Special Agent Michael Francis Reilly with President Franklin Roosevelt. Reilly headed the Secret Service's White House Detail and acted as Roosevelt's personal bodyguard. (U.S. Secret Service)

President Franklin Delano Roosevelt (in dark glasses) with members of the U.S. Secret Service White House Detail aboard the USS *Iowa* in November 1943 en route to the Cairo and Tehran summit conferences. From the left the agents are Jim Rowley, Michael Reilly, and Charley Fredericks. (U.S. Secret Service)

The presentation at the Tehran Conference of the Sword of Honour (later called the Sword of Stalingrad) on November 29, 1943. Inscribed by command of George VI, it was a gift from the British people to the Soviet defenders of Stalingrad. To the left of the British soldier holding the sword are Field Marshal Alan Brooke, Chief of the Imperial General Staff (with mustache) and Air Marshal Charles "Peter" Portal, Chief of the Royal Air Staff. To the right are Prime Minister Winston Churchill (with glasses); British Foreign Minister Anthony Eden; Soviet Marshal Kliment Voroshilov; and Josef Stalin. When Stalin subsequently handed the sword to Voroshilov, he dropped it on the floor. (U.S. Army Signal Corps)

Winston Churchill (center) enjoys a lighthearted moment with Josef Stalin during his sixty-ninth birthday party at the British Embassy in Tehran on November 30, 1943, while Franklin Roosevelt appears lost in thought. (U.S. Army Signal Corps)

With flashbulbs littering the ground, photographers and film crews record Josef Stalin, Franklin Delano Roosevelt, and Winston Churchill on the south portico of the Soviet Embassy. On the left, standing on the first step down from the porch and looking away, is U.S. Army Chief of Staff General George Marshall. Behind Marshall is Admiral Ernest King, Commander in Chief of the United States Fleet and Chief of Naval Operations (in white cap), and USAAF Commanding General Henry Harley "Hap" Arnold. The young man with the intent expression by the pillar is Soviet translator Vladimir Pavlov. Between the pillars on the right are Admiral William Leahy, Chief of Staff to President Roosevelt and Chairman of the Joint Chiefs of Staff; Soviet Marshal Kliment Voroshilov; Sir Archibald Clark Kerr, the British Ambassador to the Soviet Union (with his hand on his chin); Soviet Foreign Commissar Vyacheslav Molotov; and British Foreign Minister Anthony Eden (next to the pillar). The two men in suits beneath the cluster of officers on the steps immediately below Eden are U.S. Secret Service Agents Michael Reilly and Jim Rowley. (U.S. Army Signal Corps)

The formal Eureka Conference Big Three portrait of Josef Stalin, Franklin Delano Roosevelt, and Winston Churchill on the south portico of the Soviet Embassy in Tehran. (U.S. Army Signal Corps)

bribed. Arrangements were made for a convoy of trucks driven by men who would ask no questions.

As the sturmbannführer was suiting up to lead the retrieval operation, Merser took him aside and reminded him that it was dangerous out there. The NKVD dragnet was in full swing and Oberg didn't want to risk being caught, did he?

Oberg paused, thought it over, and agreed to let Merser be in charge of picking up the supplies.

Out at the lake bed, Merser and the Iranians watched and waited as the Ju 290 thundered overhead, and parachutes began drifting down with large metal crates. As planned, these were loaded into the Iranian trucks and driven into the capital. Not part of the plan, at least as Oberg had understood it, was a short unannounced diversion on the way to the safe house.

As Ernst Merser opened the cases for Percy Downward, the British agent was able to see for himself the extent of the arsenal that was being assembled for Operation Long Jump. There were German automatic pistols, as well as Gewehr 41 semi-automatic rifles and examples of the newly produced MP 43, a prototype weapon to the Sturmgewehr 44, which would be widely used in the final year of the war, and which is considered by historians to be the first production assault rifle. Also included were captured Allied weapons, including British Sten submachine guns, as well as Soviet Samozaryadnyj Karabin Simonova (SKS) semi-automatic rifles. These weapons were included explicitly for the infiltration mission.

What especially caught the attention of Downward was a quantity of British No. 82 grenades. Also known as "Gammon bombs," they were plastic-explosive anti-personnel weapons that were used by British airborne troops. They were light, compact, and deadly. These weapons were included explicitly for the final hit on the Big Three.

Downward now knew the details of the Long Jump arsenal, as well as the approximate number of hit men. He also knew which dry lake to watch for parachutes attached to enemy troops.

The Sonderlehrgang men landing in this location would do so under the gaze of British eyes, but those landing at Qazvin would have other problems with which to contend.

Mike Reilly had sensed that Cairo was filled with Axis agents, but he found Tehran *teeming* with NKVD agents and Soviet troops. A thousand-man contingent of NKVD agents flooded into Tehran in October, and by late November, when General Dmitri Vasilevich Arkadiev of the NKVD arrived, the number had tripled. With these men dragging their dragnet through the streets of Tehran, it would greatly complicate matters for the Long Jump teams.

As Wanda Pollack and Winifred Oberg had learned the hard way two months earlier when the Soviet presence was much less, the NKVD approach to security was straightforward and ruthless. They had come, not to protect Stalin from a *specific* threat, but to literally sweep the streets clear of *any conceivable* threats. Lacking the finesse of the British or the Americans, they went about the task as they had during Stalin's purges in the late 1930s or in occupied Poland in 1939. The NKVD set out to seize everyone who was the least bit suspicious—or the least bit *German*—as well as everyone else who happened to be in the way.

In a 1965 article in the Moscow weekly illustrated magazine *Ogoniok*, a former NKVD man named Alexander Lukin wrote that "one after the other the influential members of the German colony disappeared without leaving any trace. When the valet of one of them entered the bedroom in the morning he found nothing but a pajama button, and not a single suit had gone from the wardrobe."

Had it not been for the loose lips of Hans Ulrich von Ortel, who would soon be gathering up his parachute in the wind-blown dry lakebed of Daryacheh-ye Namak, Arkadiev and the NKVD resident agent in Tehran, Colonel Andrei Mikhalovits Vertinski, might not have been running their targeted campaign against the Germans in Tehran with such merciless furor. When he had unwittingly confided in Nikolai Kuznetsov that he would be working with Otto Skorzeny on "something big," it could have been anywhere. When he whispered to Lydiya Lissovskaya—Kuznetsov's girlfriend—that he would bring her a Persian rug, he compromised the whole operation.

The NKVD had to have known that the British had already rounded up most of the German agents in Tehran and that those Germans who remained were mainly anti-Nazis or German Jews. This, however, did not seem to matter. After the war, Laslo Havas interviewed Jakob Kupferstein, a successful clothier who was abducted along with his wife, mother-in-law, and two sons. When he told a Soviet officer that he was Jewish, the man replied that "If you are both a Jew and a German, you have two good reasons to shut up."

As Kupferstein explained, his family was "put into a single-story building belonging to the Russian barracks in the town of Meshed. There was room for 30 people at the most, but while I was there—I was released at the end of December—some 200 people were brought in. Those for whom there was no room in the building were taken away every three or four days, I still don't know where. After the war I tried to inquire at the Soviet Legation and also through the Red Cross. At the legation they said that I was mad, I had invented the whole thing.... If I am mad, someone could perhaps tell me where my wife and my mother-in-law have gone."

As clumsy as it seemed, one cannot say that the NKVD approach was ineffective. When they got their hands on Winifred Oberg, they did not know that he was part of an SD hit team out to get Stalin, but they nevertheless had him in custody and off the streets. Had it not been for the most improbable jailbreak imaginable, they would still have had him behind bars.

When Walther Schellenberg looked at Andrei Vlasov's huge anti-Bolshevik army, he was not alone in seeing an incredible opportunity.

Hitler and Himmler, however, saw a disaster waiting to happen. They were right, and Schellenberg was wrong.

The SD had thoroughly vetted the fifty Russians who were picked for the infiltration of the Soviet security detail, but not thoroughly enough. Indeed, this cadre of would-be infiltrators had itself been infiltrated by Soviet political commissars who had followed them into the German stalags when they were first captured by the Germans. This aspect of the Long Jump incursion was disclosed to the NKVD as soon as the Qazvin teams reached Tehran.

In briefing Mike Reilly at the Soviet embassy, NKVD General Dmitri Arkadiev did not mention the agents in Red Army uniforms who had landed near Qazvin but did tell him that "the Germans had dropped parachutists in the Russian-occupied area near Tehran." Arkadiev confessed that his men had "not caught any of the Germans, who, [it was] suspected, were hiding in the mountains." The "mountains" was a reference to the British zone of Iran, where it was known that Operation Franz teams were already operating with Bernhardt Schulze-Holthus, Nasr Khan, and the Qashqai. Reilly was given the impression that German sabotage teams were at large, and that he needed to rely on the assistance, readily offered, of the NKVD. Reilly believed that Arkadiev commanded some 3,000 men. Reilly would have barely more than a dozen Secret Service agents on the ground in the city. He thought it only made sense to accept help from the Soviets.

"In a few days Roosevelt, Churchill, and Stalin would be in Tehran," Reilly wrote. "The German parachutists could have been dropped for one of only two reasons: either to assassinate the Allied leaders or to sabotage the railroad between Basra and Tehran. This railroad was the life line for Russian Lend-Lease supplies shipped to the Persian Gulf from the United States."

Reilly also learned that the British had Franz Mayr in custody, and was told that "after some painful persuasion, Fritz [as Reilly called Mayr] admitted he expected the parachutists to contact him."

In Cairo, on the afternoon of November 26, Winston Churchill and Franklin Roosevelt were handed cables from Josef Stalin, telling each recipient that he would be "at your service" in Tehran in two days' time. Stalin's biographer, Dmitri Volkogonov, commented that this was "an odd phrase, coming from him, but one that was no doubt meant to project the image of a gentleman."

From the Allied embassies, to the shadowy alleyways, to the safe house on tree-lined Kakh Street, the Tehran stage was now set for the critical six days during which history would reach a turning point.

Saturday, November 27

"fog," wrote Carl Sandburg, "comes in on little cat feet."

Overnight, this nefarious weather feline, one not often associated with the North African desert, had formed upon the marshes that surround the Nile River, and had silently crept westward toward the Cairo West airfield. Lieutenant Bill Rigdon, President Franklin Roosevelt's secretary, noted in the official log that "all hands were up and ready for a 4:30 a.m. departure for the airport," but for the fog's "little cat feet" which had resulted in poor visibility.

Having sat on its silent haunches, fog "then moves on," wrote Carl Sandburg.

Wheels-up finally came at 7:07 a.m., and Roosevelt was winging his way toward Tehran.

The C-54 piloted by Major Otis Bryan carried the president; General Edwin "Pa" Watson, his senior aide; Harry Hopkins, his special assistant; Rear Admiral Ross McIntire, his doctor; Major John Boettiger, his son-in-law;

Averell Harriman, his ambassador to the Soviet Union; Admiral William Leahy, his military chief of staff, who was also the Chairman of the Joint Chiefs of Staff; Lieutenant Bill Rigdon; and Mike Reilly and the bodyguard detail that included Charley Fredericks and Roy Kellerman. Another C-54 followed with the other members of the Joint Chiefs—General George Marshall of the U.S. Army, Admiral Ernest King of the U.S. Navy, and General Hap Arnold of the USAAF—along with their respective staff officers.

An hour and a half after take-off, the passengers in Roosevelt's plane were glued to the windows as Bryan circled low over Jerusalem. The second C-54 followed suit. In his diary, Hap Arnold noted that the landscape reminded him of Death Valley, with "no trees, no green vegetation, no green grass, only desert for miles." As the Skymasters crossed Iraq and entered Iran, it would be more of the same.

Having passed into Iranian air space, the passengers returned to the windows to gaze down at the Persian Corridor and the Trans-Iranian Railway. Rigdon jotted in his notes that with "almost perfect visibility ... we sighted train loads and motor convoys loaded with U.S. lend-lease supplies, bound from the Persian Gulf port of Basra to Russia."

That, the president reminded himself, was what this remote corner of World War II was all about.

After six and a half hours, the C-54 came over the Soviet-controlled Qaleh Morgi airfield, with the immense red star painted across it to leave no doubt to anyone—especially Josef Stalin, who had landed there earlier in the day—as to who was in charge. Rigdon made note of the "large number of our Lend-Lease planes now bearing the Red Star of Russia."

The arrival was understated. As Roosevelt had requested, there was no pomp, no ceremony, no band to play "Hail to the Chief." Only Major General Donald Connolly of the Persian Gulf Service Command, U.S. Army drivers, and advance members of Reilly's Secret Service detail, were on hand to welcome the president to Tehran. Though the Big Three rendezvous in the Iranian capital was an open secret, it was still an *official* secret.

Across town at Ernst Merser's house at Kakh Street, everything had changed since the daring but foolhardy raid on the NKVD safe house. The raid had been a crucial turning point, not only for the momentum of Operation Long Jump, but also for the momentum of Merser's awkward relationship with Wanda Pollack.

As he recalled some years later to Laslo Havas, he had come to her and said frankly, "I have been in love with you from the first day we met. Perhaps I should have told you so before, but I refrained for various reasons which it would take too long to explain. However, I don't want to prolong this misunderstanding between us, and, besides, I can't bear the tension much longer. I wish to stress that your position in this house is entirely independent of what you feel and of your answer. But I should like you to know that whatever happens between us in the future depends entirely on you."

Thereupon, she tearfully embraced him in a scene which, in a romantic film, would have preceded a fade to black accompanied by a welling of violins.

But this was *not* a romantic film, and there was also the inconvenient presence of Sturmbannführer Winifred Oberg. Weeks of pacing the floor at the house on Kakh Street had propelled Oberg toward the sort of conclusion that one would expect of an action-adventure film.

At Qaleh Morgi, Roosevelt was carried down from the C-54, placed into a car and driven straight to the American embassy. For the American soldiers who met the aircraft, it was their first look at Roosevelt, and the first unanticipated realization that their own leader was a paraplegic, and could not walk off the plane under his own power. It was a subject that was never mentioned in the press nor exposed on film, and a majority of Americans did not know.

For most of the Americans in the president's entourage, it was their first look at the Iranian capital.

"Nice wide streets here," Bill Rigdon wrote in the official journal. "The roadways are paved but most of the sidewalks are not, causing the city to appear very dusty and dirty. The city's transportation system was apparently most inadequate. It consisted mainly of a very few small buses, which were invariably packed, and horse-drawn 'droshkies.'"

Arnold, Reilly, and Rigdon, as well as other Americans who kept diaries during the trip, noted that the gutters were used as open sewers.

Though the weather was clear, it was very cold. Rigdon mentioned that "some of our party required three or more blankets to keep warm at night.... Most of the buildings are heated by portable oil stoves. The Russian Embassy is the only steam heated building in the city, we were told."

At the American embassy, Roosevelt's entourage was greeted by Louis Goethe Dreyfus, the ambassador. Also on hand was Brigadier General Patrick Hurley, the president's personal troubleshooter in Russia and the Middle East who served as his diplomatic advance man for the Eureka Conference. Before he went to his room, Roosevelt sent a personal message to the Soviet embassy to invite Stalin to come to dinner that night.

The president had barely an hour to freshen up before Soviet Ambassador Mikhail Maximov arrived to officially greet the president. Stalin sent his regrets. He had endured "a very strenuous day," and could not come to dinner. Gary Kerr of the CIA, in his retrospective of the Tehran meetings, later observed that "although well rested, Stalin was determined not to ride through the streets of a foreign city, no matter how heavy his protection."

He was well aware that the boots of German agents were on nearby ground.

Kerr goes on to say that Roosevelt next phoned Churchill to invite *him*, but the prime minister explained that he had "a sore throat from talking so long at the closing ceremonies of the Cairo conference and planned to retire to bed early with a volume of Dickens. He had the consolation of Scotch whiskey, for which the Americans sorely envied him, since their cellar supply had been closed off by a ramp built for Roosevelt's wheelchair."

In his memoirs, Churchill admitted to suffering from a terrible cold, which later turned into pneumonia. He was also cranky about the well-meaning, but careless reception that he had received in Tehran, thanks to Sir Reader Bullard, the British ambassador.

While Roosevelt was able to slip into Tehran largely unnoticed, Churchill's arrival had been attended by pomp and formality, and a potentially dangerous lack of secrecy. "I could not admire the arrangements which had been made for my reception after landing in Tehran," he wrote in his memoirs. "The American Security were more clever about the President."

Bullard, who no doubt thought that he was doing the right thing, arranged for the road from Qaleh Morgi to the embassy to be lined with Persian cavalrymen every fifty yards for at least three miles.

"It was clearly shown to any evil people that somebody of consequence was coming, and which way," Churchill grumbled. "The men on horseback advertised the route, but could provide no protection at all. A police car driving a hundred yards in advance gave warning of our approach. The pace was slow. Presently large crowds stood in the spaces between the Persian cavalry, and as far as I could see there were few, if any, foot police. Towards the centre of Tehran these crowds were four or five deep. The people were friendly but noncommittal. They pressed to within a few feet of the car."

Instead of feeling special, the prime minister felt exposed. A panoply of disastrous scenarios played out in his head as he sat in traffic.

"There was no kind of defence at all against two or three determined men with pistols or a bomb," he recalled. "As we reached the turning which led to the Legation there was a traffic block, and we remained for three or four minutes stationary amid the crowded throng of gaping Persians. If it had been planned out beforehand to run the greatest risks, and have neither the security of quiet surprise arrival nor an effective escort, the problem could not have been solved more perfectly. However, nothing happened. I grinned at the crowd, and on the whole they grinned at me."

Churchill need not have been cross with Bullard. Everyone in Tehran already knew that he was coming. As Sydney Morrell recalled in his memoirs, the bazaar in Tehran "had known of the Tehran Conference days before even people in the three embassies had known. The sources of bazaar news and the manner in which it is flashed across the Middle East are mysteries which no one has succeeded in explaining satisfactorily. But bazaar gossip is the most important single influence on native life in the Middle East.... It is the center of political gossip, the heart, of intrigues and rumors.... Embassy officials, exchanging the latest official news, would invariably ask each other, 'What does the bazaar say today?'"

The only people in Tehran who were in the dark about the arrival of the Big Three were the Germans.

It was Ernst Merser who convinced the German agents in Tehran that they should lie low rather than seek out the cavalry-lined route of Churchill's progress.

The SD Sonderlehrgang teams that had landed near Qom on November 24 had been met by members of the Melliyun-I-Iran and driven into Tehran. Dmitri Arkadiev may not have known exactly where they were, but he did know they were *somewhere*. Percy Downward, meanwhile, knew the locations of most of them, because the chief rendezvous point was Winifred Oberg's base of operations at Merser's house on Kakh Street, which soon housed the teams led by Hans Ulrich von Ortel of the SD and Lothar Schoellhorn of the Abwehr.

It was entirely by accident that Merser's safe house had become the command and control center for Operation Long Jump. Had it not been for Wanda Pollack, and the crazy rescue mission that succeeded against all odds, Oberg never would have ended up on Kakh Street, nor would any of the others. Had it not been for Merser's convincing hospitality, things would have been entirely different.

Ernst Merser had become Oberg's friend and confidant, and the Long Jump advance man had gladly accepted him as the benefactor and protector of the SD Sonderlehrgang teams that came within the orbit of Merser's house. Indeed, Merser was so considerate of Oberg's need for secrecy and security that he became his only conduit to the outside world.

The newly arrived von Ortel and Schoellhorn certainly fit the role of people who were truly "evil," to borrow Churchill's phrasing. Von Ortel had the viciousness and determination that Oberg and Skorzeny considered indispensable for such an assignment as Operation Long Jump; and Schoellhorn was recruited from the criminal underworld.

In retrospect, it is amazing that such men relaxed so easily in the home of the Swiss businessman and his wide-eyed ragamuffin girlfriend, but this was part of Merser's brilliance as an intelligence operative. Of course, Oberg had fallen for Merser's cover story completely, and his endorsement certainly helped clear their host from suspicion in the minds of the new arrivals.

At the same time, Merser had used the utmost of discretion in guarding the confidentiality of Oberg's secret mission. When Oberg told him in confidence that he was on the ground as part of a plan to assassinate the Big Three, and had sworn him to secrecy, Merser agreed to tell no one, and he had told no one—except Percy Downward. He did not tell Ida Kovalska, Khalil Chapat, Mervyn Wollheim, or Peter Ferguson. They had all met Oberg on the night that they liberated him from Vertinski's prison, and they had seen him on other occasions, but they believed him to be one of the numerous German saboteurs who were widely known to be in Iran. Of course, Merser told Oberg nothing about Ferguson's association with the OSS.

With his house on Kakh Street now overflowing with Germans, Merser took a chance and asked Mervyn Wollheim if he might have room for von Ortel and his team to stay at his apartment. Wollheim agreed.

If it was strange to see a man such as Schoellhorn with his boots casually propped up on Merser's coffee table, it was also well worth a double take to see von Ortel settling in at the home of an American amateur archeologist where Peter Ferguson of the OSS regularly stopped in for a drink. As Laslo Havas later observed, von Ortel greatly enjoyed Wollheim's hospitality because for "the first time in his life he was among people who, instead of trying to prevent him from drinking, *encouraged* him."

After the war, Josef Schnabel, a member of von Ortel's team, told Havas that "the fact that they mainly spoke English did not make me suspicious. After all, we were in a distant place and I could not expect to find Germans everywhere. At home we were told that we had allies among the Americans as well as among every other people. What I could not understand, however, was how they could prepare for an action of such importance when they were dead drunk all the time."

Four miles from where Winston Churchill nursed his head cold, John Winant and Averell Harriman, the American ambassadors to the United Kingdom and to the Soviet Union, arrived to dine with Roosevelt, Hopkins, and Leahy at the American embassy.

While the president was socializing, Mike Reilly had reconnected with Dmitri Arkadiev, his "opposite number." Since they had last met forty-eight hours earlier, Reilly had learned that the NKVD had started rounding up some of the German "parachutists." Indeed, Vyacheslav Molotov, the Soviet foreign commissar, had also informed Harriman of this turn while Reilly was on his way back to Cairo to pick up the president.

Arkadiev confirmed that this was being done, and told Reilly that he had information that a total of thirty-eight Nazis had been dropped around Tehran.

"Are you sure it was thirty-eight?" Reilly asked, reacting to such a precise number.

"Very sure," Arkadiev smiled. "We examined the men we caught most thoroughly."

As Reilly later confided in his memoirs, "The way he said it made me happy I had not been present when the Nazis were questioned."

In retrospect, it would have been useful if one of Reilly's agents had interviewed the parachutists or if Reilly had interviewed Franz Mayr himself, whom he knew was in British custody.

In keeping with NKVD practice, the Germans and the turncoat Russians who had landed at Qazvin "disappeared." When bodies were found in ditches along the road from Qazvin, Norman Schwarzkopf's gendarmes investigated, but came to no conclusions.

"In a house in the road leading to the airfield, the Iranian police found the bodies of two young men," wrote Alexander Lukin two decades later of a grisly discovery made on the outskirts of town. "Their nationality was unknown, no papers showing their identity were found on them. The bodies were never identified and apparently no one regarded this as important. They had one strange identification mark in common: a tattoo mark in the left armpit, which indicates the blood group of every SS officer."

Arkadiev told Reilly only those specifics which were necessary to flesh out the narrative of an imminent threat. As the Secret Service man later wrote, the NKVD questioning "had disclosed that there were at least six German paratroopers loose in the vicinity with a radio transmitter."

This scenario coincides with the testimony of Gevork Vartanian, a then nineteen-year-old Armenian NKVD operative who was working in Tehran, and who created a global media buzz in the early twenty-first century by revealing the details of his role in thwarting Operation Long Jump.

"Our group was the first to locate the Nazi landing party—six radio operators—near the town of Qom, 60 kilometers from Tehran," he told Yury Plutenko of RIA Novosti in an interview published in 2007. "We followed them to Tehran, where the Nazi field station had readied a villa for their stay.

They were traveling by camel, and were loaded with weapons. While we were watching the group, we established that they had contacted Berlin by radio and recorded their communication. When we decrypted these radio messages, we learnt that the Germans were preparing to land a second group of subversives for a terrorist act—the assassination or abduction of the Big Three. The second group was supposed to be led by Skorzeny himself, who had already visited Tehran to study the situation on the spot. We had been following all his movements even then."

Aside from seeming to validate the theory of Otto Skorzeny's anticipated arrival on the scene, Vartanian's story indicates that while Dmitri Arkadiev and Andrei Vertinski had finished rounding up the Soviet turncoats and their German handlers coming in from Qazvin, they also knew about the other landings near Qom, possibly from British sources.

In turn, the assertion by Arkadiev that there were *exactly* thirty-eight Sonderlehrgang operatives involved in the mission roughly coincides with the Havas report that there were four Germans dropped near Qazvin, and that six teams landed near Qom. A team consisting of five or six Germans plus an Iranian translator would be in keeping with a typical Operation Franz mission, after which the Long Jump landings were modeled.

Arkadiev did not tell Reilly how many of the thirty-eight had been captured, but he implied that most—more than merely six radio operators—were still at large.

Disclosure of this distressing situation allowed the Soviets to press Reilly, General Patrick Hurley, and the president's other handlers to reconsider the idea of Roosevelt remaining at the American embassy, and to agree to accept their invitation to move into the center of the city and to stay at the Soviet compound.

Late Saturday evening, Molotov phoned Harriman and Sir Archibald Clark Kerr, the British ambassador to the Soviet Union, asking them to meet him at the Soviet embassy at midnight. The commissar, who routinely scheduled important meetings for the middle of the night, wanted to talk about the issue of getting Roosevelt closer into the city.

Though no official record of this conversation has been found, William Franklin, the deputy director of the State Department Historical Office, who edited the official history of the Tehran conference, refers to a letter that Harriman wrote to Franklin's office on May 25, 1954.

According to Franklin, Harriman said that Molotov told the two Western ambassadors very pointedly "on the basis of information which had reached him, that Roosevelt's presence at Tehran was known to German agents there, that these agents were planning a 'demonstration,' that this might involve an attempt at assassination, and that Stalin therefore urged Roosevelt to move to either the British Legation or the Soviet Embassy. A house in the Soviet Embassy compound was being made ready for Roosevelt's occupancy."

Gary Kerr of the CIA writes that Stalin's eagerness to have Roosevelt inside his compound came neither from generosity nor an interest in the president's well-being, but from a desire to eavesdrop on his American friends.

"For Stalin, bugging friend and foe was an essential part of politics," Kerr points out, citing the memoirs of Boris Bazhanov, Stalin's private secretary. "Since the early 1920s, he had kept a special telephone beneath his desk in the Kremlin for listening in on the private conversations of other Politburo members speaking on an exclusive line. Thus, all through the inner-Party struggle for succession, while leader Vladimir Lenin lay dying and for years after he died in 1924, Stalin was able to eavesdrop on all of his comrades.... Stalin magically knew all of their nighttime thoughts the next morning, outmaneuvered them every day, and eventually had most of them shot."

Naturally, the NKVD men were experienced and technically adept at this type of surveillance. As a CIA man whose business it was to know these things, Kerr notes that the "NKVD extended all manner of mechanical eyes and ears throughout the nation to reinforce the Bolshevik party's totalitarian control."

When Molotov told Harriman that a house "was being made ready for Roosevelt's occupancy," it took no stretch of imagination to suspect that not all of the wires that snaked through the place were connected to plugs and light switches.

Sunday, November 28

Averell Harriman called on Franklin Roosevelt at the American embassy about 9:00 a.m. on the morning of the president's first full day in Tehran. As Bill Rigdon noted in the official log, the ambassador told the president that "if we persisted in our refusal to accept quarters in the Russian compound we would be responsible for any injury that Marshal Stalin might suffer in driving through the town to consult with President Roosevelt. Mr. Harriman emphasized that the city of Tehran had been under complete German control only a few months before and that the risk of assassination of Mr. Churchill and Marshal Stalin while coming to visit President Roosevelt was very real."

The phrase "under complete German control" was a substantial exaggeration. Curiously, it was also used by Guy Spaman, Mike Reilly's second in command in Tehran, when he was asked in June 1945 by Frank Wilson, Chief of the Secret Service, to write an after-action report about Tehran. Spaman told his boss that "it was well known that the city of

Tehran was filled with Axis sympathizers; it had been under complete German control only a few months before and the risk of assassination of Mr. Churchill and Marshal Stalin while coming to visit the President was very real."

Because Spaman had actually been on the ground in Tehran, it is improbable that he copied Rigdon's narrative, but rather more likely that they had both heard the same message from the same source. This was almost certainly the Soviets.

"Both the Russians and the English were pressing hard for the President to move from the isolated American Legation to either the British or the Russian Embassy, which were side by side in the heart of town and were both heavily walled," Reilly recalled. "I was in complete agreement and told the President. I pointed out that Stalin and Churchill would be subjected to unnecessary danger when they came out to visit him and also that the Russian NKVD men felt FDR was risking not only his life but theirs by living outside the town."

"Do you care which Embassy I move to?" Roosevelt asked.

"Not much difference, sir."

Reilly might not have been so hasty with that assessment had he known about the contingent of turncoats in Red Army uniforms that the SD had dropped into the Qazvin area on November 22, and that the Germans had planned for an infiltration of the Soviet compound. Dmitri Arkadiev had deliberately not told Reilly about this.

One advantage of the Soviet compound noted by Reilly was that "If anything happened to the President of the United States [while he was staying at the Soviet compound] we in the Secret Service would be deeply embarrassed, but the Russian Secret Service men would be dead before nightfall." With this kind of incentive, Franklin Roosevelt could be assured of the diligence of the NKVD men who would surround him if he chose to move to the Soviet embassy.

"All right," the president declared. "It's the Russian, then. When do we move?"

The answer was as soon as the logistics were sorted out, and that took until 3:00 in the afternoon. While the president and Harry Hopkins met with Admirals Leahy and King and Generals Marshall and Arnold, Reilly met with General Connolly's Persian Gulf Service Command to set up security for the move, lining the entire route with U.S. Army troops, "shoulder to shoulder."

As Reilly recalled, "We set up the standard cavalcade with the gun-laden jeeps fore and aft, and it traveled slowly along the streets guarded by soldiers. As soon as the cavalcade left the American Legation, we bundled the President into another car, put a jeep in front of him, and went tearing through the ancient side streets of Tehran, while the dummy cavalcade wended its way slowly through the main streets with Agent Bob Holmes [masquerading as Roosevelt] accepting the cheers of the local citizens and I hope the curses of a few bewildered parachute jumpers from Germany. The Boss, as always, was vastly amused by the dummy cavalcade trick and the other cops-and-robbers stuff. I was glad it amused *him*, because it did not amuse *me* much."

Thanks to Ernst Merser, their sole source of information from out on the streets, Winifred Oberg and the SD hit teams were still oblivious to Roosevelt's arrival in Tehran.

For Reilly, the danger represented by the mysterious German agents trumped any loss of independence that Roosevelt might experience by accepting the hospitality of the generous Uncle Joe.

At his guest house within the Soviet compound, Roosevelt seemed to disregard the notion of now being under potential NKVD surveillance, or at least to discount its importance. Just as Reilly was willing to recommend this compromise to save his boss from a German bullet, Roosevelt was anxious to go to any lengths to achieve a rapport with his Soviet ally—even if it meant ignoring Stalin's dark side.

Gary Kerr of the CIA would later write that the "closed borders, internal passports, censored presses, political purges, and forced-labor camps—all of these features of the Soviet system were common knowledge in the 1930s and 1940s, [but] to keep the war effort united and to work for postwar democracy, [Roosevelt] wanted to please Stalin, whom he liked to call 'Uncle Joe.' His primary purpose was to makes friends with a man widely believed to have murdered his wife, liquidated his closest political comrades, and ordered the assassination of Leon Trotsky."

In his writings, Kerr betrayed no fondness for the Man of Steel.

Though he did not mention a concern for eavesdropping devices, Reilly and his team were well aware of being on Soviet soil. He recalled that the Soviet embassy staff made Roosevelt very comfortable, but "some of the things they did weren't any too comforting to a Secret Service agent."

"It was quite noticeable to all of us who attended the various meetings at Tehran when the Russians were present, that it wasn't the United States Secret Service who had the balance of power; it was the Russian guards," Reilly recalled in his memoirs. "The Russian Secret Service controlled everything. Even when Stalin visited the President of the United States or the Prime Minister, there were Russian guards within the building when and where Stalin was present."

He observed with wry amusement "the servants in our part of the Russian Embassy. Everywhere you went you would see a brute of a man in a lackey's white coat busily polishing immaculate glass or dusting dustless furniture. As their arms swung to dust or polish, the clear, cold outline of a Luger automatic could be seen on every hip. They were NKVD boys, of course."

The NKVD boys with their Lugers would perhaps not have been so many and so obvious had Dmitri Arkadiev not been troubled by that unknown number of German agents still out there in the dim alleyways of Tehran. The fear of the "thirty-eight Nazis," which he had instilled in Mike Reilly was a useful tool for achieving the goal of getting Roosevelt inside the Soviet compound, but it was *not* a fabrication.

Percy Downward, too, was fretting. Thanks to Merser, he had a better idea than either Arkadiev or Reilly of where the Germans were hiding, but he was nagged by the thought of those who had slipped through British fingers at Daryacheh-ye Namak. He had no idea where they were. Even though Churchill was already in town, he hesitated to make a move against any of the Germans until he knew where all of them were.

Sturmbannführer Rudolf von Holten-Pflug was the wild card, the team leader of the Germans whom the British had not been able to track. Nobody knew where he was—not the British, not the Soviets, and not any of his fellow Germans with whom he was supposed to rendezvous. Von Holten-Pflug and his men were also apparently the only German operatives in Tehran who knew that the Big Three had arrived.

Had the man who wanted to be the next Otto Skorzeny known that he and his team had stymied the Allied secret services, he would have been delighted. After the war, Skorzeny would take great pride in being labeled as "the most dangerous man in Europe," but von Holten-Pflug could have claimed the title of "the most dangerous man in Tehran"—at least for a few days in late November 1943.

But von Holten-Pflug did not realize this, nor that the whole Qazvin incursion had failed, nor that the British had eyes on *any* of the SD Sonderlehrgang teams. His team had missed making contact with the Melliyun-I-Iran reception team that was supposed to meet them in the desert, and had made their way into Tehran on their own. Their interpreter, a man named Gorechi, a member of Nasr Khan's Qashqai faction, was not especially well connected in the city, but he did have some contacts in Tehran, and he had found the team a place to hide.

Von Holten-Pflug wanted to stick with the plan and coordinate his actions with the other teams, but when they couldn't be found, Gorechi convinced him that it would be better to go it alone. They were only six men, but their Iranian friend told them that he knew somebody who could help them: Misbah Ebtehaj, the Pahlevani martial arts master who "knew everyone" in the Tehran underworld. Though he did not share the information with Gorechi, Ebtehaj knew a lot of people who were looking for von Holten-Pflug. He knew Mervyn Wollheim and Peter Ferguson, of course, and he knew that his American friends were aware of other Sonderlehrgang teams. He also knew Percy Downward, and that the British were watching everyone except von Holten-Pflug.

Franklin Roosevelt was resting in his bedroom at the Soviet compound that afternoon when he received word that a guest was on his way.

"I'll talk to him in the sitting room, Mike," the president told his bodyguard. "Stall him a second while I get ready."

At last, after months of missives back and forth, he was face to face with the leader of the Soviet Union. Churchill had met Stalin officially in Moscow in August 1942, and now Roosevelt was making his own connection with his other partner among the Big Three.

"Seeing him for the first time was indeed a shock," Mike Reilly recalled. "He came into the room, well guarded, I might add, with a most engaging grin on his face. He walked toward the Boss very slowly. Josef Stalin sort of ambled across the room toward Roosevelt, grinning, and reached down to shake FDR's hand for the first time."

"I am glad to see you," the president told the man whom he referred to in private as Uncle Joe. "I have tried for a long time to bring this about."

"Joe may or may not be a great many things, but he is certainly not dour," Reilly noted. "In fact, he laughed almost as much as the Boss."

Charles "Chip" Bohlen, the first secretary at the American embassy in Moscow, who would serve as translator and take the official notes of the president's meetings in Tehran, wrote that Stalin, "after suitable expression of pleasure at meeting the President, said that he was to blame for the delay in this meeting; that he had been very occupied because of military matters."

Roosevelt asked about the situation on the Soviet battlefront, and Stalin explained that "on part of the front, the situation was not too good; that the Soviets had lost [the city of] Zhitomir [in northern Ukraine, west of Kiev] and were about to lose [nearby] Korosten, the latter an important railroad center."

When Roosevelt "inquired whether or not the initiative remained with the Soviet forces," Stalin frankly told him that "with the exception of the sector which he had just referred to, the initiative still remains with the Soviet Armies, but that the situation was so bad that only in the Ukraine was it possible to take offensive operations."

Roosevelt told him sympathetically, through the interpreters, that he wished that it "were within his power to bring about the removal of 30 or 40 German divisions from the Eastern Front and that that question, of course, was one of the things he desired to discuss here in Tehran."

Stalin nodded in agreement. This was a sore point for Stalin. Uncle Joe had been nagging Roosevelt and Churchill for more than a year to open a second front in Western Europe that would force the Germans to divert "30 or 40 German divisions from the Eastern Front." Before the week was out, they would be able to give the Soviets a concrete promise.

"This was Stalin's first international conference outside his own country, and he was careful to watch his partners closely," Dmitri Volkogonov, Stalin's biographer wrote of the meeting. "It was all new to him. Churchill was less interesting, as he had already met him and knew him to be an unusually clever and cunning politician. But there was something about Roosevelt, with his piercing eyes and the mark of fatigue and illness on him, that appealed at once. Perhaps it was his frankness."

In the meantime, Stalin's NKVD detail and Roosevelt's Secret Service detail stood by, quietly glowering at one another. As Reilly put it, "while the two biggest men in the world talked of the destinies of millions, their personal bodyguards played a very silly game of trying to stare each other down. It resulted in a draw."

After a conversation of about forty-five minutes, Roosevelt told Stalin that he was glad to be staying where he was because it would facilitate the opportunity for he and Stalin to meet "more frequently in completely informal and different circumstances."

Peter Ferguson had spent the better part of the past three days at Mervyn Wollheim's place, boozing with Hans Ulrich von Ortel and Josef Schnabel—because they all liked to drink and Ferguson had seen in movies that you got enemy agents drunk in order to pry information from them. He missed the part about how you shouldn't drink so much *yourself.*

For Ferguson, this was a personal quirk that certainly adds color to the narrative, but it greatly endangered the lives of his friends and could easily have derailed his own objectives. With all of the drinking that was going on, it is hard to imagine that the loose-tongued von Ortel did not brag that he was in Tehran to assassinate Roosevelt, Churchill, and Stalin when they came to town. It is equally surprising that Ferguson did not let it slip that Roosevelt, Churchill, and Stalin were in town.

Perhaps they did, but if so, it was forgotten by morning.

Then Misbah Ebtehaj showed up.

When he explained that he knew someone who knew the location of von Holten-Pflug's team and why this was important, Wollheim, Ferguson, and Chapat realized for the first time the full dimensions of the secret mission that had brought these Germans to Tehran. Until then, they had no confirmation that the Germans intended to kill the Big Three.

When the Iranian had gone, they discussed what to do with this news. Mervyn Wollheim and Khalil Chapat thought that they should tell Merser, who could then convey the information to Percy Downward and the British SIS. When they told Ida Kovalska, she proposed that Ferguson should go to his contacts at the United States embassy and tell them everything. These suggestions were perfectly logical and perfectly rational.

Ferguson would hear nothing of it.

He insisted that they keep the information secret even from Ernst Merser—precisely because he *would* tell the British. Seeing himself as having been handed an opportunity to achieve heroic greatness, Ferguson had other ideas. Recalling their successful "commando action" two months earlier, he decided that they should try to capture the six Sonder-lehrgang men themselves!

Even Ida, who had been drinking the least of anyone in their little gang, agreed against her own misgivings to go along with Ferguson.

"We all felt that Peter was about to do something crazy," she told Laslo Havas after the war. "But the whole affair was so confused that we could not see clearly. Wollheim and Chapat were never sober in those days. I had no idea who Peter's contact at the embassy was, but I thought that I would go to Merser and tell him about the whole affair [however] I had known Ferguson for years and loved him. I had met Merser only a few times and I was not quite certain about the part he was playing. But it has to be admitted that, as always, Peter's enthusiasm communicated itself to us. We also thought that we could first try something on our own, and if we failed there would still be time to ask for help."

As Stalin was getting up to leave Roosevelt's cottage at the Soviet compound, the leaders were informed that Winston Churchill had arrived, having walked from the British embassy. It was decided that a spontane-ous, unscheduled first meeting of the Big Three should take place at once in a large conference room in the main part of the Soviet Embassy, where all of the formal meetings would be held.

Guy Spaman of the Secret Service later described the arrangements in his 1945 after-action report that "the street separating the Russian embassy and the British was closed off and the perimeter outside the two compounds heavily guarded. Arrangements were made for Russian interpreters to work with the [Secret Service] agents on duty at the entrance to the compound and the entrance to the President's quarters. The three heads of state were able to move between the three headquarters without entering any public streets.... The local police and the Iranian soldiers were not used at any time for guard purposes, this work being done only by American, Russian or British soldiers."

The proximity of the British embassy would make the logistics of the summit convenient. Churchill welcomed the arrangement, observing that "we were all within a circle, and could discuss the problems of the World War without any chance of annoyance. I was made very comfortable in the British Legation, and had only to walk a couple of hundred yards to reach the Soviet palace, which might be said to be for the time being the centre of the world."

At last, on a spontaneous impulse that appealed to each of them, the Big Three would all be in the same room for the first time—and surrounded by their respective military leaders. It was a truly momentous occasion.

For the Soviet personnel present, the sight of their leader—who rarely appeared in public at home—in the presence of other world leaders was impressive. The impressionable Gevork Vartanian, who was probably part of the NKVD protection detail at the summit, was duly awed.

"At that time, Stalin's authority in the world was absolute—everyone understood that the outcome of the war was being decided on the Soviet-German front," he recalled with effusive hyperbole to Yury Plutenko, still smitten with the charisma of the Man of Steel many years later. "Both Roosevelt and Churchill admitted this. Churchill recalled in his memoirs that everyone stood up when Stalin entered the hall of the conference. He resolved not to do so again. Yet, when Stalin entered the hall on another occasion, some unknown force again brought Churchill to his feet."

According to Chip Bohlen, Roosevelt spoke first, observing that "as the youngest of the three present [he was sixty-one] he ventured to welcome his elders." Stalin was then sixty-four and Churchill was two days short of sixty-nine.

He continued, according to Bohlen's notes, adding that "we are sitting around this table for the first time as a family, with the one object of winning the war.... In such a large family circle we hope that we will be very successful and achieve constructive accord in order that we may maintain close touch throughout the war and after the war."

Churchill then observed that this was "the greatest concentration of power that the world had ever seen," adding that "in our hands we have perhaps the responsibility for the shortening of this war. In our hands we have, too, the future of mankind. I pray that we may be worthy of this God-given opportunity."

The room was indeed the momentary center of the world.

Turning to Stalin, Roosevelt suggested "perhaps our host would like to say a few words."

"I think that history is indulging us," Stalin began abruptly, according to Volkogonov, who cited the official Soviet translation. "She has put very great powers in our hands and very great opportunities, I hope we will take all measures to see that this conference uses the strength and force entrusted to us by our peoples, properly and within a framework of cooperation. And now let's get down to work."

Around the table, to do that work, sat the top military brass of the Allied powers. Stalin and Molotov were accompanied by Marshal Kliment "Klim" Voroshilov, the only military member of the all-powerful five-man State Defense Committee that controlled the Soviet Union. Headed by Stalin, the committee also included Vyacheslav Molotov, the Soviet foreign commissar; Lavrenty Beria of the NKVD; and Georgi Malenkov of the Organizational Bureau of the Central Committee of the Communist Party, who acted as Stalin's political enforcer. Churchill was flanked by Anthony Eden, his foreign minister, as well as General Sir Alan Brooke, chief of the British General Staff; Admiral Sir Andrew Cunningham, chief of the Royal Naval Staff; and Air Chief Marshal Charles "Peter" Portal of the Royal Air Staff.

Roosevelt and Harry Hopkins were accompanied by Admiral William Leahy, the Chairman of the Joint Chiefs of Staff, and Admiral Ernest King, the Chief of Naval Operations. Representing the U.S. Army and the USAAF were ... *where* were George Marshall and Hap Arnold?

The two most senior generals on the Joint Chiefs of Staff were *missing*.

As aides scrambled, their hearts racing at the imagined worst case scenario, two men in a U.S. Army staff car negotiated a barely paved road far from the center of Tehran.

No one immediately conceived of a situation in which two general officers would have driven off in a car, but this is exactly what Hap Arnold recalled in both his diary and his memoirs. It was just the two of them. He wrote that they had driven out of town, stopping along a mainly deserted road to look at the primitive water system supplying the city, and to gaze north toward the majestic, snow-capped, 18,400-foot peak of Mount Damavand, the tallest mountain in the Middle East.

Hap Arnold and George Marshall, once lost, were found.

In fact, they had left word with their own staffs and were tracked down rather quickly.

"After our [morning Joint Chiefs of Staff] meeting with the President, George Marshall and I asked whether or not there was any possibility of a meeting that afternoon," Arnold wrote in his memoirs. "The President said not, so after a late lunch, Marshall and I took off in an automobile for a trip through the mountains to the north, to see if we could find out what was going on, and to see how far north we would get before we ran into the Russian Zone of Occupation. As we were returning from our trip we were met by a messenger who informed us that a conference had been called with Stalin, the Prime Minister, and the President at 4:00. Since it was then 4:15 and we were about 60 miles out of Tehran, General Marshall and I decided they would have to hold the meeting without us. Admiral King would have to represent the United States Chiefs of Staff alone."

And so he had. The lead item on Stalin's agenda was the question of when the Anglo-American Allies were going to launch that long-promised "second front," which was to be the recurring theme throughout the conference.

At this meeting, talk also turned to promises of materiel as inducements to nudge recalcitrant Turkey into the war on the side of the Allies. As Churchill later pointed out, "if we could gain Turkey, it would be possible, without the subtraction of a single man, ship, or aircraft from the main and decisive battles, to dominate the Black Sea with submarines and light naval forces, and to give a right hand to Russia and carry supplies to her armies by a route far less costly, far more swift, and far more abundant than either the Arctic or the Persian Gulf."

When the suggestion was made that this should be done sooner rather than later, ideally by the end of December, Churchill quipped that "Christmas in England was a poor season for Turkeys."

Stalin didn't get the joke, but when it was explained to him, he said he "regretted that he was not an Englishman."

Roosevelt said that "should he meet the President of Turkey [Ismet Inonu] he would, of course, do everything possible to persuade him to enter the war, but that if he were in the Turkish President's place he would demand such a price in planes, tanks and equipment that to grant the request would indefinitely postpone Overlord."

Churchill observed that the Turks would be "crazy" to turn down such an offer, to which Stalin added "there are some people who apparently prefer to remain crazy."

For the formal dinner that night, it had been decided that Roosevelt would take the first turn as host, so the cook staff from his presidential yacht, who had been traveling with him, took over the kitchen, producing what Mike Reilly described as a "first-class spread for the bigwigs."

He added that Roosevelt "had been well briefed on Russian hospitality customs and demands, so the bourbon flowed like vodka and FDR was every bit as canny as the Marshal in the business of handling the endless stream of toasts. And, of course, his Britannic Majesty's First Minister [Churchill] could easily drink toast for toast with any given battalion of Russians."

As the party was breaking up, Reilly noted an interaction between Churchill and Stalin which illustrated the Soviet leader's bitter impatience for Operation Overlord. When Churchill asked if he could arrange an inspection tour of the Soviet battlefront, Stalin told him coldly, "Maybe it can be arranged sometime, Mr. Prime Minister. Perhaps when *you* have a front that I can visit, too. Good night."

Monday, November 29

At the Soviet embassy, the second full day of the Big Three parley followed the pattern set on Monday. A conference of the military leaders, this time with all three countries represented, was convened mid-morning, followed by a Roosevelt-Stalin meeting after lunch, with the main Big Three meeting, attended by the military leaders, scheduled for late afternoon.

As before, Operation Overlord dominated the morning meeting, with General Brooke presenting an extensive technical briefing. Roosevelt had earlier pointed out that "the English Channel was a disagreeable body of water and it was unsafe for military operations prior to the month of May, and that the plan adopted at Quebec [the Quadrant Conference between Roosevelt and Churchill in August 1943] involved an immense expedition [Operation Overlord] and had been set at that time for May 1, 1944."

To this, Churchill interjected that "the British had every reason to be thankful that the English Channel was such a disagreeable body of water."

When Brooke completed his presentation, a petulant Marshal Voroshilov took exception to the target date, implying that the outline offered by the chief of the British General Staff was just a series of excuses for the Allies taking another six months to open a second front. He told Brooke that he understood that "crossing the Channel was more difficult than crossing a large river, [but pointed out] that during the recent Soviet advances to the west they had crossed several large rivers, the most recent of which was the Dnieper. In the latter case the ordinary difficulties of a river crossing were greatly increased by the high, steep western bank and the low eastern bank, but with the help of machine gun, mortar and artillery fire and the employment of mine throwers it had been found possible to lay down a fire so intense that the Germans could not endure it."

In an attempt to break the tension in the room, General Marshall interjected that his military education "had been based on roads, rivers, and railroads and that his war experience in France had been concerned with the same. During the last two years, however, he had been acquiring an education based on oceans and he had had to learn all over again … prior to the present war he had never heard of any landing craft except a rubber boat. Now he thinks about little else."

"If you think about it, you will do it," Voroshilov told him tersely.

"That is a very good reply," Marshall said. "I understand thoroughly."

Voroshilov's dictum, "if you think about it, you will do it," applied in a big way to Peter Ferguson. The adrenaline pumping in his veins, he was dead-set determined to launch a surprise attack on the Sonderlehrgang team commanded by Rudolf von Holten-Pflug.

As so often with even best laid plans, there was a wrinkle or two in the scheme. Misbah Ebtehaj was happy to cooperate with Ferguson, but not merely through the kindness of his heart. He had been forthcoming with the information that von Holten-Pflug and his men had arrived in Tehran—but he had not told Ferguson *where* they were hiding.

The Iranian knew that this was valuable information, and valuable information had a price. In this case, he said that it would cost Ferguson the equivalent of more than a quarter of a million dollars in today's value.

When Ferguson gasped, Ebtehaj pointed out that Ferguson, as an OSS man, was an agent of the United States government, an entity with limitless resources. What, he asked rhetorically, was the life of President Roosevelt worth to the United States government?

Placed in such terms, Ebtehaj calculated that the price he asked was a mere pittance.

Ebtehaj explained that he would need his money by Monday night. He was certain that von Holten-Pflug would stay put until then, but he did not explain exactly how he knew this.

Ferguson had realized right away that he could not lay his hands on that kind of money in such a short time. What was he going to do? Walk into the American embassy in the midst of a hush-hush presidential visit and ask for a quarter of a million dollars?

"What for?" Ferguson would be asked.

If he told the truth, someone else would certainly take over the operation and Ferguson would be cheated of his magnificent opportunity for heroism on a historic scale.

He needed a Plan B.

He and the other members of his gang racked their brains for an alternative. The best they could come up with was to beg, cajole, or trick the information out of Ebtehaj. As Plans B go, it was pretty weak, but it was the best they could come up with on the spot.

"After endless debates [Ferguson] agreed that if, within a certain time limit, he discovered where the Germans were, we would help him carry out the action," Ida Kovalska later recalled to Laslo Havas. "If not, Ferguson would ask competent people for help."

Normally, she was the most level-headed of the group, the moderating influence upon Ferguson—both Khalil Chapat and Mervyn Wollheim were as prone to action as Ferguson—but her affection for him clouded her better judgment. She had now been caught up in the OSS man's infectious lust for glory and dangerous adventure.

———————

General Hap Arnold, the USAAF commander, with whom Marshall had been field-tripping the previous day, skipped the Monday morning meeting of the Big Three. Instead, Arnold and Harry Hopkins accepted an invitation from U.S. Army General Donald Connolly, who offered to show them around the 400-year-old Grand Bazaar, an eight-square-mile "city within a city" in the heart of Tehran. As Arnold described it in his diary, the bazaar was "miles and miles of small, cubbyhole stores under roof behind the Mosque. Dirt, filth, all kinds of humanity, walking, talking, jabbering. Copper, brass, silver, rugs, meat, meal, bakeries, shoe leather, jewelry, hardware goods from all over the world. Prices about four times as high as they should be; [Persian] rugs are cheaper in New York."

"We became separated," during the tour, he confided in his diary recalling how he and Hopkins apparently lost Connolly and their guide in the labyrinthine maze of alleyways and twisting corridors. "After we wandered around about an hour they were convinced that we were lost, hence a search party. We came out about a mile from where we went in."

———————

The Big Three luncheon at the Soviet compound was not without a bit of excitement. After lunch, Winston Churchill announced that he wished to make a presentation of a gift from King George VI to Marshal Stalin, and the assembled group made their way to an adjacent reception room.

Mike Reilly recalled that, as a British honor guard wheeled in a large wooden case, "from nowhere, in marched a detachment of Russian troops. They were all big and husky, none of them over 25 or 26 years of age, and all of them dressed as immaculately as the poor character of the Russian uniform would permit, all with the same kind of boots, the same cut of trousers, the same shade of uniform. Each had in front of him a [PPSh-41 submachine] gun which he carried across his chest. The [weapons were] loaded and the finger of each man was on the trigger."

Opening the case, Churchill withdrew what he called the "Sword of Honour"—later called the "Sword of Stalingrad"—a jewel-encrusted edged weapon that had been forged and inscribed as a memento to commemorate the defenders of the Russian city that had suffered so severely at the hands of the Germans a year earlier. He handed it to Stalin, who muttered a humble "thank you," kissed the blade and passed it to Roosevelt who commented that the Stalingrad defenders had "hearts of steel," a dual reference to the metal of the blade and to Stalin's persona as the Man of Steel.

As the formalities concluded, Stalin passed the sword to Voroshilov, who promptly dropped it on the floor—much to the visible embarrassment of the Man of Steel.

When Roosevelt got together with Uncle Joe after the sword presentation for their second à deux meeting without Churchill, he brought up his interest in the idea of a postwar "United Nations." The term had been in use since the "Declaration by United Nations" in 1942 to describe nations who were united in opposition to Nazi Germany and who envisioned a postwar organization of the same name.

In particular, Roosevelt wanted to talk about an idea that he called the "Four Policemen," four countries who would use their might and muscle to maintain postwar peace and "deal immediately with any threat." In addition to the Soviet Union, the United States, and Great Britain, Roosevelt wanted to include China, but Stalin objected. He considered China's armed forces—those commanded by Chiang Kai-shek—to be weak, ineffective, and poorly led. Roosevelt concurred, but was especially prescient in his reply that they should think about China's immense population and the inevitability of its importance in the future. Left unmentioned was Stalin's longstanding support for Mao Zedong's Chinese Communist insurgency. Stalin wanted to see Mao ruling China after the war.

Less than an hour after the two men adjourned their face-to-face meeting, they reconvened in the large conference room with Churchill and their respective military leaders.

Again, as in earlier meetings, Stalin expressed his restlessness over the long-delayed Overlord and Soviet frustration with Churchill's continued talk of Anglo-American military operations in the Balkans and Eastern Europe, which he interpreted as an unwillingness to confront the Germans in western Europe and others interpreted as Stalin's not wanting their interference in what the Man of Steel perceived as a Soviet postwar sphere of influence.

Though it was widely suggested in the Western media, and certainly belabored by Stalin at Tehran, that Churchill favored Balkan operations to the exclusion of Overlord, the prime minister dismissed this as "nonsense."

As the long shadows of the afternoon faded into twilight, Peter Ferguson received a visitor. The deadline had arrived and Misbah Ebtehaj had come for his money.

When the OSS man found that he could not outwit the martial arts master and coax him into revealing the whereabouts of the elusive Germans, he finally relented. Ferguson admitted that he did not have the money *tonight*, but he would go to the United States embassy in the morning and get it.

Ebtehaj reluctantly agreed to extend the deadline.

What Ferguson had not said was that he planned to try one last ploy. He would attempt to borrow the money from the deep pockets of Ernst Merser.

That evening, Merser was in his secret wireless room with Winifred Oberg, preparing to communicate via short wave, for the first time in several days, with Walther Schellenberg in Berlin. Allowing him to use the wireless had gone a long way toward establishing Merser's *bona fides* with Oberg, and it added to his credibility that he permitted the sturmbannführer only limited access.

The word from Berlin was startling. Oberg was told to his amazement that Schellenberg's Cairo agents had learned of the departure of both Roosevelt and Churchill from the Egyptian capital on Saturday. The agents had not confirmed their destination, but other intelligence, including decryptions of Allied radio traffic, indicated Tehran. Merser feigned surprise.

One would have expected Oberg to propose that he and Lothar Schoellhorn of the Abwehr swing immediately into motion, but he did not. Instead, he wanted to confirm Berlin's intelligence, and he accepted Merser's suggestion that Swiss businessman should use his own local contacts to find out.

Meanwhile, there was no shortage of drama at the Soviet embassy on Monday night. It was Stalin's turn to play host for the Big Three dinner, which did not get underway until almost 9:00 p.m. When it came to the raising of glasses, Mike Reilly recalled "no American above the rank of Congressman or corporal was overlooked in the toasts."

Chip Bohlen, meanwhile, recalled that "Marshal Stalin lost no opportunity to get in a dig at Mr. Churchill. Almost every remark that he addressed to the Prime Minister contained some sharp edge, although the Marshal's manner was entirely friendly. He apparently desired to put and keep the Prime Minister on the defensive." Included in these digs was an accusation that Churchill had delayed a second front for so long because he "nursed a secret affection for Germany and desired to see a soft peace."

In his memoirs, Churchill reports that he did not "at all resent [this teasing] until the Marshal entered in a genial manner upon a serious and even deadly aspect of the punishment to be inflicted upon the Germans. The German General Staff, he said, must be liquidated. The whole force of Hitler's mighty armies depended upon about 50,000 officers and technicians. If these were rounded up and shot at the end of the war, German military strength would be extirpated."

Stalin had undertaken executions on this scale against his own officer corps during the Great Purge of 1937–1938, so it was not outside the realm of the believable. Churchill knew that thousands had been executed, though it was not until NKVD files were opened in the 1990s that a death toll in excess of 600,000 was revealed.

Churchill turned to Stalin and told him pointedly that "the British Parliament and public will never tolerate mass executions. Even if in war passion they allowed them to begin, they would turn violently against those responsible after the first butchery had taken place. The Soviets must be under no delusion on this point."

Churchill conceded that it was "perhaps only in mischief," but Stalin retorted tersely that "Fifty thousand *must* be shot."

"I would rather," Churchill said angrily, "be taken out into the garden here and now and be shot myself than sully my own and my country's honour by such infamy."

At the time, Churchill was also aware of what the Soviets had done in the Katyn Massacre, though not the full extent of the death toll of more than 21,000. While the massacre was not finally confirmed for decades, the Red Cross had looked into it and there were many, including Churchill, who had heard enough to believe that it had taken place. He also believed, that given a chance, this could happen again. Stalin had just said so.

Roosevelt, hoping to diffuse the situation by casting Stalin's suggestion as a joke, proposed that only "49,000 Germans" be executed. Churchill interpreted his comments as cordial agreement with Stalin's plan. Churchill grew angrier and angrier, and finally stood up and went into another room.

"I had not been there a minute before hands were clapped upon my shoulders from behind," Churchill recalled. "There was Stalin, with Molotov at his side, both grinning broadly, and eagerly declaring that they were only playing, and that nothing of a serious character had entered their heads. Stalin has a very captivating manner when he chooses to use it, and I never saw him do so to such an extent as at this moment. Although I was not then, and am not now, fully convinced that all was chaff and there was no serious intent lurking behind, I consented to return, and the rest of the evening passed pleasantly."

Tuesday, November 30

Peter Ferguson arose early. Tuesday was going to be a big day—perhaps even *the* big day. Yesterday, he had promised Ida Kovalska that this morning he would drive out to the American embassy and tell them the whole story.

However, as they sipped their morning coffee, he admitted that he was going to make one last attempt to obtain the means of running a commando operation of his own. She raised her eyebrows as he told her he was going to ask Ernst Merser for the money to pay off Misbah Ebtehaj and learn the location of Rudolf von Holten-Pflug. She told him that the Germans had likely changed locations, but Ferguson was insistent: he was going to see Merser.

"I'm going with you," Ida said.

At Kakh Street, Ferguson maneuvered Merser out of earshot of the German agents and explained that he needed to borrow money for something of "indispensable consequence to the war effort."

Merser was surprised by the astonishing sum that Ferguson requested, but said calmly that he would need to know more before he helped finance an endeavor so expensive. He did not have that kind of money, but he would try to get his hands on it—*if* he knew what it was for.

"You and your friends are hiding numerous Germans in town, waiting for the appropriate moment to arrest them," Ferguson asserted, referencing Merser's close cooperation with the British SIS. "Until now I did not know what the whole thing was about, in spite of the fact that two Germans are staying with my friend Wollheim. Now I know. The Germans are preparing an attempt on the lives of Roosevelt, Churchill, and Stalin. No one has taken the trouble to inform me of this, so you cannot expect me to trust you more than you trusted me."

How could he know this? Until now, Merser had assumed that Ferguson and his colleagues were as unaware of the objectives of Operation Long Jump as Oberg was of Merser's being a double agent. Had von Ortel or one of his team members talked?

Merser grasped that Ferguson, for all of his unprofessional bravado and blundering, actually had a line on information unknown to either the British or himself—the location of the missing Sonderlehrgang team.

"Nobody knows, nobody except myself, that a German commando unit succeeded in slipping through the net, became suspicious, and decided not to contact the others," Ferguson explained.

"And you know where they are hiding out?" Merser queried guardedly.

"If I knew I would have acted," Ferguson admitted, adding that if he had the money by the end of the day, he could get this information.

Merser then asked the obvious question—why didn't Ferguson simply go to his OSS handlers at the United States embassy? They had money on hand for contingencies like this.

Ferguson had no way to answer this except the truth, and in refusing to tell the truth, he stammered, stumbled, and allowed Merser to figure out his ulterior motive. Merser understood. He had been in on the foolhardy raid on the NKVD holding facility in September. He had seen Ferguson in action and knew that the OSS man was a cowboy at heart.

"The man I have to pay will hand over the Germans only to me and to no one else," Ferguson insisted, not identifying Ebtehaj by name. "If this were not the case I should already have asked for help from official quarters. But what would be the advantage of sending out a whole army? It would only frighten off my man, and by the time a conventional police action gets under way it might be too late."

Merser relented. He promised Ferguson that he would get the money before the end of the day, but that he would have to be present when Ferguson handed it over to "the man."

Ferguson agreed, and they made arrangements to reconvene at Mervyn Wollheim's apartment at 10:00 p.m. that night.

After Ferguson and Ida left, Merser phoned his bank—but *first*, he phoned Percy Downward.

While the British and American chiefs of staff met early in the day at the British embassy, Franklin Roosevelt remained at his quarters a block away in the Soviet compound, where he spent the morning in as close proximity to Iran and Iranians as he would get while he was in the country.

Roosevelt was wheeled into what his daily log described as a "branch post exchange." Donald Connolly's Persian Gulf Service Command had set up what amounted to a temporary curio stand where Americans who were part of the president's entourage could get their hands on locally produced souvenirs. Realizing that the day was Winston Churchill's birthday, Roosevelt bought a decorative bowl from Kashan, due south of Tehran, to give him later as a birthday gift.

At 11:30 a.m., the president had his first and only meeting with Mohammed Reza Pahlavi. The young Shah called on Roosevelt, presenting himself at the president's quarters in the Soviet compound with his prime minister, Ali Soheili, as well as with his London-educated foreign minister Husain Ala, and Sa'ed Maragheh'i of the foreign office.

The State Department Historical Office believes that no official minutes were taken, and relies for the record on accounts of several people who were present, including Patrick Hurley, Elliott Roosevelt, and Ambassador Louis Goethe Dreyfus. In their accounts of the Tehran conference, they each allude briefly to the session, mentioning that the principal topics of conversation were the Shah's economic concerns, and requests for American aid. Mysteriously, Arthur Chester Millspaugh, the American economist who was then functioning as Iran's Administrator General of Finances, was not included in the meeting, although he did meet briefly with Roosevelt the following day.

Roosevelt's mind was on his 1:30 lunch meeting in his quarters with both Churchill and Stalin.

After the caustic interaction between Churchill and Stalin the night before, Chip Bohlen's notes reveal a more congenial atmosphere, with Stalin confirming that the Red Army would coordinate a major offensive of its own with Operation Overlord, and Churchill speaking sympathetically about the Russian yearning for warm water ports that dated back to the days of the Czars, before there was a Soviet Union.

The day's principal plenary session among the Big Three and all of their supporting characters—nearly thirty of the highest ranking Allied leaders—convened at 4:00 that afternoon in the big conference room at the Soviet embassy. The meeting began with talk of the all-important Anglo-American invasion of northern France, with Stalin once again pledging that "the Red Army would launch simultaneously with Overlord large scale offensives in a number of places for the purpose of pinning down German forces and preventing the transfer of German troops to the west."

Churchill wanted to move to another topic. He proposed that "since the military business of the conference was concluded, there were some political matters of extreme importance which remained to be decided. He hoped it would be possible for the three Heads of State to meet on the first and second of December and not to leave Tehran until December 3. He said it would be well if they remained until all questions of importance had been decided."

Both Roosevelt and Stalin concurred.

Ernst Merser met Percy Downward at one of the little cafes where they often met in order to get away from Merser's houseguests. Downward was especially keen to learn that the "missing" Sonderlehrgang team had been located, even if they did not yet know exactly where.

Merser also did not yet know that "the man" to whom Ferguson would pay the cash was Misbah Ebtehaj, nor did Ebtehaj know that the money would now be hand-delivered by Merser. Of course, the two knew one another, and Merser knew that Ebtehaj was on Percy Downward's payroll. The fact that the martial artist was engaging in this freelance shakedown of an OSS agent—especially involving such a staggering sum—was way out of line, though not really out of character.

Merser and Downward had to have expressed concern that the missing Sonderlehrgang team could potentially strike at any time, but Downward nevertheless held to the strategy of not acting until the location of *all* the Germans was known. It now seemed reasonable that this objective could be met by the end of the day. The SIS had all of the German contingents except one under constant surveillance, and around 10:00 that night, SIS teams would be following Ferguson and his merry band of gunslingers—accompanied by Merser himself—to this last elusive quarry.

When Merser returned to Kakh Street that evening, however, Oberg and Schoellhorn were pacing the floor and insisting on another short wave conversation with Berlin. The coded message from Schellenberg's headquarters this time was that the Big Three *were* in Tehran.

Walther Schellenberg had been confirming this intelligence from multiple international sources—including his enigmatic "No. 2 organization" in Istanbul. The Turk, the Egyptian, and the Arab who ran this operation all agreed. The Big Three *were* in Tehran.

Oberg argued that he had no information on the ground to support this. He glanced to his host for confirmation, and Merser nodded. Merser told Oberg, "I have no such facts."

Schellenberg demanded action. Merser intervened, saying he would bring all the German teams together at Kakh Street for a meeting at 3:30 p.m. the following day. It was one last stalling tactic, made at almost exactly the same moment that both Roosevelt and Stalin had agreed to Churchill's proposal for the Big Three "not to leave Tehran until December 3."

With Roosevelt and Stalin having hosted the formal dinners on Sunday and Monday, it was now Churchill's turn, and he chose to host it at the British embassy rather than at the Soviet compound, which had been the venue for the first two. Tuesday was also the prime minister's sixty-ninth birthday, so none would begrudge him his choice.

This did not mean, however, that the Soviets would abdicate any responsibility for security. Clearly still fearful of the German hit men who lurked in the shadows outside, the NKVD, according to Churchill "insisted on searching the British Legation from top to bottom, looking behind every door and under every cushion, before Stalin appeared; and about 50 armed Russian policemen, under their own General, posted themselves near all the doors and windows. The American Security men were also much in evidence."

Not counting the respective security details, there were more than forty dinner guests who began filing into the hall at around 8:30. Stalin arrived in good spirits, and Roosevelt smiled broadly as his wheelchair was wheeled into the room.

"This was a memorable occasion in my life," Churchill recalled of his birthday dinner. "On my right sat the President of the United States, on my left the master of Russia. Together we controlled practically all the naval and three-quarters of all the air forces in the world, and could direct armies of nearly 20 millions of men, engaged in the most terrible of wars that had yet occurred in human history."

Roosevelt opened the evening with the traditional first toast to King George VI, adding that he did so because Churchill had granted him the privilege, and because he had entertained the king during his visit to the United States before the war.

Churchill responded by calling Roosevelt "a man who had devoted his entire life to the cause of defending the weak and helpless, and to the promotion of the great principles that underlie our democratic civilization."

Next, the prime minister toasted Stalin, noting that he was "worthy to stand with the great figures of Russian history and merited the title of 'Stalin the Great.'"

Despite feeling poorly because of the onset of pneumonia, Churchill had been, and continued to be, in his usual sardonic form. As he recalled in his memoirs, "my cold and sore throat were so vicious that for a time I could hardly speak. However, Lord Moran [Dr. Charles McMoran Wilson, Churchill's personal physician] with sprays and ceaseless care enabled me to say what I had to say—which was a lot."

According to Major John Boettiger, all of the speeches on Tuesday night "took the form of toasts, following the Russian custom and the policy established at the Stalin dinner." The official minutes for the dinner meeting were taken, not by Chip Bohlen, but by Boettiger, the husband of Roosevelt's journalist daughter Anna, who was on leave from his civilian job as publisher of the *Seattle Post-Intelligencer*.

Churchill noted that "many informal toasts were then proposed, according the Russian custom, which is certainly very well suited to banquets of this kind."

Hap Arnold called it a "remarkable party [with] toasts and more toasts, everyone toasting his opposite in rank and position in the armed forces of the other countries. The Prime Minister did very well at that birthday party. One speech followed another. Churchill extolled the President, glorified Stalin, then the United States, our armies, our air forces, our navies, and the Red Army. In turn, everyone had to get up and make his little toast. The President seemed more reserved. He listened, talking when he thought it was necessary, but he never opened up to the extent the Prime Minister did."

Captivated by the charisma of the Soviet leader, Arnold recalled Stalin as "apparently fearless, brilliant of mind, quick of thought and repartee, ruthless, a great leader, and having the courage of his convictions. How much English he understood … I don't know, but his answer came so closely after any remark from Churchill or the President that it appeared he knew more English than he was given credit for. When he talked about the British, the Prime Minister, and the Chief of the Imperial General Staff, [General Sir Alan] Brooke, he was half humorous, half scathing."

It was Stalin's toast to Brooke, interrupting that of Roosevelt, that came as the most awkward in the otherwise cheerful gathering.

As described in our Prologue, Stalin rose to say that Brooke had failed to show real feelings of friendship toward the Red Army.

An uncomfortable hush came over those in the room as the translation was articulated.

Stalin continued, saying that he hoped in future Brooke would show greater comradeship towards the soldiers of the Red Army.

"I was very much surprised by these accusations, as I could not think what they were based on," Brooke later recalled.

Having risen to his feet to thank Roosevelt for his toast, Brooke remained standing, recalling later that "I had seen enough of Stalin by then to know that if I sat down under these insults I should lose any respect he might ever have had for me, and that he would continue such attacks in the future."

Brooke replied that the Man of Steel had "failed to observe those feelings of true friendship which I have for the Red Army, nor have you seen the feelings of genuine comradeship which I bear towards all its members."

Stalin told Churchill that he liked the general, adding "he rings true ... I must have a talk with him afterwards."

This apparently diffused the situation.

Later, when some of the parties had retired to another room to continue drinking, Stalin toasted Brooke, telling him that "the best friendships are those founded on misunderstandings."

As Churchill wrote in his memoirs, "it seemed to me that all the clouds had passed away, and in fact Stalin's confidence in my friend was established on a foundation of respect and good will which was never shaken while we all worked together."

The party finally ended sometime after 2:00 a.m., and the Big Three and their hangers on finally went their separate ways. Churchill wrote that "I went to bed tired out but content, feeling sure that nothing but good had been done. It certainly was a happy birthday for me."

Wednesday, December 1

The rendezvous between Peter Ferguson and the mystery man at Mervyn Wollheim's apartment did not occur until the early hours of Wednesday, because Ebtehaj was late. When he arrived, the German agents Josef Schnabel and Hans Ulrich von Ortel were sleeping off a drunk in another room.

Merser was appalled when he saw that Ebtehaj was Ferguson's mystery contact, and castigated the Iranian martial artist for extorting Ferguson while he was already being paid by the SIS. He then demanded to know why Ebtehaj was several hours late. Ebtehaj's answer to that was shocking: his men had *already* seized Rudolf von Holten-Pfulg and his Sonderlehrgang men because they had been getting ready to move. Ebtehaj and nearly two dozen of his friends and family, including Ebtehaj's son, had captured them.

Many of the Iranians who had burst into the safe house around midnight were people von Holten-Pflug knew. He thought they were pro-German Melliyun-I-Iran who were favorably disposed to "Hitler-Shah" and willing to aid the SD as they had been doing for the past week. In fact, they *were* and they *had been*, but they answered the higher calling of Misbah Ebtehaj—a man who was about to come into some money which he had promised to share.

While Merser, Ferguson, and Ebtehaj were bickering, Ebtehaj's son arrived to confirm that his men had von Holten-Pflug and company wrapped and ready for pickup. Ferguson had been cheated out of his dream of a heroic gun battle with Nazi assassins, but he could pick the Germans up, turn them in, and *still* be a hero.

———

Having been up until the wee hours themselves, the Big Three slept late. Franklin Roosevelt did not get to his daily official mail pouch until after 11:00. Having found that there were no Congressional matters requiring his immediate attention, he wheeled over to make his second visit to the "branch post exchange" that had been set up in the Soviet embassy, and purchased several items to take back to Washington as gifts.

In the meantime, a Persian carpet arrived for Roosevelt as a gift from the Shah. Having inspected it, the president dashed off a note, thanking the monarch for this gesture and for his hospitality. "I shall leave Iran with regret at not having had an opportunity to extend my acquaintance with you and to have seen more of your country and your people," he wrote. "Iran has always occupied a warm spot in American hearts, more than ever now that we are brothers in arms. We know the part Iran is playing in the common struggle and our hope is that when peace at last comes, the spirit of working together that now exists between our two peoples will continue unchecked in peaceful labors."

Roosevelt also autographed a photo of himself, had it put into a silver frame and asked Louis Dreyfus to take it to the Shah after the summit. The president may or may not have been aware of the infamous autographed photo of Adolf Hitler that had been given to the Shah's father, and which was still on display at the Shah's Sahebgharanie Palace.

It was almost noon when Arthur Millspaugh, Iran's American fiscal manager, arrived for his brief conference with Roosevelt and Harry Hopkins. Millspaugh had been pushing the Majlis for an income tax bill, while battling with the Shah over the monarch's spendthrift desire for a larger army, which was simply, for the Shah, a matter of prestige, as the Shah had no intention of engaging in actual combat operations against the Axis.

"Because of fifteen years of dictatorship, because of the War, and because of the Allied occupation, Iran and the Iranians are at present in a condition of inconceivable disorganization, demoralization, and corruption," Millspaugh told Roosevelt, and confirmed in a memo that he sent over later in the day. "If American assistance is withdrawn at the end of four years, our effort will be largely wasted. To do a permanent job, fifteen or twenty years will be required."

Millspaugh added that he supported the American aid for which the Shah had asked Roosevelt the day before. He said he thought this was in line with Roosevelt's postwar worldview for an interventionist American foreign policy.

In a letter to Hopkins six weeks later, Millspaugh summarized the meeting, writing that "Iran, because of its situation, its problems, and its friendly feeling toward the United States, is (or can be made) something in the nature of a clinic—an experiment station—for the President's postwar policies—his aim to develop and stabilize backward areas; that the present American effort in Iran is actually a means of implementing those policies, a means of helping nations to help themselves, with negligible cost and risk to the United States; and that a similar effort might well be made in other regions."

As Roosevelt and Hopkins bade farewell to Millspaugh, they were handed a critical memo that would terminate the Big Three summit earlier than expected. After a week of clear, sunny days, the weather was turning. By Friday, the day of the scheduled departure, meteorologists predicted an approaching cold front could shroud the mountain passes with clouds. Departing aircraft would have to fly at a higher altitude than the president's doctor would approve.

As Bill Rigdon, the president's secretary, explained, "it was decided to make every effort to complete business on Wednesday in order that the President might leave Tehran Thursday morning." Otherwise, the president's departure might be delayed indefinitely.

———

Misbah Ebtehaj had come to Wollheim's apartment confident that von Holten-Pflug and his men were all but tied with a bow, and that he had earned his fee. He was sure that nothing could have gone wrong. After his son showed up at Kakh Street to confirm this, the elder Ebtehaj was so sure of himself that he agreed to remain at Wollheim's with Ida Kovalska until the others returned.

Percy Downward was in one of the cars following Ferguson and Merser as they wound their way through Wednesday morning Tehran traffic with Wollheim and Khalil Chapat. Thanks to Merser, the British had the addresses of the other safe houses where the Sonderlehrgang were hiding. The still-groggy von Ortel and Schnabel would be nabbed at Wollheim's within the hour. Winifred Oberg and Lothar Schoellhorn were being watched, and would be the last to be picked up.

Unfortunately, at the safe house where von Holten-Pflug had been staying, there had been a reversal of fortune. The Iranian gang, a small army of them, had easily overpowered von Holten-Pflug and his five-man Sonderlehrgang team. What the gang hadn't noticed was that the Germans' Iranian translator, the man named Gorechi, was *not* among them.

Having successfully completed the task assigned to them by Ebtehaj, they went home to go to sleep, leaving two men to guard the prisoners until Ferguson arrived with his men. Gorechi, however, got there first, shot the two guards, and freed the Germans.

When Merser, Ferguson, and their companions arrived, the room was empty except for two Iranians lying in pools of their own blood. When Downward arrived, he was furious, and the SIS took Ferguson, Wollheim, Chapat, and Ebtehaj into custody. They were not exactly under arrest, but under the circumstances Downward felt that Tehran would be a safer place without them on its streets.

As Franklin Roosevelt was scrawling his name on a picture of himself and preparing to discuss the future of Iran with Arthur Millspaugh, there was an armed cadre of killers on the streets of Tehran, untracked by any Allied agency, who were gunning for him.

At lunch, the Big Three were in generally good spirits, though Stalin's teasing of Churchill continued. They did, however, manage to agree to send a message to the American and British ambassadors in Ankara asking them to invite Turkish President Ismet Inonu to fly down to Cairo to meet Roosevelt and Churchill over the coming weekend.

Late in the afternoon, Roosevelt took Stalin aside for a final private meeting, in which he raised the very delicate issue of Soviet intentions in postwar Poland, which was of great concern to Roosevelt and Churchill. In the spirit of tripartite harmony, the subject had been allowed to lurk as a shadow in the corner of the room. Essentially, Stalin wanted to keep the swath of eastern Poland which the Soviet Union had been granted under the Hitler-Stalin pact of 1939, install a pro-Soviet government in the remainder of Poland, and annex the previously independent, but now Soviet-occupied Lithuania, Latvia, and Estonia. To Stalin, all this was non-negotiable. But the Americans and the British officially recognized Poland's prewar borders and government. Indeed, the Polish government in exile was in London, and Poles loyal to that government were fighting valiantly on the Allied side.

Roosevelt approached the topic through a back door, framing it as a domestic, rather than international issue. As Chip Bohlen wrote, Roosevelt confided in Uncle Joe that "we had an election in 1944 and that while personally he did not wish to run again, if the war was still in progress, he might have to. He added that there were in the United States from six to seven million Americans of Polish extraction, and as a practical man, he did not wish to lose their vote.... [He] went on to say that there were a number of persons of Lithuanian, Latvian, and Estonian origin [and] the big issue in the United States, insofar as public opinion went, would be the question of referendum and the right of self-determination."

Stalin then replied that Lithuania, Latvia, and Estonia "had no autonomy under the last Czar [the countries were then part of greater Russia] who had been an ally of Great Britain and the United States, but that no one had raised the question of public opinion, and he did not quite see why it was being raised now."

Roosevelt told Stalin that "it would be helpful for him personally if some public declaration in regard to the future elections" could be made.

Stalin replied that there would be "plenty of opportunities for such an expression of the will of the people."

As it turned out, Lithuania, Latvia, and Estonia remained inside the Soviet Union until 1990; and the swath of Poland that the Soviets gained through their pact with Hitler in 1939 was never returned.

Ernst Merser arrived home Wednesday afternoon and told Winifred Oberg and Lothar Schoellhorn that the meeting with the Sonderlehrgang teams scheduled for 3:30 at his house would now have to take place elsewhere, so they should grab their coats. He had discovered, he said, that Roosevelt, Churchill, and Stalin were already in town.

He saw that Oberg had been using his wireless equipment and had already confirmed this himself. The text of a message Oberg had sent to Berlin a few hours earlier was jotted down on a sheet of paper.

"Guests are here," it read, according to Merser's later recollection. "This afternoon we confer. Execution of Operation Long Jump foreseeable within 24 hours."

When the final three-way meeting of the Eureka Conference convened at 6:00 p.m., Roosevelt continued to press Stalin on the subject of Poland and Eastern Europe, as Stalin had earlier pressed Roosevelt and Churchill on the subject of Operation Overlord and the second front in Western Europe. The president told the Soviet leader that he hoped for an early resumption of diplomatic relations between the Soviet Union and the Polish government in exile.

Stalin bit back, telling Roosevelt that "the Polish Government in exile were closely connected with the Germans and their agents in Poland were killing [pro-Soviet] partisans."

Churchill reminded Stalin that "it would be difficult not to take cognizance of the fact that the British people had gone to war [in 1939] because of Poland," implying that the British people had gone to war over the violation of Poland's prewar boundaries, both east and west.

Stalin replied that the Soviets were "in favor of the reconstitution and expansion of Poland at the expense of Germany and that they make distinction between the Polish government in exile and Poland. He added that they broke relations [in April] with Poland not because of a whim but because the [government in exile] had joined in slanderous propaganda with the Nazis."

What Stalin meant by that was that the Polish government in exile had called on the International Committee of the Red Cross to investigate the Katyn Massacre.

The subject was changed, and the Big Three moved on to summarizing those issues upon which they had achieved agreement.

That afternoon, Merser took Winifred Oberg and Lothar Schoellhorn not to a meeting with the Sonderlehrgang teams, but to Percy Downward and arrest by the SIS.

After two months in Tehran, relaxing and waiting for his big moment, Winifred Oberg beheld the abrupt and unforeseen end to his career with the SD. Lothar Schoellhorn, who had been riding the wave of building momentum on an adrenaline surfboard, suddenly slammed into a brick wall. It was, they both learned, all over.

All of the German conspirators were now in custody, except for Rudolf von Holten-Pflug and his team. Von Holten-Plug's Iranian translator, Gorechi, had taken him to the Tehran police—not to be arrested, but because Gorechi had a friend there who could help them.

Sadraq Movaqqar was a police lieutenant, part of the Melliyun-I-Iran, and loyal to the cause of "Hitler-Shah." He welcomed von Holten-Pflug to a new safe house—his own.

Movaqqar also had a wealth of information about the Big Three from the Allied security services and Schwarzkopf's gendarmes, including the fact that they would be leaving Thursday morning.

If Movaqqar could discover the routes the three targets would take on their way to the airport, the Germans could catch them at some vulnerable point. Von Holten-Pflug asked Gorechi whether he could find Iranians to assist them in the operation.

Yes. Gorechi would make a call—to Misbah Ebtehaj, of course.

Because Ebtehaj had not personally participated in the earlier ambush at the safe house, neither von Holten-Pflug nor Gorechi knew he had already sold von Holten-Pflug out.

With Oberg and Schoellhorn in custody, Downward decided to release the Ferguson gang, including Wollheim, Chapat, and Ebtehaj, which meant that Ebtehaj was at home when Gorechi came calling.

After Gorechi revealed von Holten-Pflug's plans for Thursday morning, Ebtehaj said the job was too big and he did not want to recruit a mini-army to help the SD assassination squad.

Gorechi pleaded, telling him that all the Germans needed was a little logistical support. The Germans would do all the shooting. If anything went wrong, none of Ebtehaj's men would be in the line of fire. Nobody would get hurt. The convincing argument finally came in the form of a substantial wad of currency.

It was finally agreed that Operation Long Jump would begin in earnest at 6:00 a.m. Thursday morning.

Misbah Ebtehaj later claimed that he had meant to call the British SIS right away, though he did not do so until much later.

His next caller was an irate Peter Ferguson. It seemed that everyone at the SIS was blaming Ferguson for the mishandling of the von Holten-Pflug capture—and Ferguson blamed Ebtehaj.

What, Ebtehaj asked, could he do to help him?

"Find the Germans," Ferguson demanded. He had given Ebtehaj a fantastic sum of money and he wanted the Germans that he had paid for.

Ebtehaj refused and tried to kick him out, but Ferguson poured him something to drink and tried to bring him around in the same manner that he had tried to get him to betray von Holten-Pflug's previous safe house earlier in the week. They had been arguing for ten minutes when Wollheim, Chapat, and Ida Kovalska arrived.

"Peter said that he could not continue to live with such a blot on his name," Ida later explained to Laslo Havas. "As usual, against our better judgment we allowed ourselves to be drawn into his senseless adventures." And indeed they were drawn in. So too was Misbah Ebtehaj.

After the fireworks at Churchill's birthday banquet on Tuesday, the final dinner meeting of the Eureka Conference was anticlimactic. Indeed, no minutes were taken and the principal business transacted was to finalize a tripartite Declaration on Iran.

This echoed Roosevelt's earlier communications with the Shah by stating that the three parties "recognize the assistance which Iran has given in the prosecution of the war against the common enemy, particularly by facilitating the transportation of supplies from overseas to the Soviet Union. The Three Governments realize that the war has caused special economic difficulties for Iran, and they are agreed that they will continue to make available to the Government of Iran such economic assistance as may be possible, having regard to the heavy demands made upon them by their worldwide military operations and to the worldwide shortage of transport, raw materials, and supplies for civilian consumption."

Sydney Morrell interpreted that the declaration was actually motivated by a simmering distrust that existed between the three Allies.

"Which power distrusted another first and with what justification it is irrelevant to discuss," he reported, projecting their motivations into what each then imagined for the postwar geopolitical reality. "The British suspected the Russians intended to retain north Iran under one pretext or another; the Russians suspected that the British realized their postwar position would be weak and were attempting to embroil America in Middle East affairs; the Americans were not yet ready to be embroiled. All three sets of suspicions were there, and the result was an attempt to put back the clock, an announcement of the intention to withdraw the armies from Iran, to put back the frontiers, destroy the zones of influence, restore the Middle East vacuum. How Stalin must have smiled when he signed it!"

Morrell was right insofar as the postwar Middle East and postwar Iran would be far more complicated than any of the Allied leaders could imagine—but Stalin would not have the last laugh.

Thursday, December 2

Don Holten-Pflug planned to divide his six-man hit team into thirds, each targeting one of the Big Three, striking as their targets were en route to the airport. The two-man teams would be supported by Iranian getaway drivers and lookouts.

Roosevelt had spent the night at the American post at Camp Amirabad on the edge of town. As the Tehran street had no secrets, the Germans had learned from Misbah Ebtehaj that Stalin and Churchill were still at their embassy compounds and would be driven through the crowded byways of central Tehran.

The Sonderlehrgang killers were well armed with MP40 submachine guns and gammon bombs. If they could get close enough, their chances of doing lethal damage were very good.

Von Holten-Pflug and his men *planned* to escape by losing themselves in the confused crowds of Iran's narrow streets, but they were well aware that they were embarking upon what would likely be a suicide mission.

At their 6:00 a.m. meeting, Ebtehaj led the Germans from his house to a separate building in a nearby alley, where they were to meet their Iranian volunteers. But as Rudolf von Holten-Pflug descended the narrow passage to the cellar of this second building, he felt a painful blow to the back of his head.

As his wits returned, he discovered that he and the rest of his team had been bound hand and foot by Mervyn Wollheim, Khalil Chapat and some of Ebtehaj's men. Peter Ferguson stood over him pointing a revolver at his head.

Gorechi, left alone at Ebtehaj's house, was bored and curious. He decided to follow the Germans.

His arrival, which was not part of the plan, startled Peter Ferguson.

Gorechi immediately realized that he had led von Holten-Pflug into a trap sprung by the devious Ebtehaj.

Ferguson went for his gun.

Gorechi went for the gammon bomb he had in his pocket.

Ferguson was quicker.

K'pow! K'pow! K'pow!

The pistol shots were deafening in the confined space of the cellar.

Gorechi fell, dead before his face smacked into the dirt floor, but as the gammon bomb tumbled from his grasp, the others in the room realized that he had pulled the retainer pin to arm the fuse.

Peter Ferguson, having been trained by the OSS to know about such things, immediately recognized that they had but a matter of seconds before the creeper spring released the striker that would hit the percussion cap within the weapon.

The cellar collapsed with a loud, crashing thud as Ferguson and his companions leapt through the door, back into the alley.

"This place is a good deal like home," Franklin Roosevelt told the troops in the American hospital at Camp Amirabad. "I landed about ten days ago—way over in Morocco. This is the nearest thing to the United States that I have seen yet. I wish the people back home could all see what we are doing here and how well we are doing it. I want you boys, all of you, to remember that back at home we are thinking about you. I know that you wish to get out of the hospital as soon as possible, and come back to the United States as soon as we lick the Nazis.... It is good to see you. I wish I could stay longer. Today it is good to see a lot of fellow Americans even in Persia. Get well as soon as you can, and come back home."

Having left gifts of cigarettes and chocolate for the staff who cared for the needs of himself and his staff at the Soviet compound, Roosevelt spent his last night in Tehran as a guest of General Donald Connolly and the Persian Gulf Service Command at the American base. He rose early on Thursday to tour the facility and meet with some of the men who lived and worked there.

Riding in the front seat of a jeep, he posed for photo ops with the American troops, flashed the infectious Roosevelt grin, and dropped into the hospital for a quick pep talk.

After a second address to a large group of troops, Roosevelt left the base at about 9:10 a.m., and transferred from the jeep to a staff car outside the Amirabad gates for the twenty-minute drive to Qaleh Morgi airport.

Bill Rigdon, keeper of the official log, recorded wheels-up at 9:46 a.m. Winston Churchill was also on the move. The two of them would be dining at Ambassador Alexander Kirk's villa in the shadow of the pyramids that evening.

Stalin remained long enough to be the only one of the Big Three to call on Shah Mohammed Reza Pahlavi at his palace. Gevork Vartanian was apparently a member of the NKVD contingent that accompanied Stalin, along with Klim Voroshilov and Vyacheslav Molotov.

"When the Soviet leader entered the throne room, the Shah ran up to Stalin and tried to kiss his hand," Vartanian recalled. "But Stalin did not let him and raised him to his feet."

If this account is to be believed, the last official engagement of the Big Three summit was certainly a cinematic moment, and an embarrassing one for Iran.

What Might Have Been

"President Roosevelt and Prime Minister Churchill have completed a long conference in Cairo and are now en route to somewhere in Iran to meet Premier Stalin, it is known here definitely," reported the Reuters correspondent in Lisbon on November 30.

The outside world, or at least most of it, knew nothing about either the Sextant Conference or the Eureka Conference until the latter was nearly over. The reporters who had covered the first phase of the Sextant conference in Cairo had agreed not to release the news until after the Big Three departed from Tehran, but someone slipped it to Reuters in Lisbon, who broke the story two days early.

What if the news that day had been not simply a meeting in a distant locale but a triple assassination? One can imagine the confusion if the people of the United States, the Soviet Union, and the British Empire suddenly learned that their leaders had been killed in faraway Iran.

The intention of Operation Long Jump had been to decapitate the Allies, to render them momentarily leaderless. But what would that have actually achieved? Adolf Hitler may have wished to exploit the situation to the fullest extent possible, but on the battlefronts of December 1943, there were no immediate opportunities for a significant offensive beyond what the Germans were already doing. On the Eastern Front, there was a stalemate in the grip of winter. In Italy, the Allied offensive, which had moved with difficulty since the September invasions, had struck an impasse north of Naples in the form of the impregnable Gustav Line. If Hitler was incapable of a decisive blitzkrieg in December 1943, neither was he immediately susceptible to one. Meanwhile, the triple assassinations would likely have only strengthened the resolve of the Allied people and their leaders—which brings us to the question of who those leaders would have been.

What if the Allied powers had been suddenly leaderless? In neither the Soviet Union nor the United Kingdom was there any mechanism of leadership succession, as there is in the United States. Neither Stalin nor Churchill had a statutory successor.

In the Soviet Union, all meaningful power had resided in Stalin for the better part of two decades. All of his serious adversaries had, he thought, been liquidated in the purges. Stalin was the General Secretary of the Communist Party in a state where the party leader was the head of government. He had also given himself the military rank of Marshal of the Soviet Union. Stalin was surrounded by sycophants and rivals (who were often the same people) but he had no equals and no one dared to assert himself publicly as an heir apparent.

The institutions which had ruled the Soviet Union before the war, the Central Committee of the Communist Party and the Supreme Soviet were no longer either central or supreme. They had been downgraded and superseded since June 1941 by the omnipotent Gosudarstvennyj Komitet Oborony (State Defense Committee, or GKO), which ruled all facets of military and civilian life in the Soviet Union. Stalin was its chairman, and it functioned as his "war cabinet." The members of the GKO were the most powerful men in the country. The deputy chairman of the GKO was Vyacheslav Molotov, who was also the deputy chairman of the Council of Ministers and the Foreign Commissar. Marshal Klim Voroshilov, a former commissar of defense, wore the uniform of the Red Army and chaired Sovnarkom, the Council of People's Commissars. Georgi Malenkov was a party insider who directed the bureaucracy of the Communist Party and managed aircraft production. Lavrenty Beria was Commissar of Internal Affairs and head of the dreaded and ubiquitous NKVD.

It is into the GKO that we look first for Stalin's possible 1943 successor. If anyone was Stalin's heir apparent, it was Molotov. He would have raised few eyebrows inside or outside of the Soviet Union had he moved into Stalin's office. He was as well connected as anyone within the Soviet hierarchy and would have had as much support as anyone. Internationally, he was fully engaged diplomatically, while Stalin was, by comparison, a recluse.

It is well known that Molotov had been the steady hand on the tiller during the disastrous days of the German invasion in June 1941, while Stalin shut himself away in a paroxysm of panic and indecision. There is little doubt that Molotov would have had the wherewithal, both personally and politically, to have risen to the occasion of Stalin's assassination.

However, in the event of a simultaneous attack on the Big Three, such as we have suggested in our Prologue, Molotov himself would likely have also perished. Voroshilov, likely another victim in a serious Sonderlehrgang strike, would have been an unlikely successor. According to the dictator's biographer, Dmitri Volkogonov, Stalin had little respect for Voroshilov.

The sinister Beria, as head of the NKVD, wielded great and intimidating power; he was feared by all, except perhaps by Stalin. There is a saying about "knowing where the bodies are buried"; in the Soviet Union, no one knew this better than Beria—because for the most part, he had literally *put them there.*

Not one for the limelight, he was an individual who preferred the shadows, always the man behind the curtain, more a kingmaker than a potential king. However, it can be said with certainty that no one could have succeeded Stalin without Beria's support.

Malenkov, a colorless functionary and old-guard Bolshevik, kept himself close to Stalin—especially during the purges when it was more than career suicide to be Stalin's perceived foe. The Man of Steel had recently named Malenkov as a "Hero of Socialist Labor" when he put aircraft production on track after September 1943. Ultimately, when Malenkov went on to become Stalin's *actual* successor in 1953, he lasted only about a week before he was compelled to share power with the younger and more ambitious Nikita Khrushchev.

Beyond the GKO, another possible competitor within a leadership power struggle might have been Mikhail "Kalinych" Kalinin, who chaired the Presidium of the Supreme Soviet, which gave him great nominal, though little practical, power. He kept his head down during Stalin's great purges—although his wife was arrested for being a "counterrevolutionary" and spent World War II in the gulag archipelago. Stalin and Beria "liked" Kalinin so much that they had him under surveillance by NKVD "bodyguards" twenty-four hours a day.

It was perhaps among the leadership of the Soviet armed forces that the paranoid Stalin had seen the greatest source of potential rivals, but the great purges of the 1930s had eliminated a substantial number. Among those who remained to lead the Red Army against the Germans after 1941, the ones whose battlefield success had made the heroes among the Soviet people were in no position to engage in Kremlin intrigues. They were on the battlefield.

Most notable among Soviet military men was Marshal Georgi Zhukov, who had played key roles in the successful defense of Leningrad, Moscow, and Stalingrad, and who had gone on to lead the Red Army to victory at Kursk in March 1943. He had recaptured Kiev from the Germans only two weeks before Stalin went to Tehran.

As Volkogonov wrote, "Stalin knew that Zhukov conceded nothing to him in toughness of character." Stalin trusted Zhukov as his chief surrogate within the armed forces because "he trusted him to carry out his orders, however harsh they might be and come what may. Zhukov's immense contribution to the defeat of the Germans at Moscow, in the salvation of Leningrad, at Stalingrad and a host of other operations, is widely recognized. Characteristically, as the war progressed and Zhukov's popularity rose, so Stalin's attitude towards him grew more reserved.... He had no intention of sharing the glory of the victory with anyone else, certainly not as popular a war leader as Zhukov."

Volkogonov wrote that "Stalin did not have favorites. He simply relied on some people more than on others. Apart from Beria to some extent, he took little notice of what his entourage told him about individuals." Indeed, it was Beria's job to know these things and to take care of any potential threats to Stalin.

If the dominating force of Stalin had been suddenly removed from the Soviet Union by assassination, would the Soviet war effort have proceeded apace, or would the new Communist leader have sought a separate peace with Germany, as the Bolsheviks had done in the First World War? Would he have chosen to concentrate on consolidating his power rather than carrying the war across Soviet borders and into Hitler's Reich as Stalin was to do in 1944–1945?

It seems most likely that the war effort would have continued unabated. Not only had the harshness of German occupation and the brutality of the struggle hardened Russian feeling against the Germans, but no one with the ruthlessness necessary to succeed Stalin would have varied far from the merciless treatment that he had imagined for postwar Germany. Nor is it probable that any new Soviet dictator would have been any less determined than Stalin to extend a buffer of satellite communist states in Eastern Europe. The Soviet Union had always intended to be an expansive power, seeking world revolution. There was nothing new in this.

Still, there is the remote possibility that a new Soviet dictator, assessing the staggering losses that the Soviet Union had experienced up to that time, might have been tempted to consider a negotiated settlement with

Germany, provided that Hitler's secret opponents succeeded in eliminating the Führer himself.

Since 1940, when Britain had teetered on the abyss of defeat, Winston Churchill had been the glue that held his island nation together. "We shall not flag or fail," he told the British people. "We shall defend our Island, whatever the cost may be, we shall fight on the beaches, we shall fight on the landing grounds, we shall fight in the fields and in the streets, we shall fight in the hills; we shall never surrender."

Though a fickle electorate would turn him out of office in 1945, he still stood tall in 1943 as the indispensable leader of the British Empire at its "finest hour." It would have been a profound and far-reaching shock for the British people to have awakened to a somber BBC newscaster describing the details of his violent death.

Churchill had an heir apparent in Anthony Eden, who had served as foreign secretary between 1935 and 1938, and had returned to the post in Churchill's cabinet in 1940. Like Churchill, he was a member of the Conservative Party, though Churchill's War Cabinet did contain members of the opposition Labour Party. Before joining the cabinet, Eden had his differences with Churchill, but afterward he became his loyal supporter— at least in public—and was groomed by Churchill as his eventual, though at some distant date, successor. Privately, the foreign minister was professionally frustrated by the prime minister's insistence on handling foreign affairs personally with Britain's most important ally through the "special relationship" that Churchill had formed with President Roosevelt.

But what if Eden too had been killed in Operation Long Jump?

John Wheeler-Bennett recalled in his biography of King George VI that Churchill had written to the king to inform him that it was "the Prime Minister's duty to advise Your Majesty to send for Sir John Anderson in the event of the Prime Minister and the Foreign Secretary being killed."

Anderson had been the lord president of the Privy Council in the War Cabinet, and was well known domestically for having previously served as home secretary and minister of home security, which gave him ongoing responsibility for civil defense. In late September, two months before Tehran, he had been given the portfolio as Chancellor of the Exchequer after the sudden death of Sir Howard Kingsley Wood.

While it is likely that Anderson, a man whose experience in the management of the war was limited, would have become prime minister in the immediate aftermath of the assassinations, there is an additional wrinkle. It is important to recall Britain's wartime coalition government included Clement Attlee, the leader of the opposition Labour Party, as Churchill's deputy prime minister. Had King George been prevailed upon to hold general elections in the wake of the Tehran assassinations, Attlee would certainly have carried his party banner against either Eden—if he had survived—or Anderson. As we know from history as it actually played out, Attlee *did* succeed Churchill as prime minister when the king called for elections in July 1945, two months after Germany's defeat. The Labour Party victory at that time is seen as having been, not a referendum on Churchill's wartime record, but as a referendum on what sort of government the British electorate wanted after the war (and the answer, at least initially, was a welfare state that would look after Britain's returning veterans and worn out civilians).

Could Attlee and Labour have won in 1943 while the war was still ongoing? It is impossible to know. Eden's stature and extensive foreign policy experience might have seen him through. Anderson, though, was a far lesser figure. In his actual premiership, Attlee pressed for a dramatic shift toward public ownership of key industries and institutions. Within three years, the Bank of England, as well as civil aviation, the railways, telecommunications, and the coal industry were nationalized, and the publicly funded National Health Service was created. It seems unlikely that during wartime he would have pursued such policies for at least three reasons: first, he was regarded as a "consensus" politician and he would have needed an overwhelming mandate to pursue such policies while the war against Hitler raged on; second, the war had already placed extensive powers in the hands of government bureaucrats; and third, had such a massive restructuring taken place during 1944 and 1945, the bureaucratic confusion alone would have been seriously disruptive to the war effort. An Attlee government, while having socialist policies as its goals, would very likely have had to have waited until the defeat of Hitler to begin enacting them.

In foreign policy, Churchill distrusted the Soviets, while Attlee was much more favorably disposed to Stalin and the Soviet Union and did not see the Soviet Union as a potential postwar threat. Churchill was willing to set aside differences to work with Stalin to defeat Hitler, but he had always been an aggressive anti-Communist worried about Soviet expansion. Attlee would have dismissed such worries and been much more optimistic about continued close relations with the Soviet Union than the wary Churchill; and it is possible that the results of such a policy might have led to long-lasting Soviet influence in Greece, Turkey, and Italy.

The biggest changes that would have been wrought by the Tehran assassinations would have come from the abrupt end of the "special relationship" between Churchill and Roosevelt. United States President Henry Agard Wallace would have found a kindred spirit in Clement Attlee, but Wallace's relations with Eden or Anderson would have been much cooler.

But what if, as in our dramatic prologue, not only Roosevelt, Churchill, and Stalin had been killed, but also the Anglo-American Combined Chiefs of Staff, including Admiral William Leahy, who chaired the American Joint Chiefs of Staff; the service chiefs, General George Marshall, Admiral Ernest King, and General Hap Arnold; British Air Marshal Charles Portal, Field Marshal Sir Alan Brooke, Admiral Andrew Cunningham, and Field Marshal John Dill?

The important decisions effecting the reorganization that would define Allied operations against Germany for the remainder of World War II had not yet been made. This was all to have taken place—and did take place—in Cairo as the Sextant Conference reconvened immediately after Tehran. But the deaths of all the principals would have left a gaping void in the command structure. The creation of the Supreme Headquarters, Allied Expeditionary Forces (SHAEF) in Europe, and the appointment of General Dwight Eisenhower as Supreme Allied Commander, had been discussed, but not yet formalized. The planning for Operation Overlord had a momentum of its own, so the Normandy invasion would have taken place, although possibly not under Eisenhower's command and possibly not in June 1944.

The biggest question is: What would have happened to the doctrine of Unconditional Surrender which was promulgated by Roosevelt at Casablanca, quickly embraced by Churchill, and immediately controversial? Critics, of whom there were already many in 1943, maintained that it would prolong the war unnecessarily. As things turned from bad to worse for Germany in 1944, there were numerous secret feelers extended toward the Allies seeking the possibility of a negotiated end to the war. If these had been accepted, the war might have ended much earlier than May 1945, though, of course, with Germany undefeated and still in control of much of Europe.

The biggest opponent of any negotiations to end the war was Adolf Hitler, not only because he manically still expected to win the war or to bring utter destruction to a Germany that had failed him, but because he knew that there would be no place for him in a conditional surrender acceptable to the Allies.

But the Führer well knew there was a gradually growing groundswell of clandestine support within the Wehrmacht and elsewhere for cutting a deal with the Anglo-American Allies. Even Heinrich Himmler and Walther Schellenberg attempted to open a dialogue with the Allies by way of Sweden, although not until the spring of 1945.

Allen Dulles, the future director of the CIA, who was the OSS station chief in Switzerland during the war, became a virtual clearinghouse of entreaties from numerous German government officials. Among these were the conspirators of the July 20, 1944, plot to assassinate Hitler.

The most consequential outcome that might have flowed from the success of Operation Long Jump was a weakening of Allied resolve, and a willingness to accept a negotiated end to the Second World War. Much would have depended on who would have taken the reins of government in the Soviet Union, Britain, and the United States. Henry Wallace, the American vice president, would have become an intriguing world leader, under whom the path of postwar history would have followed a very different course.

The Common Man

While we can only speculate about what might have happened to the leadership of the Soviet Union or the United Kingdom had Josef Stalin and Winston Churchill been killed in Tehran, there is no question what would have happened in the United States. Article II of the U.S. Constitution states categorically that the role of President of the United States "shall devolve on the Vice President." In November 1943, that man was Henry Agard Wallace, who had been elected in 1940 as Franklin D. Roosevelt's third term running mate.

But who *was* Henry Wallace?

We obviously know a great deal about Roosevelt's *fourth* term running mate, Harry Truman, who *did* become president, but Wallace is today a largely forgotten figure.

Wallace was a third-generation Iowa farmer and farm journal publisher, though he and his father had spent more time behind their publisher's desk than behind a plow. Henry Cantwell "Harry" Wallace had served as Secretary of Agriculture in the Harding administration, as Henry Agard Wallace served in the same post for seven years under Roosevelt.

Henry Wallace had a life-long interest in agronomy and breeding high-yield hybrid corn. Using his wife's inheritance, he started the Hi-Bred Corn Company, which is now part of DuPont. Though raised as a Presbyterian, Wallace flirted with Theosophy during the 1930s, and was for several years a devotee and pen pal of Nicholas Roerich, a strange Russian mystic and self-styled spiritualist, who eventually became an embarrassment to the vice president and the Democratic Party.

Wallace was also very much a disciple of Roosevelt's New Deal social initiatives, and his loyalty as Secretary of Agriculture led to Roosevelt's picking him as a running mate in 1940. Wallace's biographers, John Culver and John Hyde, described him as "a genuine New Dealer [with] a strong geographic base and the support of an important constituency." Nevertheless, his leftist leanings made Wallace a controversial choice, and he was booed at the 1940 Democrat Convention before being narrowly approved.

On the campaign trail he was outspoken and untactful, commenting that Republican presidential nominee Wendell Wilkie was "not an appeaser and not a friend of Hitler.... But you can be sure that every Nazi, every Hiterlite and every appeaser is a Republican."

After the United States entered World War II, Wallace played virtually no role in strategic planning. The president used him mainly for domestic projects where his New Deal credentials were useful. Roosevelt did name him to chair the newly created Board of Economic Warfare, concerned mainly with labor relations and the management of procurement and resources for the war effort. Through the end of 1943, Wallace's only war-time overseas trip had been a rambling five-week goodwill tour of Latin America.

In May 1942, Wallace defined his vice presidency—and his potential presidency—in speech he delivered at a Free World Association banquet in New York. There he called for a "Century of the Common Man." Henry

R. Luce, the influential publisher of *Time* and *Life* magazines, had written that the years following World War II would be defined as the "American Century." Wallace meant to challenge this notion with a more proletarian vision.

"Some have spoken of the 'American Century.'" Wallace observed. "I say that the century on which we are entering—the century which will come out of this war—can be and must be the century of the common man. Everywhere the common man must learn to build his own industries with his own hands in a practical fashion. Everywhere the common man must learn to increase his productivity so that he and his children can eventually pay to the world community all that they have received."

The idea of "increasing productivity" in order to "pay to the world community all that they have received" reminded many commentators on both left and right of the doctrine of "from each according to his ability, to each according to his need," promulgated by Karl Marx in the nineteenth century as a basis of Marxism.

While Roosevelt had formed his "special relationship" with Winston Churchill and was optimistic about American-Soviet relations, Wallace was much more enamored with the Soviet Union and socialism than the president, and voiced a deep distrust of Winston Churchill, whom he saw as emblematic of the evils of "British imperialism."

Wallace had most memorably staked out his foreign policy position in November 1942 at the immense "Tribute to Russia" rally held in Madison Square Garden and sponsored by the Congress of American-Soviet Friendship. Roosevelt had urged Wallace to accept an invitation to speak at the event in order to provide moral support for the Soviet people.

Wallace began innocently enough, grandly telling the audience that "it is no accident that Americans and Russians like each other when they get acquainted. Both peoples were molded by the vast sweep of a rich continent. Both peoples know that their future is greater than their past."

Wallace, however, continued: "Some in the United States believe that we have over-emphasized what might be called political or Bill of Rights democracy. Carried to its extreme form, it leads to rugged individualism, exploitation, impractical emphasis on states' rights, and even to anarchy. Russia, perceiving some of the abuses of excessive political democracy, has placed strong emphasis on economic democracy. This, carried to an extreme, demands that all power be centered in *one man* and his bureaucratic helpers." Many thought that Wallace's own preferred policies tended more towards the Soviet model than the American one.

In the interest of not having both the president and vice president out of the country simultaneously, Wallace never joined Roosevelt for any of his overseas conferences, but he did sit down with Churchill for two meetings when the prime minister came to Washington for the May 1943 Trident Conference.

When Churchill talked of perpetuating the Anglo-American special relationship into the postwar world, Wallace disapproved.

Churchill wrote in his memoirs that "finally, I said [to Wallace] I could see small hope for the world unless the United States and the British Commonwealth worked together in fraternal association. I believed that this could take a form which would confer on each advantages without sacrifice."

Wallace recalled in his diary that day that "I said bluntly that I thought the notion of Anglo-Saxon superiority inherent in Churchill's approach would be offensive to many nations of the world, as well as to a number of people in the United States."

Culver and Hyde wrote that "Wallace came away from the luncheons charmed by Churchill socially and appalled by his philosophy."

In an interview that was part of an oral history project conducted by Columbia University after the war, Wallace said that "as far as the war is concerned, we owe him [Churchill] a great debt of gratitude. As far as the peace is concerned, he's one of the architects of World War III."

Had Wallace succeeded Roosevelt in the wake of a successful Operation Long Jump and defeated Republican candidate Thomas E. Dewey in the November 1944 election, his presidency would have diverged significantly from the course followed by Roosevelt and Truman.

It is likely that regardless of the war—or even because of the war—he would have moved aggressively in the direction of "economic democracy" over "Bill of Rights democracy" and pursued policies of government economic control that went well beyond Roosevelt's New Deal; this was, after all, his primary political interest, and he would have had Democratic majorities in both houses of Congress. However, many Democrats were themselves suspicious of Wallace. They had only narrowly nominated him in 1940, and he was, in reality, dumped from the Democratic ticket in 1944 for being too far to the left.

Wallace despised Nazi Germany and would have pressed for its destruction. But would he have continued the policy of Unconditional Surrender? The answer to that would seem highly dependent on who succeeded Churchill and Stalin. On whether President Wallace would have made the decision to use nuclear weapons against Japan, we have Wallace's own unenlightening testimony.

"I just don't remember how I felt at the time," Wallace told the Columbia University oral history project. "Perhaps these massive events numbed me."

Culver and Hyde commented that "to his credit, Wallace did not criticize—either then or later, publicly or privately—Truman's decision. Present at the inception of the project, Wallace had helped persuade Roosevelt 'it was something to put money into.' To have second-guessed Truman when the weapon was actually used would have been intellectually dishonest."

It was his view of the Soviet Union which colored Wallace's postwar international perspective, and which would have guided the foreign policy of a Wallace presidency.

In his diary on August 10, 1945, he wrote that "It is obvious to me that the cornerstone of the peace of the future consists in strengthening our ties of friendship with Russia. It is also obvious that the attitude of Truman, [Secretary of State James] Byrnes, and both the War and Navy Departments is not moving in this direction. Their attitude will make for war eventually."

In 1943, Wallace had seen Churchill as "one of the architects of World War III." Two years later, he was casting Harry Truman in that role.

By this time, Wallace was no longer vice president, but Secretary of Commerce, and his views placed him in a minority within the Truman administration.

Soviet empire-building in Eastern Europe was causing international alarm. In one country after another, "liberation" by the Red Army brought imposition of one party, pro-Soviet rule, with the NKVD taking up the places recently abandoned by the Gestapo. Wallace continued to give the Soviets the benefit of the doubt, and generally said nothing when Estonia, Latvia, and Lithuania were not actually liberated, but incorporated directly into the Soviet Union.

Poland, like Wanda Pollack, the poor Polish refugee, had been ravished by both the Germans and the Soviets. Wallace made no comment when in March 1945 the Soviets invited sixteen Polish leaders—including Leopold Okulicki, commander of the underground Home Army, and Jan Jankowski, deputy prime minister of the Polish Underground State—to a meeting, where they were promptly arrested by the NKVD and whisked off to Moscow for a quick trial and jail sentences. Only two were still alive six years later. Both Okulicki and Jankowski were murdered in prison and their bodies burned.

After the war, Wallace's continued fascination with the idea of the Soviet Union as a sort of theme park of economic democracy blinded him to the brutal reality of the totalitarian regime and its aggressive ambitions.

Henry Wallace never backed down. Neither did Harry Truman. On September 1946, he asked for Wallace's resignation, telling the media that he could not permit Wallace's position on foreign policy "to jeopardize our position in relation to other countries."

Wallace wrote back that he would "continue to work for peace" and invited the president to join him.

Wallace made a run for the White House in 1948 under the banner of the Progressive Party. Dogged by rumors that the party was controlled by the Communist Party and loyal to the Soviet Union, Wallace came in fourth—behind Truman, the Republican candidate Thomas Dewey, and Dixiecrat candidate Strom Thurmond, who took four states.

President Wallace, like private citizen Wallace, would have ignored the mistreatment of Poland and the gulag archipelago. He would have opposed the Marshall Plan and NATO. In 1949, he told Texas Democrat Tom Connolly, Chairman of the Senate Foreign Relations Committee that he feared NATO because it might turn the Soviet Union into "a wild, desperate cornered beast." It is certain that the Cold War would have taken a much different course under a Wallace presidency that did not challenge Soviet adventurism. One wonders whether or not a President Wallace would have come to grips with the plight of the "common" men and women who were suffering under Soviet rule.

22

The Tide of History

"In a place like Tehran there are hundreds of German spies, probably, around the place," Franklin Roosevelt told the news conference in Washington on December 17. "I suppose it would make a pretty good haul if they could get all three of us going through the streets."

The president laughed it off and the official transcript records that there was general laughter in the room. There were no follow up questions. As is so often the case, there were no investigative journalists who picked up and followed a fragile thread that might have led to a tantalizing story while it was still fresh in the minds of those who had been there. The reporters, with a great deal to consume their attention, allowed the story fade away unexplored, and the tide of history moved forward.

The Big Three lived to fight another day. They lived to watch their armies drive the Wehrmacht from the Soviet Union, from the beaches of northern France, and into a headlong retreat through the heart of the Third Reich itself.

They lived to meet again. In February 1945, fourteen months after Tehran, at the Argonaut Conference in the Livadia Palace near Yalta in the Soviet Crimea, Roosevelt, Churchill, and Stalin came together to plan, not a strategy for winning a war, but a plan for shaping a postwar world. In retrospect, we know that it was an imperfect strategy, just as it was to be an imperfect world which emerged from World War II, one marred by a near half century of Cold War.

Only one of the Big Three would still be at the helm of his government when World War II finally came to an end. Franklin Roosevelt attended the Yalta Conference a sick and dying man, and was dead a little more than two months later. Winston Churchill met Josef Stalin again, at Potsdam in suburban Berlin after the defeat of Nazi Germany, only to discover during the conference—to his humiliation—that he too had been defeated, not by an enemy at war, but by the British electorate whom he had served.

Churchill nevertheless returned to power in 1951, and outlived Stalin by a dozen years. Stalin died a terrible and ironic death in his own bedroom in 1953. He suffered a stroke, and lay dying—alone, immobile, and unaided by his doctors for more than twenty-four hours—because he had left orders not to be disturbed, and nobody dared to disobey Stalin's commands. Churchill passed at the age of ninety with his wife and three children at his side. A spokesman said that he "died in peace and without pain."

The ambassadors who had represented Britain, the United States, the Soviet Union, and the Third Reich in Tehran during those days each survived the war. Sir Reader Bullard retired in 1946 and lived out his life in Oxfordshire. Louis Goethe Dreyfus left Tehran in 1944, but returned to Southwest Asia in 1949 as ambassador to Afghanistan, where he served until his retirement in 1951. Andrei Andreyevich Smirnov worked his way up to the job of deputy foreign minister by 1946, and he later served for a decade as Soviet ambassador to West Germany before being assigned to Turkey in 1966.

The German ambassador Erwin Ettel never had a chance to serve as Germany's military governor of the Middle East, the post that Foreign Minister Joachim von Ribbentrop had promised him, but he did spend time in Istanbul as a handler of Mohammed Effendi Amin el-Husseini, the anti-British, anti-Jewish Grand Mufti of Jerusalem. Ettel left von Ribbentrop's Ministry of Foreign Affairs in 1944 to serve the remainder of the war with the Waffen SS. Between 1950 and 1956, he worked as an editor for the German national weekly newspaper *Die Zeit* under the pseudonym "Ernst Krüger," writing about espionage and current affairs from the perspective of the unrepentant former Nazi that he was.

In the months following the Tehran summit, the two agencies directly involved in the planning of Operation Long Jump, the Abwehr and SD-Ausland—as well as their respective leaders, Wilhelm Canaris and Walther Schellenberg—continued on a collision course. The Abwehr, the intelligence apparatus of the German armed forces—like the Wehrmacht at large—possessed a growing number of anti-Nazis. Meanwhile, the steadfast Nazis of the rival SS, and its constituent SD and Gestapo, suspected as much, and were only too willing to work toward ferreting out the traitors within their competing service.

Beginning in the autumn of 1943 and paralleling the run-up to Long Jump, the Gestapo infiltrated dissident groups within the military, turning up tangible links to traitors within the Abwehr ranks in the process. By early 1944, it was evident that Canaris was personally involved in opposing Hitler. This led to his dismissal from the Abwehr, and his being placed under house arrest by Hitler's direct order. On February 18, Hitler formally abolished the Abwehr, transferring its intelligence functions to the Reich Main Security Office (RSHA) where it was merged into the operations of the SD. Here, none other than Walther Schellenberg was now in charge of virtually the whole Reich intelligence apparatus.

Canaris remained under house arrest for a year, where he missed being involved in the infamous July 20, 1944, plot by German military officers which almost succeeded in killing Hitler. Early in 1945, Hitler decided that

Canaris was of no more use and ordered him court-martialed. Naturally, when the Führer ordered a court martial, the verdict was predetermined, and the 58-year-old admiral was executed in April 9, 1945, at the Flossenbürg concentration camp in Bavaria, shortly before the area was captured by the Americans. Adolf Hitler committed suicide three weeks later on April 30, 1945. Himmler followed suit on May 23.

Schellenberg remained a fervent Nazi almost to the very end, finally offering moral support for Heinrich Himmler's last minute armistice overtures to the British and Americans. When the Third Reich collapsed, Schellenberg fled first to Denmark and later surrendered to the British. He languished in custody for years, and while he was not tried before the International Military Tribunal at Nuremberg, he testified there against his former colleagues and fellow Nazis. In 1949, Schellenberg was finally put on trial when a U.S. military court took up the cases of those who had been part of the RSHA and other Reich ministries involved in war crimes. He was sentenced to six years, but served only two, during which time, he wrote his memoirs. Released because of terminal liver cancer, he lived out his final months in the Italian town of Verbania Pallanza, dying a painful death in March 1952.

Schellenberg's notorious Albanian double agent, Elyesa Bazna, "Cicero," who worked as a valet for the British ambassador to Turkey, continued to supply SD-Ausland with sensitive British documents until the spring of 1944. After that, his work became more difficult because of a new alarm system at the British embassy, and because Turkey was now officially distancing itself from the Reich.

As Schellenberg recalled in his memoirs, by that time, "Cicero's documents showed clearly that the continued neutrality of Turkey would be short-lived. Step by step the Turks were going over into the Allied camp. The Turkish diplomats proceeded carefully and according to plan—almost exactly as Knatchbull-Hugessen had described in his dispatches to the Foreign Office."

When Turkish president Ismet Inonu met with Roosevelt and Churchill at Cairo in December 1943, he promised to enter the war against

Germany—although he did not break off diplomatic relations with the Reich until August 1944 and declared war only in February 1945, as a formality to allow Turkey into the postwar United Nations.

As Schellenberg wrote of Cicero, "I never discovered his motives, whether greed, hatred, or just love of adventure—but often during my many journeys my thoughts would turn again to this strange case. Again and again I wondered whether perhaps there lay behind Cicero the shadow of the Turkish Secret Service. The more I thought about this, the more likely it seemed to me that through his material, Turkey had tried to warn Germany and prevent her from continuing on her path to total destruction. At the same time, she would be warning us of the almost inevitable transference of her loyalty to the camp of the western Allies, and would thus be safeguarding herself against the oppressive menace of Russia."

After the war, Cicero moved to Istanbul, where he planned to retire on the $1.8 million (in today's dollars) that Schellenberg had paid him during the war. However, much to his surprise, he discovered that the British banknotes he had been given were counterfeit! He even tried vainly to sue the postwar West German government.

Over the ensuing decade or so, the man who had become a legend of espionage folklore had to get by with such odd jobs as selling used cars, while he hoped to make back his losses by peddling his story. His handler, Ludwig Carl Moyzisch, beat him to the punch, however, with his 1950 book *Operation Cicero*. The 1952 20th Century Fox film adaptation, entitled *5 Fingers*, was directed by Joseph L. Mankiewicz, and starred James Mason as Cicero. It was not until 1962 that Bazna's own book, *I Was Cicero*, was finally published. By the mid-1960s, he was living in West Germany, declining interviews and waiting for Hollywood to come knocking at his door. He died in Munich in 1970 without a movie deal.

On the other side, there was the almost mythical double agent Nikolai Ivanovich Kuznetsov, who had assumed the identity, among others, of Lieutenant Paul Wilhelm Siebert. As the drinking companion of Hans Ulrich von Ortel, he learned all of the sturmbannführer's secrets, turned them over to the NKVD and therefore gave the Soviets the heads-up that Long Jump was in the offing. He was allegedly killed in a shootout with anti-Soviet Ukrainian nationalists in March 1944. Though part of his story is known, there is much more that remains secret. Kuznetsov's complete file reportedly still exists, but remains classified, within the archives of the Rossiyskoy Federatsii (FSB), the Russian successor to the Soviet NKVD and KGB.

George Lenczowski, the well-connected press attaché at the Polish embassy in Tehran, whose memoirs are an invaluable source on the prewar and war years in Iran, chose not to return to Soviet-dominated postwar Poland and emigrated to the United States. He landed a job as an assistant professor at Hamilton College in Clinton, New York. In 1949, he published his book *Russia and the West in Iran*, which offered a great many details about the German influence in Iran between the World Wars, and provided much information about Franz Mayr and the SD's Operation Franz missions into the country during the war. In 1952, he relocated to the University of California at Berkeley, where he spent the remainder of his career. He served as a professor of political science, and founded the Center of Middle Eastern Studies at the university. His son John became a foreign policy advisor to President Ronald Reagan.

Michael Francis Reilly continued to travel the world as Franklin Roosevelt's bodyguard. He was with him on his trips throughout the United States, especially during the long presidential campaign in 1944. He was also at his side for the Pacific Strategy Conference with Admiral Chester Nimitz and General Douglas MacArthur, and Reilly accompanied Roosevelt to the Big Three summit at Yalta in February 1945. Along with Dr. James Paullin and Lieutenant Commander Howard Bruenn, the president's cardiologist, Reilly was in the room with Roosevelt at the "Little White House" in Warm Springs, Georgia, when he died. He instinctively checked Roosevelt's pulse, recalling in his memoirs that a Secret Service man "must check all credentials. Even Death's."

As Michael Sampson of the Secret Service explained to this author, "after President Roosevelt's death in 1945, [Reilly] and other members of the White House Detail were [re]called to active duty. Reilly regained a commission in the U.S. Navy, which he had had to forego to remain as a member of the White House Detail, and oversaw Intelligence work." He later served as president of the Southern California Aircraft Corporation, a company doing airplane modifications at the Ontario Airport. In June 1973, he died in Butte, Montana, not far from where he had been born sixty-three years earlier.

Norman Schwarzkopf did not return home when the war ended. He remained in Iran, still in charge of a force of around 20,000 gendarmes. In 1946, Schwarzkopf uprooted his son, the future general, on his twelfth birthday and brought him to Tehran to live. Two months later, his wife wired that she too was coming, and bringing their two daughters. As the younger Norman recalled in his memoirs, "When Soviet and British troops withdrew from Iran's outlying provinces in the spring of 1946, a few months before I arrived, it was Pop's gendarmes who filled the vacuum, keeping order in the countryside, confiscating guns, and backing up local police when antimonarchy demonstrations got out of hand. So my father became a target for Soviet propaganda. Tass published reports denouncing him, and when Iranian communists staged demonstrations, there were always 'Down with Schwarzkopf' signs. That was fine with Pop, who made no bones about the fact that he was anticommunist and prided himself on helping to keep Iran out of the Soviet bloc."

In 1948, Norman Schwarzkopf and his family relocated to Germany, where he became deputy provost marshal in the American occupation zone. In 1953, he returned to Iran on a top-secret mission. When the British and Soviet occupation troops pulled out in 1946, Iran had reverted to its prewar political turbulence. At the political extremes, were the increasingly assertive pro-Soviet Tudeh Party and the former members of the pro-German Melliyun-I-Iran. By 1950, a political crisis had arisen over growing demands for nationalization of the British-controlled Anglo-Iranian Oil Company. In 1951, the Majlis nominated, and the Shah confirmed, the appointment of Mohammed Mosaddegh (a.k.a. Musaddiq), a veteran left-leaning politician as prime minister. Shortly thereafter, Anglo-Iranian was nationalized, creating a squabble that culminated in the breaking of relations between Britain and Iran.

The Shah, still young and inexperienced, remained a weak leader, and Mosaddegh moved to consolidate his own power, while curbing that of the monarchy, a move that was popular on the Tehran street. Though not a Tudeh man himself, Mosaddegh depended to a great extent upon their support and that of the mullas, especially Ayatollah Abol-Ghasem Kashani who became speaker of the Majlis.

By 1953, Britain and the United States began to fear that the Tudeh factions, given the power they held over Mosaddegh, were on the verge of pushing Iran into the Soviet orbit. The SIS and CIA then initiated Operation Ajax, of which Schwarzkopf was a part, which was aimed at convincing the Shah—who had fled the country and was living in Rome—to fire Mosaddegh before Mosaddegh formally deposed him. Though he was intimidated by his own popular prime minister, the Shah finally replaced Mosaddegh with General Fazlollah Zahedi. Operation Ajax was Schwarzkopf's last great overseas adventure. He died in 1958, two years after his son graduated from West Point. The younger Schwarzkopf, of course, achieved fame as a four-star general in command of American forces in Operation Desert Storm in 1991.

General Zahedi was a familiar face from the Melliyun-I-Iran, who had worked closely with Franz Mayr and Bernhardt Schulze-Holthus during the early years of World War II when a German victory was thought probable. Zahedi served two years as prime minister before moving to Geneva as Iran's ambassador to the United Nations, a post he held until his death in 1963. Mosaddegh died under house arrest four years later.

The timid young Shah who had presented himself humbly to the Big Three in 1943, and who had run from his country in fear in 1953, found his nerve at last in the wake of the Mosaddegh affair and became what history recalls as a tyrant. In 1967, he declared himself an emperor and later watched Iran grow fantastically wealthy as oil prices skyrocketed. In

1979, Iran, a former international diplomatic backwater, underwent an Islamic revolution of global consequences, and the Shah was deposed by Ayatollah Ruhollah Khomeini. The Shah died of cancer in exile a year later.

As 1943 faded into 1944, the tide of history had already washed away the last vestiges of the German operational presence in Iran—except in the mountains of Qashqai country where Bernhardt Schulze-Holthus was still running free along with SS-Obersturmbannfuhrer Martin Kurmis and his Sonderlehrgang team. With the Wehrmacht in retreat across the steppes of the Soviet Union, the Qashqai had given up on Hitler-Shah and any hope that the Germans would deliver them from the British and the Soviets.

Relations between the Germans and the tribal guerilla armies had grown strained, and the Operation Franz teams were stymied. Kurmis had requested that they be extracted, and assurances had been made. Kampfgeschwader 200 was coming to get them, it was promised, but not until the middle of January 1944.

"Christmas arrived," Schulze-Holthus wrote in his memoirs. "It was a dismal feast. On Christmas Eve we all went to the [wireless] station. It had snowed, the moon shone on the snow, and we were all in a melancholy mood. Each of us wanted to send our personal greetings to our families in Germany. The [generator] motor started and keys began to rattle under Piwonka's fingers. Then there was a sudden terrible bang, a cloud of smoke came from the set and the gay rattle of the keys fell silent."

The explosion destroyed the generator and left the men with no way of contacting Germany. Kampfgeschwader 200 would not be coming.

On January 2, 1944, an emissary came from Nasr Khan.

"Allah strengthen your hearts for the news I bring you," he said as he sat down on the carpet and lit his hookah.

"What's the matter?" Schulze-Holthus asked as the man puffed a few clouds of smoke into the air. "Is it something to do with Nasr Khan?"

"Unfortunately, yes. Nasr Khan has demanded your surrender."

The Qashqai leaders promised that they would not turn the Germans over to the Allies, but insisted that they should be taken into Qashqai detention. After much negotiating, the Germans wound up in a mountain village unreachable by motor vehicles, where they remained until the Persian New Year in late March, treated as much like guests as prisoners. After the New Year's feast, they were taken on a long journey that ended with their being turned over to the British. Reflecting upon the demise of the last German agents at large in Iran, Sydney Morrell wrote that during the feat the Germans were "pounced on by the tribesmen and overpowered. Three of them, obviously weary of the whole game, gave in at once, but the fourth, a typical tough young Nazi, fought like a cat and had to be bound. They were brought down to Bushehr on the coast and were handed over to the British."

While in custody, Martin Kurmis slashed his own wrist, and wound up in the hospital, where he completed his attempted suicide by grabbing a guard and jumping through a second-story window.

Schulze-Holthus and the others were taken to Palestine, where they were placed in a prisoner of war camp at Emmaus in the Judean Hills about ten miles from Jerusalem. Ironically, the Nazis were in the same camp that the British would later use for interning Zionist underground fighters. It was here that Schulze-Holthus was reunited with Franz Mayr.

Early in 1945, Schulze-Holthus was traded for a British SIS officer and repatriated into the dying Third Reich by way of Switzerland. As the world remembered Lawrence of Arabia and forgot Wilhelm Wassmuss of Persia after World War I, almost nobody today remembers Bernhardt Schulze-Holthus of Iran. Having kept his head down during the immediate postwar years, he published his memoirs in Germany in 1952. They were later translated into English as *Daybreak in Iran*. He did not say what ultimately became of Mayr.

Otto Skorzeny, who never made it to Iran, continued his career as the most celebrated special operations officer of the Third Reich. In October 1944, Skorzeny led Operation Panzerfaust. The operation involved abducting Miklos Horthy Jr., the son of Admiral Horthy, the regent of Hungary. On his father's behalf, Miklos had been trying to negotiate an armistice with the Soviets. By kidnapping Miklos, foisting a coup against Admiral Horthy, and then blackmailing him (his son was now in a concentration camp) into publicly renouncing the negotiated armistice and supporting the new government, the operation kept Hungary in the pro-Nazi camp.

Two months later, Skorzeny spearheaded Unternehmen Greif, or Operation Griffon, an infiltration of Allied lines during the Battle of the Bulge. This action involved the reprise of an aspect of Operation Long Jump—an attempt to either kill or kidnap General Dwight Eisenhower.

After the war, Skorzeny was picked up and held as a war criminal on charges of murdering unarmed American prisoners during the Battle of the Bulge. He was also charged with violating the rules of war for putting his SS teams into American uniforms during the Battle of the Bulge. He was acquitted on the latter charge after a British operative testified that the SOE had used German uniforms to infiltrate German lines. In 1948, Skorzeny's reputation as a special operations mastermind was further enhanced when he staged a daring escape from Allied custody—which involved captured American uniforms.

Skorzeny was never recaptured. He lived for a time in Austria—and was photographed by a news photographer relaxing at a sidewalk cafe in Paris—before going into the private security business as an international soldier of fortune. He traveled to Argentina as a bodyguard to Eva Peron, and he set up a team of former SS officers to advise the Egyptian army. Finally "denazified" in absentia by the West German government in 1952, Skorzeny continued to operate his international private security company, the Paladin Group, from its base in Spain. After some years of deteriorating health, he died of lung cancer in July 1975.

Among the former Sonderlehrgang special ops men who had yet to get enough adventure in their lives, many wound up in organizations such as Skorzeny's. Others were recruited by the mercurial General Reinhard Gehlen, who had set up a clandestine organization of former German intelligence operatives to work for the CIA against the KGB during the Cold War.

Gehlen's background was with neither the Abwehr nor the SD, but as the head of an organization within the Wehrmacht's Foreign Armies East (Fremde Heere Ost, FHO), that was tasked with developing extensive intelligence information about the Soviet Union before and during the war. As the conflict was winding to an end, Gehlen decided to preserve all of his files and to place them, as well as his organization and personnel, at the disposal of the United States. During the early part of the Cold War the "Gehlen Organization" became home to dozens of former SS and Abwehr hired guns who were not ready to call it quits.

In 1956, with the Cold War growing colder, the West German government embraced Gehlen and his organization, and brought it out of the shadows, transforming it into the Bundesnachrichtendienst (BND), West Germany's—and later reunified Germany's—official intelligence service.

Those former SS officers with too much blood on their hands for Gehlen or even Skorzeny simply tried to disappear. Some escaped Europe, aided by Nazi sympathizers still active throughout the world, and others passed though channels oiled by the mysterious—and allegedly apocryphal—SS alumni association known as the Organization der Ehemaligen SS-Angehörigen (ODESSA), which facilitated their slipping the noose of postwar justice for new lives in the Middle East and South America. Notable among the SS escapees were Obersturmbannführer Adolf Eichmann, who was eventually caught, and Hauptsturmführer Josef Mengele, who died of a stroke while swimming in the Atlantic off a Brazilian beach in 1979.

Neither Walther Schellenberg nor Otto Skorzeny mentioned Operation Long Jump in their respective postwar autobiographies, but that is understandable. Schellenberg wrote his memoirs while he was in Allied custody, and he was unlikely to have admitted, under such circumstances, to the attempted murder of Roosevelt, Churchill, and Stalin. Skorzeny, meanwhile, was technically still a fugitive from justice when his memoirs were published in 1957.

For a man who took immense pride in having been labeled by the Allies "the most dangerous man in Europe"—a phrase he used in the subtitle of his memoirs—Skorzeny was curiously evasive, when not silent, about Operation Long Jump. For years, he denied knowledge of the operation, but later amended that to denying *direct* involvement in it. Perhaps "the most dangerous man in Europe" was reticent about mentioning Operation Long Jump because he never made it to Tehran himself—or perhaps because it had failed.

Epilogue

Success has many fathers, it has often been said, but failure is an orphan. Perhaps the single most important element in Operation Long Jump having faded to historical obscurity was that it failed.

That it failed through quirk of happenstance, and not through heroic effort, made it something better forgotten than celebrated by its intended victims. For the Germans, it was a defeat, an embarrassment, but for the Allies, the fact that it had come so precariously close to success was no victory.

After a deep sigh of relief, nothing more was said of this deeply troubling near miss. Three weeks later, when Franklin D. Roosevelt laughed it off, quipping to the media that there was "no use going into details," the press corps, lacking today's post-Watergate cynicism, did not. The president laughed, and the press corps laughed with him. Nothing had happened in Tehran, so there indeed seemed to be "no use going into details." This was the height of World War II, and there were too many other, far more serious matters to consume the attention of press and public.

As the journalists of 1943 had bigger fish to fry, so too did the first generation of postwar biographers and historians. Given that World War II was a unique epoch, defined by a great tableau of world-changing events, it was only natural that an obscure and failed conspiracy should be overlooked, especially during the war and in its immediate aftermath.

Meanwhile, of course, obfuscation was and remains an institutional way of life in the world of espionage and covert operations. This is illustrated by the continuing classification of Nikolai Kuznetsov's file, and by the British Official Secrets Act of 1939, which mandated severe penalties involving jail time for disclosing designated official secrets. No one talked about anything—for a very long time. Information about Ultra, the cryptographic program that had broken the German Enigma code, and which has been heralded for decades as one of the most important Allied intelligence successes of World War II, remained unmentioned until 1974 because of the strict provisions of the Official Secrets Act. What then of other secrets, whose institutional memory has faded before their successes could be celebrated?

Even the Americans were anxious to keep the lid on. American journalists in Tehran and Washington were certainly aware of the "hundreds of German spies" to which Roosevelt alluded in his press conference two weeks after the fact. However, what if they had *ignored* the president's suggestion that there was "no use going into details?" Had they returned to Tehran to do some digging, they would have been stymied by the lack of official cooperation and the walls of censorship erected by the Soviets, the British, and even by the *Americans*. Perhaps there were some who tried. If so, they would have failed. Though the Persian Gulf Command was principally an engineering operation, General Donald Connolly was as strict on censorship as the British, and possibly even the Soviets.

"This was a cause for despair, for only a visiting journalist, possessed of some discernment, could write truly of the situation," wrote British agent Sydney Morrell, who was himself in the business of putting a spin on information, but who sympathized with the plight of journalists. "Even so, it would have had to be written from outside the country, and, even under such conditions, the obstacles were formidable enough, for under a War Department ruling all stories referring to the [Persian Gulf] theatre, wherever written—whether in Tehran or New York—had to be submitted to Connolly's staff for approval."

George Lenczowski, who was also sympathetic to eager journalists despite being an *official* press attaché, noted the frustration with censorship that was experienced even by people associated with the Office of War Information (OWI), which functioned as the official United States government news source. In Tehran, he knew Morrell, and he got to know the OWI men, former reporters, and understood their frustration.

"The Office of War Information did send some men to Iran," Lenczowski wrote in *Russia and the West in Iran*, "The first was Harold Peters, former United Press correspondent. He was entrusted with the task of editing an American newspaper in Teheran which would satisfy the needs of American soldiers there and also serve as a general information organ for local consumption. Unfortunately Peters' status was ill-defined. He was not granted a diplomatic post as press attaché at the Embassy, nor was he put into any clear position vis-a-vis the Persian Gulf Command. Local rivalry existed between the army and the Embassy, and both were none too kind toward the OWI. The net result was that Peters found himself suspended in air, unable either to publish a newspaper or to start any normal activity among Iranian newspapermen. He was leading a shadow existence on the fringes of the Teheran diplomatic colony. Peters was succeeded in due time by James Downward [not to be confused with *Percy Downward*], also of the OWI. Downward was similarly unable to accomplish anything. He became involved in difficulties with the Persian Gulf Command and after a few months was recalled."

"There was, indeed, tension between General Connolly's staff and the local American embassy," wrote Sydney Morrell of Connolly and Peters in his wartime memoir *Spheres of Influence*. "I knew of the control which an American army commander exercises in his theatre in time of war. His power far exceeds that of the local diplomatic representative, even to the point where no American, not even a representative of the State Department, can enter a theatre without the express permission and request of the military commander.

"Approximately two years earlier, while in Washington, I had assisted in the preparations of plans by OWI for staffing the Iran theatre. The OWI outpost chief in Tehran at that time was a one-time United Press man, Harold Peters, an American who was interested in the country, cared for its future, and believed that America had a general role to play. Eighteen months later the OWI withdrew Peters, whom I met in Cairo on my way to Tehran. He was full of warnings at the sinister influence of the United States military forces on Iranian affairs, but at the time I was disposed to pay little heed to them, believing that Harold Peters' quarrels were no concen of mine."

As anyone associated with military secrecy knows, and as this author has discovered first hand on many occasions, those who have sworn not to reveal confidentialities consider it a mark of duty and honor to never talk, even decades after the fact. In such an environment, it is easy to understand how years of inattention allowed so many secrets to be forgotten and to fade quietly from the historical memory of World War II. Memories and unspoken truths passed into oblivion with the passage of time and the passing of lives. Many wartime secrets are gone forever.

By the 1960s, the legend of Long Jump still remained, but in the form of rumors being whispered in obscure corners of popular culture. Occasionally, those whispers appeared in print on a back page here or there, mentioned by such writers as Alexander Lukin and Viktor Egorov in the Soviet Union, Kyril Tidmarsh in Britain, and Laslo Havas, a Hungarian journalist working in Paris.

In 1965, Lukin, a former NKVD man who became a writer after the war, published a short but enticing article entitled "Operatsiya Dalyni

Prazhok" (Operation Long Jump) in the Moscow weekly illustrated magazine *Ogoniok*. It attracted little attention at the time, nor did the story gain any traction in the Western media. Three years later, Egorov published his *Zagovor Protiv Evriki: Broshenny Portfel* (*The Plot Against Eureka: The Lost Portfolio*), and later in 1968, Tidmarsh published an article in the *Times of London* entitled "How Russians foiled Nazi plot to kill Tehran Big Three."

After this brief flurry of activity, the story again went quiet, until fragments of information from long-sealed archives began trickling from the former Soviet Union. In 2003 both Yuri Kusnez and Pavel Sudoplatov published books in Russia that detailed secret and long forgotten aspects of the Soviet role in thwarting Long Jump. In his book, *Special Operations: Lubyanka and Kremlin*, Sudoplatov provided much new information about Nikolai Kuznetsov, whose discovery of Hans Ulrich von Ortel had been a pivotal element in alerting the Soviets to Long Jump.

Gevork Vartanian, perhaps the last surviving participant in the affair, garnered a great deal of attention with his subsequent revelations in an interview with Yury Plutenko for the RIA Novosti news service that was published on October 16, 2007.

"We were lucky, we never met a single traitor," he said proudly of his life as an NKVD man in Tehran. "For us, underground agents, betrayal is the worst evil. If an agent observes all the security rules and behaves properly in society, no counter-intelligence will spot him or her. Like sappers, underground agents err only once."

The file on Gevork Vartanian "was declassified only on December 20, 2000," Yury Plutenko reminded his readers in his interview. "He and his wife Goar, a member of his group, immediately [after the war] received five decorations: [including] the orders of the Great Patriotic War, Battle Red Banner and Red Star."

Vartanian was later widely interviewed in the West, but conceded cryptically that he had not told all, and he took some of his secrets to his grave in 2012.

In Paris during the early 1960s, when the trail was still warm, journalist Laslo Havas heard rumors of the mysterious conspiracy and tried to track down some of the players who had been involved.

Little is remembered today of Havas, who moved in the same postwar Paris literary and intellectual circles as Louis Pauwels, with whom he coauthored the 1969 book *Les Derniers Jours de la Monogamie* (*The Last Days of Monogamy*). Pauwels was a well-known contributor to numerous French literary and mass-market magazines in the 1950s and 1960s, and perhaps best known as the founder of the literary magazine *Planète* (later *le Nouveau Planète* or *New Planet*), as well as for having collaborated with Jacques Bergier on the 1960 book, *Le Matin des Magiciens* (*The Morning of the Magicians*), a diverse anthology of tales of ancient wisdom, forgotten lore, and occult theories. The book was popular and widely translated, becoming an iconic text of the 1960s counterculture. Pauwels also did a great deal of work documenting the occult underpinnings of Heinrich Himmler's SS, the agency that provided Operation Long Jump with its momentum. It was likely through Pauwels, because of his work with obscure German wartime mysteries, that Havas was put on the track of the Operation Long Jump participants.

Havas went to Argentina, where Skorzeny had served as a bodyguard and advisor to the Juan and Evita Peron. On a back street in Buenos Aires, he found Rudolf von Holten-Pflug, Skorzeny's acolyte and understudy. The man who had wanted to *be* Skorzeny, and who had come closest to achieving Long Jump's climactic success, was working not as a mercenary nor as a commando, but pouring drinks at a small cantina that he owned. The Hungarian journalist and the Prussian hit man chatted, sipping fernet and Coke, as older men occasionally dropped by to drink and chat in German about earlier times. Havas later recounted von Holten-Pflug's continued exasperation that he and the operation had come so close to success, only to be frustratingly foiled.

Havas crossed the Andes to Chile, where he managed to locate Winifred Oberg. The erstwhile Long Jump advance man was then living a comfortable life as a legal advisor to North American companies doing business at the opposite end of the hemisphere. Unlike those with an SS pedigree who sought to hide their past as a member of Himmler's cadre of dark knights, ex-sturmbannführer Oberg was proud of the role that he had played in the SD. When talk turned to Long Jump, however, Oberg became evasive. Like his old boss, Walther Schellenberg, who avoided mention of it in his memoirs, Oberg wanted not to be recalled by history as a would-be assassin of such high-profile targets. It would have been bad for business.

Havas caught up with Otto Skorzeny in Madrid, where he was running his private security firm. He found the infamous "most dangerous man in Europe" more reflective than he had expected, and cautiously willing to discuss matters he had not revealed in his memoirs a decade earlier.

"Throughout our first meeting he remained very much on the defensive," Havas reported. "He had never been questioned [by the Allies] on the Tehran affair. Subsequently he did admit that he had been put in charge of Operation Long Jump. He gave us the details, but omitted the names of his colleagues. The old spirit of loyalty was not yet dead. Skorzeny was the same man he had always been, a political adventurer in the grand style, a romantic, courageous and true to those who trusted in him, still loyal to a worthless cause and even today reluctant to admit it."

Having read George Lenczowski's recollections of Tehran in the 1940s, Havas was well aware of Operation Franz. His knowing about this apparently impressed Skorzeny, who readily fleshed out more detail on the skeleton of what Havas had previously known.

Other Germans proved more elusive. After twenty years, many who had sought to disappear had succeeded. Havas heard rumors that former Abwehr agent and underworld enforcer Lothar Schoellhorn was continuing his strong-arm trade in Africa and the Middle East. There were stories that he had worked as a mercenary for Moise Tshombe in the former Belgian Congo, but Havas was unable to confirm this. He also failed to find any trace of SD officer Roman Gamotha. Strangely, Havas does not mention having looked for Franz Mayr, whose presence in Tehran was confirmed in numerous published narratives, such as those of Bernhardt Schulze-Holthus, George Lenczowski, and Michael Reilly—as well as in the much later stories told by Gevork Vartanian. After he was last seen by Schulze-Holthus in Palestine in 1945, Mayr seems to have disappeared, possibly into the Gehlen Organization.

Havas did track down Josef Schnabel. In 1943, Schnabel had been a young SS untersturmführer drinking to excess in the Tehran home of an American amateur archeologist and plotting against Roosevelt, Churchill, and Stalin. Two decades later, he was living in Hamburg, where he owned a construction company and held a seat in city government as a Social Democrat. Like so many of his generation, he had joined the Nazi Party as a young man—an obvious prerequisite to SS membership—but had long since put his youthful indiscretion behind him to become active in a modern mainstream party.

Naturally, the "new" Schnabel was reluctant to talk about "those years," but Havas won him over by explaining that the story was going to be told with or without him and this would be an opportunity for Schnabel to put his own spin on the narrative. Schnabel cooperated and identified characters new to Havas, including Ernst Merser and the real name of the woman we know as Ida Kovalska. She was living in Israel and married to a man in the government. When Havas tracked her down, she agreed to tell him everything she knew, provided that her husband would be unable to deduce that she was the "Ida" in the story.

It was left unsaid whether Havas used pseudonyms for others in his narrative, such as Percy Downward and Khalil Chapat, or for the Americans, Peter Ferguson and Mervyn Wollheim. One is inclined to think that he might have. In the case of the Swiss double agent, "Ernst Merser" might have been his real name, or perhaps it was merely the alias that he used in

Tehran and at other times in his career. Vasile Dumitru Fulger, writing in 2012 in *Periscop*, the quarterly journal of the association of Romanian reserve military and foreign information service personnel, provided additional information about Merser's career with the Schweizer Nachrichtendienst, as well as with the German and British services—mentioning him by that name. In 2014, when we tried to reach Mr. Fulger through his publisher, we learned that they had had "no news" from him for more than two years.

From the woman he identified as Ida Kovalska, Havas learned the fate of poor Wanda Pollack, whose life before Tehran had been one of unspeakable pain and horror—and whose life in Tehran had been punctuated by incarceration in an NKVD torture chamber. With the onset of the cold, bleak Tehran winter, she apparently sank into a deep depression. Three months after the excitement surrounding the failure of Operation Long Jump, she swallowed a fistful of sedatives. Apparently, it was an impulsive act that she regretted almost immediately, and she called for help. She was taken to a hospital, but it was too late. Ida was with Wanda when her friend passed away.

"Ernst should have told her a little more often that he loved her," Ida Kovalska said of Merser's relationship with Wanda. "Merely reassuring her about her past was not sufficient. But Ernst is the most modest, the most reserved man I have ever known. I felt sure he would kill himself, also. I hold it against him, just a little bit, that he did not."

Quite to the contrary, the man we know as Ernst Merser survived and flourished. By the 1960s, he maintained homes in Geneva and in the South of France. The man who had foiled Long Jump by keeping its would-be perpetrators incommunicado in the safety of his safe house, continued into the Cold War as a freelance secret agent. Havas mentioned his having worked for at least six countries.

Like Skorzeny, Merser was initially reluctant to talk, but on Ida Kovalska's recommendation, he finally agreed to a meeting. Havas sent his wife to meet with the Swiss spy in Nice, to tell him what they had learned to date, and ask him to fill in the missing pieces. He listened, but said little. Ten days later, however, Merser phoned to invite Havas and his wife to join him aboard his yacht for a sail along the Mediterranean coast of France and Spain.

Havas recalled that they talked about little more than the weather for several days, but then one day, Merser handed Havas a typed manuscript he had written about his wartime activities. It contained 200 pages about Tehran. Havas was allowed to read it and to use parts of it as a reference— with the caveat that Merser planned to get it published later and he did not want Havas to lean on it too extensively.

"I should like it to be published after my death, or perhaps, not at all," Merser explained. "But since you seem determined to drag me into your story, it's just as well you got your facts straight. Not everything you'll read in this manuscript is publishable, of course."

The book was never published, and the manuscript, not seen again since, has presumably been lost.

As they coasted along the Costa Brava for two weeks, Merser spoke quite candidly of that week in 1943 when the world almost changed.

"Sometimes the unmasking of an agent demands years of unflagging work," he said. "Our German agents in Tehran simply walked into prison. It would have been different had the Abwehr sent them to me. But remember, I found Oberg by accident and we were able to control all the others through him."

Naturally, talk turned to the "might have been" scenarios. Merser was quite willing to indulge his interviewer.

"It is silly to play at 'what would have happened if,' but it is difficult not to wonder. What would have happened had we not found Oberg at the Russian headquarters? What would have happened had Berlin left me out of this operation? What would have happened had 40 Germans remained at liberty in Tehran with its childish [Allied] security measures? They could not, perhaps, have come anywhere near Stalin, but what of the other two? Or what would have happened had the last commandos, von Holten-Pflug's men, not picked Ebtehaj, or at least, not approached him for a second time against all logic?"

The journalist asked what became of the others. Merser told him that Ferguson and Wollheim had returned to the United States, but Wollheim had died in Los Angeles shortly after the war. Misbah Ebtehaj was also deceased, though he lived until 1964 and had become a wealthy business-man in Tabriz, the city where the Abwehr's Bernhardt Schulze-Holthus had served a vice-consul before the war. Khalil Chapat had returned to Beirut, where he too, became a successful businessman. Percy Downward, Merser explained, was still with British intelligence in the 1960s, "some-where" in the Far East. Merser would have known this, as he was still working actively with the SIS.

While Downward remains an obscure figure, his wartime Tehran colleague, Sydney Morrell, who had been recruited in New York by the SIS in 1940, returned to Manhattan, and made a name for himself on Madison Avenue. For a time, he was an executive vice president with the advertising firm McCann Erickson, and started his own a public relations consulting firm, Sydney Morrell & Company, in 1963. If he knew anything about Long Jump, he apparently never said so publicly.

"Downward thought nothing of Schellenberg but had a very high opinion of Canaris," Merser said, recalling how he and the British agent had tried to sort out the German organization for Long Jump. "It was funny in itself that the Abwehr and the RSHA should both participate in the action. Even after all the Germans had been questioned, Downward failed to see clearly, but in the face of every piece of evidence he refused to believe that Canaris had shared in the directing of the operation."

"We have nothing to be proud of," Downward had told Merser. "Nat-urally, everyone is pleased that it is all over and nothing happened. But it is no thanks to us that there was no trouble, at least, no thanks to me."

At last, when the sun was low in the sky, with its golden light shim-mering on the Mediterranean, Ernst Merser and his guests sipped pinot noir as he reflected upon what had transpired during those weeks in

Tehran two decades earlier. Gazing thoughtfully toward the distant horizon, he told them, "The whole affair was somehow...somehow irregular. I realize that in subversive warfare there are no fixed rules, each case creates its own, but this was like nothing we had experienced before, or since. The whole thing was somehow insane."

About the Author

Bill Yenne is the author of more than three dozen non-fiction books, mainly on historical topics, as well as ten novels, including the Raptor Force adventure series and the Bladen Cole Westerns. General Wesley Clark called Mr. Yenne's biography of Alexander the Great the "best yet," while the *New Yorker* wrote of *Sitting Bull*, his biography of the great Lakota leader, that it "excels as a study in leadership." General Craig McKinley, president of the Air Force Association, wrote that in Mr. Yenne's *Hap Arnold: The General Who Invented the US Air Force*, he had done "a superior job helping the reader better understand General Arnold both as an individual and as a military leader."

Mr. Yenne has contributed to encyclopedias of both world wars, and has appeared in documentaries airing on the History Channel, the National Geographic Channel, the Smithsonian Channel, and ARD German Television. He lives in San Francisco, and can be found on the web at www. BillYenne.com.

Bibliography

Azimi, Fakhreddin. *Iran: The Crisis of Democracy: From the Exile of Reza Shah to the Fall of Musaddiq.* New York: Palgrave Macmillan, 1989.

Bamberg, J. H. *The History of the British Petroleum Company,* volume 2, *The Anglo-Iranian Years.* Cambridge: Cambridge University Press, 1994.

Blake, Kristen. *The U.S.-Soviet Confrontation in Iran, 1945–1962.* Lanham, MD: University Press of America, 2009.

Churchill, Winston. *The Second World War,* volume 4, *The Hinge of Fate.* Boston: Houghton Mifflin Company, 1950.

———. *The Second World War,* volume 5, *Closing the Ring.* Boston: Houghton Mifflin Company, 1951.

———. *The Second World War,* volume 6, *Triumph and Tragedy.* Boston: Houghton Mifflin Company, 1953.

Colvin, Ian. *Admiral Canaris: Chief of Intelligence.* London: Colvin Press, 2007.

———. *Flight 777: The Mystery Of Leslie Howard.* London: Evans Brothers, 1957.

Congress of the United States. *Congressional Record*, volume 89, 1943. Washington, DC: Congress of the United States, 1943.

Culver, John C., and John Hyde. *American Dreamer: The Life and Times of Henry A. Wallace.* New York: W.W. Norton & Company, 2000.

Egorov, Viktor. *Zagovor protiv Evriki: broshenny portfel'* [*The Plot Against Eureka: The Lost Portfolio*]. Moscow: Sovetskaya Rossiya, 1968.

Foreign Office of the United Kingdom, Political Intelligence Department Political Warfare Executive. *Political Intelligence Department Papers, 1939–1946.* Kew, Richmond, Surrey: The National Archives, 1938–1973.

Franklin, William M., with William Gerber, Robert C. Hayes, and Donald M. Dozer. *Foreign Relations of the United States Diplomatic Papers, The Conferences at Cairo and Tehran, 1943.* Washington, DC: United States Department of State Historical Office, 1943.

Goss, Chris. *Bloody Biscay: The Story of the Luftwaffe's Only Long Range Maritime Fighter Unit, V Gruppe/Kampfgeschwader 40, and Its Adversaries, 1942–1944.* London: Crécy Publishing, 2001.

Gunther, John. *Inside Asia.* New York: Harper & Brothers, 1939.

Havas, Laslo, translated by Kathleen Szasz. *Hitler's Plot to Kill the Big Three.* London: Transworld, 1967, revised 1971.

Höhne, Heinz. *Canaris: Hitler's Master Spy.* London: Secker & Warburg, 1979.

Jangravi, Mehdi. *Occupation of Iran.* Tehran: The Institute for Iranian Contemporary Historical Studies, 2012.

Kapuscinski, Ryszard. *Shah of Shahs.* London: Penguin Books, 2006.

Kern, Gary. *A Death in Washington: Walter G. Krivitsky and the Stalin Terror.* New York: Enigma Books, 2003.

———. "How 'Uncle Joe' Bugged FDR." Langley, VA: Center for the Study of Intelligence, Central Intelligence Agency, 2007.

Kusnez, Yuri Lvovich. *Tehran 43: The Collapse of Operation Long Jump.* Moscow: Eksmo, 2007.

Lenczowski, George. *Russia and the West in Iran, 1918–1948: A Study in Big-Power Rivalry.* Ithaca, NY: Cornell University Press, 1949.

Maclean, Fitzroy. *Eastern Approaches.* London: Penguin Global, 1999.

Millspaugh, Arthur. *Americans in Persia.* Washington, DC: The Brookings Institution, 1946.

———. *The American Task in Persia.* New York: Arno Press, 1925.

Montefiore, Simon Sebag. *Stalin: Court of the Red Tsar.* New York: Random House, 2005.

Morrell, Sydney. *Spheres of Influence.* New York: Duell, Sloan and Pearce, 1946.

Motter, T. H. Vail. *The Persian Corridor and Aid to Russia.* Washington, DC: Center Of Military History United States Army, 1952.

O'Sullivan, Donal. *Dealing with the Devil: Anglo-Soviet Intelligence Cooperation in Iran.* New York: Peter Lang, 2010.

Pauwels, Louis, and Havas, Laslo. *Les Derniers Jours de la monogamie.* Paris: Mercure de France, 1969.

Piotrowski, Tadeusz. *The Polish Deportees of World War II: Recollections of Removal to the Soviet Union and Dispersal Throughout the World.* Jefferson, NC: McFarland, 2007.

Reese, Roger. *Why Stalin's Soldiers Fought.* Lawrence, KS: University Press of Kansas, 2011.

Reilly, Michael F. As told to William J. Slocum. *Reilly of the White House.* New York: Simon and Schuster, 1947.

Roosevelt, Franklin D. (Comments, quotes, and press conferences). *Public Papers of the Presidents of the United States.* Washington, DC: United States Government Printing Office, various dates.

Sadr, Muhsin. *Khatirat-i Sadr-ul Ashraf.* Tehran: Vahid, 1985.

Schulze-Holthus, Bernhardt. *Daybreak in Iran: A Story of the German Intelligence Service.* London: Staples, 1954.

Skorzeny, Otto. *Skorzeny's Special Missions: The Memoirs of "The Most Dangerous Man in Europe."* London: Robert Hale, 1957.

Smith, Richard Harris. *OSS: The History of America's First Central Intelligence Agency.* Guilford, CT: Lyons Press, 1972.

Stalin Archive, Central Party Archive of the CPSU. *The Tehran, Yalta & Potsdam Conferences Document.* Moscow: Progress Publishers, 1969.

Sudoplatov, Pavel, and Anatoli Sudoplatov, with Jerrold L. and Leona P. Schecter. *Special Operations: Lubyanka and Kremlin, 1930–1950.* Moscow: Olma-Press, 2003.

———. *Special Tasks: The Memoirs of an Unwanted Witness: A Soviet Spymaster.* Boston: Little, Brown & Company, 1994.

Thorpe, James Arthur. *The Mission of Arthur C. Millspaugh to Iran, 1943–1945,* volume 2. Madison: University of Wisconsin Madison, 1973.

United States Department of State. *Foreign Relations of the United States Diplomatic Papers: The Conferences at Cairo and Tehran, 1943.* Washington, DC: Government Printing Office, 1961.

Wallace, Henry Agard. *The Price of Vision: The Diary of Henry A. Wallace, 1942–1946.* Boston: Houghton Mifflin, 1973.

West, Nigel. *Historical Dictionary of World War II Intelligence.* Lanham, MD: Scarecrow Press, 2008.

Wheeler-Bennet, John. *King George VI: His Life and Reign.* London: Macmillan, 1958.

Index